STUDIES IN IMPERIALISM

general editor John M. MacKenzie

Established in the belief that imperialism as a cultural
phenomenon had as significant an effect on the dominant
as on the subordinate societies, Studies in Imperialism
seeks to develop the new socio-cultural approach which
has emerged through cross-disciplinary work on popular
culture, media studies, art history, the study of education
and religion, sports history, and children's literature.
The cultural emphasis embraces studies of migration and
race, while the older political, and constitutional,
economic and military concerns will never be far away.
It will incorporate comparative work on European and
American empire-building, with the chronological focus
primarily, though not exclusively, on the nineteenth and
twentieth centuries, when these cultural exchanges were
most powerfully at work.

STUDIES IN
IMPERIALISM

General editor John M. MacKenzie

'Benefits bestowed'?

EDUCATION AND BRITISH IMPERIALISM

edited by J. A. Mangan

The Fifth Stage of Empire

'And then a shift, into a worthier Schoolmaster's
pride, of benefits bestowed and gratitudes ...'

(From James Morris, *Farewell The Trumpets:
An Imperial Retreat*, Penguin, 1981, p. 388)

MANCHESTER
UNIVERSITY PRESS
Manchester and New York
Distributed exclusively in the USA and Canada
by ST. MARTIN'S PRESS

Copyright © Manchester University Press 1988

Whilst copyright in the volume as a whole is vested in Manchester University press, copyright in individual chapters belongs to their respective authors, and no chapter may be reproduced wholly or in part without express permission in writing of both author and publisher.

Published by M A N C H E S T E R   U N I V E R S I T Y   P R E S S
Oxford Road, Manchester M13 9PL, UK
and Room 400, 175 Fifth Avenue,
New York, NY 10010, USA

Distributed exclusively in the USA and Canada by
S T . M A R T I N ' S P R E S S I N C . , 175 Fifth Avenue,
New York, NY 10010, USA

British Library cataloguing in publication data
'Benefits Bestowed'?: education and British imperialism. — (Studies in imperialism)
1. Education — Social aspects — Commonwealth of Nations — History
I. Mangan, J. A.   II. Series
370.19'34'09171241   LC191

Library of Congress cataloging in publication data
'Benefits bestowed'?: education and British imperialism/J. A. Mangan, editor.
   p. cm. — (Studies in imperialism)
   Includes index.
ISBN 0-7190-2517-6 : $35.00 (U.S. : est.)
1. Education—Great Britain—History—19th century. 2. Education—Great Britain—
Colonies—History—19th century. I. Mangan. J. A. II. Series: Studies in imperialism
(Manchester (Greater Manchester))
LA631.7.B46 1988
370'.941—dc19

ISBN 0-7190-2517-6 hardback

Printed in Great Britain
by Bell & Bain Limited, Glasgow

CONTENTS

[v]

LIST OF ILLUSTRATIONS

NOTES ON CONTRIBUTORS

J. A. Mangan, (editor), Head of Education Section, Jordanhill College of Education, Glasgow. Publications include *Athleticism in the Victorian and Edwardian Public School*, 1981, and *The Games Ethic and Imperialism*, 1986.

Richard Aldrich, Senior Lecturer in History of Education, University of London Institute of Education. Publications include *Sir John Pakington and National Education*, 1979, and *An Introduction to the History of Education*, 1982.

Mark Connellan, sports master of the preparatory school of Trinity Grammar, Sydney, Australia. At present, he is researching the history of organised games and athleticism in Australia.

John Coolahan, Professor of Education, Maynooth University College, Ireland. Publications include *Irish Education, its History and Structure*, 1981, and *The ASTI and Post-Primary Education in Ireland*, 1984.

Patrick Dunae is an Archivist at the British Columbia Archives, Victoria, British Columbia, Canada. Publications include *Gentlemen Emigrants*, 1981, and *Ranchers' Legacy*, 1986.

Deborah Gaitskell, History Tutor, Morley College, London, and WEA (part-time). Publications include 'Upward all and play the game ...' in *Apartheid and Education* (ed. Peter Kallaway), 1984. Is also an Editor of the *Journal of Southern African Studies*.

Pamela Horn, Part-time lecturer in History, Oxford Polytechnic. Publications include *Changing Countryside in Victorian and Edwardian England and Wales*, 1984, *Rural Life in England in the First World War*, 1984, and *Life and Labour in Rural England, 1760–1850*, 1987.

Donald Leinster-Mackay, Associate Professor in Education, University of Western Australia. Publications include *The Rise of the English Prep School*, 1984, and *The Educational World of Edward Thring, a Centenary Study*, 1987.

Phillip McCann, Professor of Education, Memorial University of Newfoundland, Canada. Publications include *Blackboards and Briefcases: Personal Stories by Newfoundland Teachers, Educators and Administrators*, 1982.

Roger Openshaw, Senior Lecturer in Education, Massey University, New Zealand. Publications include *Reinterpreting the Educational Past* (with D. Mackenzie), 1986.

Paul John Rich, Head of Supervisory Programs, Department of Training and Career Development, State of Qatar. Is presently working on a history of the British political residents in the Arabian Gulf and their role in education.

NOTES ON CONTRIBUTORS

G. *Sherington*, Senior Lecturer in Education, Sydney University, Australia. Publications include *Australia's Immigrants 1788–1978*, 1980, and *English Education, Social Change and War, 1911–20*, 1981.

Clive Whitehead, Senior Lecturer, Department of Education, University of Western Australia. Publications include *Education in Fiji*, 1981.

GENERAL EDITOR'S FOREWORD

Imperialism was more than a set of economic, political, and military phenomena. It was a habit of mind, a dominant idea in the era of European world supremacy which had widespread intellectual, cultural, and technical expressions. The 'Studies in Imperialism' series is designed to explore, primarily but not exclusively, these relatively neglected areas. Volumes are planned on the scientific aspects of imperialism, on education, disease, the theatre, literature, art, design, and many more. But in redressing the balance in favour of these multi-disciplinary and cross-cultural studies, it is not intended that the economic, political, and military dimensions should be ignored. The series will also contain books in these fields and will seek to examine colonial and imperial developments in a variety of periods and in diverse geographical contexts. It is hoped that individually and collectively these works will illumine one of the more potent characteristics of modern world history.

The diffusion of and reactions to British cultural ideas and values through the educational process have received insufficient attention in imperial history. While there have been some missionary and local studies, there have been few attempts to examine education as a transmitter of the dominant culture in a variety of institutional, geographical and ethnic contexts. This volume attempts to explore imperial education at several levels: experiential, curricular, institutional, structural, ideological and political. It has, *inter alia*, chapters on the teaching of imperial history, the growth of the imperial idea, the influence of freemasonry, and British colonial education policies in general, ranging from Ireland to South Africa, Newfoundland to New Zealand, and Australia to Canada. These essays, it is hoped, will stimulate discussion on both the origins and evolution of educational systems, and the relationship between education and religious, social, cultural and political patterns within the Commonwealth.

John M. MacKenzie

INTRODUCTION

Imperialism, history and education

I

In his Introduction to *Imperialism and Popular Culture*, John MacKenzie suggests that the central role of imperialism must now be noted in all debates about culture, media and society between the 1870s and the 1940s.[1] Sound advice, yet surely incomplete. In the full context of empire, the list should certainly include education.

Imperialism, both as a concept and a reality, has influenced the formal educational systems of Britain and her imperial possessions, directly and indirectly and to a greater or lesser extent, for over three hundred years. In the late nineteenth and early twentieth centuries – the period of the so-called 'New Imperialism' – as several contributors to this volume demonstrate,[2] its influence was especially significant. The extent of this influence has been nowhere near adequately considered. It is certainly time it received fuller attention, was more exhaustively explored, more comprehensively analysed. There is much still to discover about the past *and* present impact of British imperialism on the educational systems of Britain, dominion and colony and, by extension, on their societies and cultures. *Ipse dixit* the roots of current attitudes to 'race' and colour lie deep in the imperial past. Happily, research is now under way, some of it interestingly revisionist, which will go some way to offset apparent past indifference. This volume contains an early cross-section.

Imperialism, we are warned, is a word to be used with extreme caution. It is as likely to confuse as clarify, lacks an agreed meaning, and is open to many interpretations.[3] By way of a general definition, we will follow Nadel and Curtis: 'the extension of sovereignty or control, whether direct or indirect, political or economic, by one government, nation, or society over another together with the ideas justifying or opposing this process'.[4] This definition is arguably the clearest and most succinct available. However, it is doubtful whether it subsumes the variety of meanings, sometimes peripheral rather than central, that the contributors to this set of essays attribute to the term. For example, Nadel and Curtis provide no scope in their definition for the consideration of imperialism as a cultural 'umbilical cord', not so much stimulating impulses of domination as acting as a means of unification within a dominion, as Sherington and Conellan describe in Chapter 7. This fact should not necessarily be a source of despair, irritation or criticism. Imperialism was an extraordinarily complex phenomenon. Only by acknowledging the multiple meanings attached to it, can a full appreciation of its role in British and overseas affairs — and education — be obtained.

We will travel further with Nadel and Perry and argue that, for our purposes as for theirs, whether imperialism was a form of widespread benevolence or an unmitigated evil is beside the point. 'Such judgements,' as they remark, 'belong to individual conscience.'[5] In the following pages, imperialism in its relationship to socialisation is treated as a fact requiring explanation rather than a phenomenon inviting censure or support.[6] Our purpose is neither excoriation nor eulogy. Our task is exegesis not polemics. The odd thing is that while the British empire is emphatically, in the words of A. P. Thornton, 'at one with Nineveh and Tyre', it is also true, as he adds, that 'among academics, the reading public and television viewers it now enjoys a popularity it never had the luck to draw upon while it lived'.[7] This has been the case for some time, and fuller inquiries into imperial education might have been attempted sooner.

It has been pointed out that historians of ideas in Victorian England have tended to ignore education.[8] We must add that historians of British imperialism in their numerous and frequently renowned studies, and with their careful attention to the complex interrelationship between social institutions, seem to have had little interest in education *per se* and, more puzzling perhaps, in its relationship to the politics, economics, religion and culture (high and 'low') of an imperial past. On occasion, this lack of interest is inexplicable. By way of illustration, in *Studies in Mid-Victorian Imperialism*, first published in 1924 (and re-issued in 1968), C. A. Bodelsen stated modestly that his intention was to attempt to describe the emergence and growth of an imperial spirit in England as reflected in contemporary literature, in public debate and in the press.[9] His effort was all the more modest for his neglect of the literature on the upper-middle-class educational system and its role in this revolution. It was left to E. C. Mack, who ranged far beyond the theme of imperialism, in his splendid two-volume work *Public Schools and British Opinion* fourteen years later, to make good Bedelsen's omission.[10] Time has made little difference to such neglect. The recent collection of essays in C. C. Eldridge's *British Imperialism in the Nineteenth Century* (1984), for example, chosen to provide 'a stimulating introduction to the study of certain aspects of British expansion in the nineteenth century',[11] excludes education as a subject in its own right and makes sparse reference to it.[12] The subject of British expansion, Eldridge tells us, 'has lost none of the vitality Sir John Seeley first breathed into his lectures on *The Expansion of England* one hundred years ago',[13] but he was unable to find space for a consideration of the vigour of educationalists in their dissemination of British Christian culture or of indigenous populations in accepting, adapting or opposing these efforts. And some on both sides were mightily energetic.[14] In between times, A. P. Thornton in *The Imperial Idea and its Enemies: A Study in British Power* (1955), which set out *inter alia* 'to account for those changes in attitude toward the British Empire which had been adopted by ... public opinion in general during the past hundred years', considered that school history texts current in 1890 or in 1920 were as valuable in this exercise as the more scholarly historical theses,[15] yet it is our loss he wrote little about text-books, classrooms or schooling in Britain and its empire and their role in shaping imperial and anti-imperial attitudes, except for standard reflections on the English public-school system. And on this subject, as we shall discuss in due course, he might usefully have gone beyond orthodoxy. It would be tedious to heap example upon example of the tendency of many historians to treat education in general histories of imperialism as of little or no consequence, but those interested in taking the matter further, and discovering how far preoccupation with other themes can go, will read with interest Robert A. Huttenbach's *The British Imperial Experience* (1966) and *A Concept of Empire* (1967) edited by George Bennet. A last lament for lost perspectives and a variation on the theme of neglect: in *The Victorian Empire: A Pictorial History 1837–1901* (1970), Dennis Judd sought 'to capture the substance of a vanished epoch'[16] without a single illustration of imperial education proselytisers at home or abroad, of those influential cradles, crèches and foster homes of imperial Britain — the preparatory and public schools, of plain and basic straw-roofed 'Winchesters' in Africa or ornate and elegant domed 'Etons' in India, of sun-baked scholastic playing fields on the South African veld or in the Australian suburbs, of elementary school festivities on Empire Day in Battersea or Camden Town: odd omissions: rich opportunities for evocation missed: indifference compounded.[17]

Imperialism in its relationship to education, it should be noted, has not fared much better at the hands of educational historians. Many distinguished contributors frequently seem to posture as 'little Englanders'.[18] Most general histories of British (and English) education can be read without any realisation of the fact that Britain was an imperial power in the eighteenth, nineteenth and twentieth centuries. Possibly this reflects the influence of the author's 'intellectually formative years' or their liberal persuasions. Perhaps they wished to see imperialism as 'essentially an irrelevance to domestic British history'.[19] Certainly they write as if it were. In A. C. Barnard's *A History of English Education from 1760* (2nd edition, 1961), imperialism fails to appear either as a concept in the text or as a term in the index. J. A. Adamson's *English Education 1798–1902* (1930) devotes attention to internationalism but not imperialism. S.J. Curtis, in his *History of Education in Great Britain* (7th edition, 1967), finds space for reference to the Imperial College of Science and Technology but not for the subject of colonialism. The same is true of H. C. Dent, *1870–1970: A Century of Growth in English Education* (1970); S. J. Curtis and M. E. A. Boultwood, *An Introductory History of English Education Since 1800* (1970 edition), and Keith Evans, *The Development and Structure of the English Education System* (1975). W. H. G. Armytage, in his *Four Hundred Years of English Education* (2nd edition, 1970), discusses religious missions in the Old Kent Road and Camberwell[20] but not the numerous British missionary societies and their imperial educational enterprises. He also briefly considers H. B. Gray's *Public Schools and Empire* (1913) and his *Eclipse or Empire* (1916) co-authored with Samuel Turner, but only to point to the fact of low academic standards in the public schools and not to reflect directly on Gray's anxiety that the public-school system was failing to produce suitable products able to ensure the development, maintenance and survival of the British Empire, or on the schools' assumed responsibilities in this matter.[21] In British journals devoted wholly or in part to the history of education, in most cases there is surprisingly little on empire and education. Only the *Journal of Educational Administration and History* has consistently published articles on the subject.[22]

In sum, given, as Ronald Hyam reminds us, that to the Victorians ' ... the spread of education was credited with almost miraculous powers to create a prosperous and enlightened community',[23] and that imperialists of the stamp of Raffles in Singapore and Bentinck in India considered it the pre-eminent metropolitan donation to these possessions, its role in the imperial scheme of things would seem to have received less attention than it merits from British general imperial and educational historians. Detailed studies of regions and institutions exist of course, but much work has not been integrated into imperial overviews. Part of the problem, of course, has been that historians of all persuasions have paid too little attention to socialisation, as opposed to social change.[24] Certainly, few academic stormtroopers have launched a major assault, and only very few sharp-shooters have mounted a vanguard in analytical attacks on socialisation, education and imperialism.

Different paradigms have concerned them, and of course there have been many to arouse their concern. From their pens, in many instances, have come works of distinction which have filled large gaps in our knowledge and become definitive statements on imperial or educational issues. With their work ably done, to utilise a common metaphor, it is surely now time to turn to barer patches on the imperial canvas, still sizeable and still significant, and begin to fill them in.

II

At the most general level, socialisation may be considered to be the total process by which the culture of a community, or section of a community, is passed on from one generation and assimilated, in whole or part, by the next. Our concern is political socialisation which, to shorten the rather cumbersome definition in the *International Encyclopedia of the Social Sciences*, may be considered as tuition, formal and informal, planned and unplanned, explicit and implicit, involved in the adoption of appropriate political perceptions, the acquisition of associated cultural beliefs and the learning of related social attitudes.[25]

Clearly, such instruction embraces both formal and informal education. We concentrate essentially on the ideologies, processes and practices of formal education that shaped and were shaped by imperial values, attitudes and behaviour in Britain and its empire: 'When a culture builds the content and regulations of its schools and universities,' observes Martin Kaplan, 'it institutionalizes and thereby legitimizes a particular myth or vision of itself.'[26] This volume is concerned with myths and visions of imperialism, and deals *inter alia* with the nature and extent of ethnocentric attitudes, declared and undeclared, in this building process, with the use of formal education as a means of disseminating and reinforcing imperial images, with the changing concept of imperialism as reflected in the ideological emphases of period educational literature, with the different perceptions of imperialism in the various social and ethnic strata of metropolitan and overseas communities and their respective educational systems, with the assimilation, adaptation and rejection (partial if not complete) of metropolitan educational models and with the vexed issue of formal imperial education as enlightenment, hegemony and control.

It is also concerned, therefore, with certainties, confidence and success but also with doubts, inadequacies and failures, with ambiguities, compromises and adjustments and with the unexpected and the unanticipated. Policies, of course, are not always closely argued and clearly defined; processes, of course, are not always well-constructed and ends are seldomly wholly achieved. It should be added that we do not intend, if we can help it, to commit the sin of naïve or deliberate reductionism and define education exclusively in terms of formal construction. The wider aspects of education, which we firmly include under the heading 'socialisation', will receive particular consideration in a forthcoming volume on *socialisation and imperialism*, to be published in due course.[27] We endorse Bernard Barlyn: the history of education should embrace 'the entire process by which a culture transmits itself across the generations'.[28]

One fact emerges with great force from this set of essays — the close and continuing association between British imperialism and the public-school system.[29] It was direct and substantial and this is reflected in several contributions.[30] Dominion and colony took ethos, trappings and organisation; freemasonry recruited its pupils and former pupils and established a privileged imperial network of 'old boys' within a wider network of privileged 'old boys'; preparatory schools across Britain and the empire adopted the instruments and techniques of imperial training, reinforcing an upper-middle-class obsession with games and games fields; the Colonial College in Suffolk offered its public school clientèle a restricted and favoured practical training for colonial success in stock-rearing and agriculture, while simultaneously attempting to ensure that the emotional link between schools and empire was strengthened and made more durable in the process. This 'special relationship' could scarcely have escaped the notice of historians in the former empire interested in education and they have summed up its significance particularly well. In his *History of St Andrew's College, Grahamstown*, R. F. Currey wrote succinctly and correctly that the public-school movement 'grew to be a flood; and it mightily affected the history of the British Commonwealth', adding shrewdly of the 1950s: 'it is still flowing'.[31] In *Growing up British in British Columbia: Boys in Private Schools*, Jean Barman was more specific in her observations and just as ambitious in her conclusions: ' ... given the role played by little more than half a hundred boys' schools in one isolated corner of Empire, then that of perhaps three thousand institutions of this kind across the Empire — and even beyond — may well have been critical to the maintenance of British influence in these societies, both before and after the demise of formal political authority'.[32]

In the course of time, unfounded assertions regarding the relationship have arisen. Curious judgements have been made. Lasting mythologies have been created. In *Victorian Tragedy*, Esmé Wingfield Stratford was of the view that in the late nineteenth century:

The barbaric scale of values, that exalts physical prowess above the truth, passed from the fathers to the sons, and the aim of public school discipline was more and more diverted from the production of scholars to that of sportsmen and athletes ... The strength of the public school system lay in the training it provided for the younger sons of the aristocracy ... it was of inestimable value in the work of empire building that was now proceeding apace. The squire's son easily adapted himself to the open air life of the colonies.[33]

This ringing assertion has produced later echoes.[34] There is a great deal of romantic nonsense in this passage. When was the public-school system ever devoted to the production of scholars? How many younger sons of the aristocracy and squirearchy would it have taken to fill the many public schools of late Victorian England? And assertions about the role of the younger sons of the landed gentry in the administration of empire have been called into question in the case of at least one important possession.[35] Furthermore, as many of the time were well aware by the end of Victoria's reign, the open-air life of the colonies could prove hard-going for the sons of all backgrounds, younger or otherwise, from the public schools. The anxieties of H. B. Gray regarding the inadequate preparation of public schoolboys for imperial careers have been referred to earlier. Charles Bryce, in *Macmillan's Magazine* in 1905, wrote on the subject:

> The Bishop of Rochester has recently declared that one of the saddest things to be seen in Australia is the number of well-educated men, sons of the clergy and professional men, not a few of them of high birth and connection, in a state of destitution. And this is not due to moral failure, but because their education has never taught them to look the realities of life in the face, to think out what they are going to do, to feel the necessity of fitting themselves for the work of the world. In almost every part of our empire public schoolboys and university men may also be found in the same perilous condition.[36]

Patrick Dunae in *Gentlemen Emigrants* has recently shown how right Bryce was to be concerned.[37]

After reviewing the myths and slogans of traditional imperial historiography, Hyam and Martin concluded, 'much remains untouched and the business of demolition even on a small scale is protracted'.[38] In fact, the *reconstruction* of principles and practices as well as the demolition of myths and slogans is required. The sparse references to education in the general histories of imperialism discussed above concentrate for the most part on the leadership training that the public schools provided for imperial administrators, soldiers and missionaries. Bernard Porter offers a good example: 'the public schools, too, were geared to the empire's needs. Many of the ideals they aimed at, the qualities they worked to instill in their words — notions of service, feelings of superiority, habits of authority — were derived from, and consequently depended upon, the existence of empire: of colonial subjects to serve, feel superior to and exert authority over.' He concluded: 'To this extent the upper and middle classes and the schools which nurtured them, had a vested interest in empire.'[39] This narrow focus on preparation for the exercise of executive authority is typical. It has become a cliché of the general text-books of imperialism.[40] It is time to remind ourselves that the empire was served by technicians, technologists and scientists of all kinds. Many were educated in the public schools. Their specialist skills in the maintenance of the infrastructure of empire deserves recognition and requires examination. There were also training establishments for young, prospective imperialists, wholly overlooked by Porter and others. Far removed in tradition and practice from the English public schools, however hard they tried to emulate them, Scotland's 'science schools', for example, such as Allan Glen's in Glasgow, provided the empire with a continuous stream of scientists, technologists and technicians throughout the late nineteenth and early twentieth centuries — engineers, chemists, doctors, agricultural advisers and the like. This interesting and not insignificant aspect of imperial education still awaits its recorder.[41] Again, no one, as yet, has bothered to examine the role of the grammar school in winning middle-class allegiance to the cause of imperialism or catalogued the grammar-school imperialists in the empire and their various contributions. In the matter of schools and empire, A. J. P, Taylor's more general observation has acute local relevance. There has been too much of a tendency to concentrate on the history of the English upper classes.[42]

At the same time, it must be recognised that the history of upper-class education and imperialism has scarcely been exhausted. The file cannot yet be closed. Before we leave the public-school system and its influence on empire and vice versa,[43] we might note further gaps in our knowledge. It is seldom recognised that we know extraordinarily little about attitudes to imperialism within actual public schools, and even less about variations in emphasis between them, although we talk and write as if we knew so much. As I have written elsewhere:

> Intensive, comprehensive and comparative studies of general attitudes to imperialism within the schools are required; to locate the disseminators and the responses to their dissemination, to establish the nature and extent of

[8]

dissent, to discover the ritualistic and symbolic instruments of persuasion, to examine the relationship between the various mechanisms of propaganda and their relative efficacy, to trace the nature of the association between public school and state school in the promulgation of imperial enthusiasm, and to discern the changing nature of school attitudes to imperialism as the twentieth century progressed.[44]

Then again, we have no comparative studies of the nature, role and significance of the public-school system as it has evolved in Africa, Australia, Canada, India, New Zealand, South Africa and elsewhere, nor have we any comparative studies of the ideological and curricular emphases and content of the imperial public schools of Anglican, Catholic and Dissenter. In fact, we have remarkably little on the curriculum of the imperial public school – or any other type of school for that matter.[45] And the question might usefully be asked as to the long-term, post-colonial effect of that evangelical tradition given over to the education of Africans, Asians and others, as one writer has euphoniously put it, 'in English modelled public schools where [indigenous] sin could be exorcized by Christianity, caning and compulsory games'.[46]

There are many questions regarding imperialism and education still to be answered. Some were asked by Stafford Kay and Bradley Nystrom in the restricted context of imperialism in Africa in 1971.[47] They are relevant to the wider imperial scene. Few British academics appear to have addressed them in the interim. Kay and Nystrom expressed dissatisfaction with much comment on African colonialism[48] and education: complex issues had been simplified, the views of the colonised had been insufficiently considered, the nationalist 'fault-finding' or 'deprecatory' schools of Fanon and others had proved 'indiscriminating and unilluminating'. A more adequate examination of adjustment, adaptation and initiative on the part of native peoples – 'neither pawns nor queens in the imperial drama; their moves established lines along which colonial education developed',[49] fuller scrutiny of evolving and differing missionary attitudes,[50] investigation of the influence of non-official colonialist – settler, trader and plantation owner – on official educational policy, more searching studies of period research into native ability and the labelling consequences of such terms as 'pre-logical societies', 'cultural stages' and 'African intelligence',[51] inquiries into the influence of one imperial power upon another, are among their requests, still pertinent fifteen years on.[52]

And what of the relationship between higher education and imperialism in Britain and overseas? There is, of course, Richard Symond's recent *Oxford and Empire* (1986), but what of Cambridge, London and the Scottish universities? What has been the role of the university in promoting nationalism and imperialism in dominion and colony?[53] Then again, we lack sufficient studies of what Rahman has called 'academic colonialism' in a post-colonial age[54] — the practice of teaching former colonial children and their descendants about metropolitan climate, environment, culture, literature and history, and the effect that this has had on Third-World cultures, their educational development and national self-image.[55] And we have very little on the education of girls in colonial or post-colonial eras. Phillip Altback has added further thoughts to those of Rahman on the subject of neo-colonialism and education and its relevance to imperialism, and requests greater concentration on the reactions of the colonised in preference to the intentions of the colonialist — shades of Kay and Nystrom.[56] Brian Simon's words are apposite here: a history of education written exclusively from a European standpoint comprises 'a deficient account of the world of yesterday'.[57]

Finally, on the issue of research shortfall, Terence Ranger has pointed out one further route to future lode-bearing veins. The historian of Africa, he observes, can be in no doubt of the interrelationship of educational and political developments and their significance. The school, he argues, is central to the study of African nationalism. In so far as the recent politics of Africa may be viewed in terms of the allocation of resources, processes determining the number of schools and their development are of central importance, and in so far as leadership patterns[58] merit attention, information about leaders' schools and their ideological influence are of considerable value. His remarks too have a wider imperial relevance. His conclusion that political historians are paying more and more attention to educational history is welcome.[59] It makes sense. We shall return to this point.

III

The images of imperialism in this book are purposefully various: a political ambition at one moment moral and desirable, at another immoral and contemptible; an alien cultural imposition to be rejected and replaced at the earliest opportunity; an instrument of siren-like propaganda leading youth persuasively to the holocaust of the Great War; a means of controlling nascent proletarian consciousness through the use of carefully-chosen and evocative national rituals and symbols; an educational rationale for an upper-middle-class games addiction; an occupational sustenance for a self-selected mafia of the privileged; a crucible melting down ethnic differences and boiling away 'racial' hostilities; a source of outdoor relief for less than bright public-school boys keen to assimilate patriotism and practical husbandry at one and the same time; a perspective, together with gender expectations, determining the parameters of educational provision for black girls and, finally, a synonym not so much for single-minded exploitation as confused philanthropy.

Diversity of imagery, national background and professional discipline give unusual breadth to these essays. Richard Aldrich discusses the development of history as an academic discipline in British education over the last hundred years and the place of imperial history within it, from Seeley, *The Expansion of England* (1883) to Edgington, *The Role of History in Multi-Cultural Education* (1982). He traces the stages of a collective historical consciousness enveloping the concept of imperialism and plots the progress of a national process of relatively unassertive socialisation achieved through history in the curriculum of primary, secondary and higher education: a progress, he argues, loosely controlled 'by centrally prescribed syllabuses, text books and teaching methods', allowing both opposition and indifference as well as endorsement and enthusiasm and, in the 1980s as a consequence of a dramatic change of national role, resulting in radical historians teaching a radical imperial history. Narrow conviction and patriotic assertiveness have now quite disappeared, he tells us, and modern teaching on imperialism draws on the views of both ruled and ruler and covers both pre- and post-colonial periods.

Pamela Horn, for her part, is concerned with the assured propagandists of imperialism in the period before the Great War and their certainties and influence on elementary schooling. Their objective, she explains, was to instil a patriotism and physical fitness which would enable the elementary pupil to sustain Britain's empire. From the late 1870s, through curriculum and organisation, these patriots set about developing the imperial virtues of diligence, obedience, self-denial, endurance and pluck in the children of the working classes. Albeit less thorough and intensive than European rivals such as France, this effort at proselytism, Horn claims, was endorsed at every level from government department to school classroom. Education officials, schoolteachers, private citizens, publishers and philanthropic organisations formed a doctrinal alliance aimed at creating, in Springhall's expression, a 'Holy Trinity' of citizenship, empire and patriotism. Flags, maps, dances, songs and celebrations such as Empire Day were the powerful and symbolic means by which messages of loyalty and duty were pressed home. A happy by-product was the provision of medical care and school meals for needy children; a less sanguine outcome, suggests Horn, was the jingoistic euphoria of Kitchener's recruits to the Great War.

Ireland was England's first colony. John Coolahan records English efforts to promote an imperial culture 'and to reduce the cultural distinctiveness between Irish and English and its failure to meet with any significant level of success'.[60] Schools were the main location of this political socialisation. An optimistic belief in the power of the school to foster allegiance to the Crown and counteract the teaching of nationalists, argues Coolahan, produced a highly-organised scheme to create a common loyalty and cultural identity. From 1831, the Board of Commissioners for National Education was responsible for the schooling of children of all denominations. By 1870 it was 'by far the more prominent form of schooling'. Its purpose was deracination. To achieve this, attempts were made to control entry to teaching, courses of study and the content of textbooks. Irish school readers, for example, were imperialist, racist and 'devoid of material dealing with Ireland and its heritage, landscape and traditions'. Such efforts at control proved counter-productive, stimulating resentment and alienation. In the case of Ireland, imperial education was ineffective. Policies, strategies and tactics failed. The Irish independence movement was the first to break the link in the chain of empire. The Irish Free State in turn attempted to indoctrinate its young with equal force 'but in the reverse direction'. As Coolahan remarks, 'the wheel had come full circle'.

If Ireland proved intractable, Newfoundland was amenable. The Newfoundland School Society, discussed by Phillip McCann, was established in 1823. It had a bluntly imperial purpose: to ensure that the children of the island understood and appreciated 'their connection with and interest in the moral as well as national greatness of their mother country'.[61] The Society, McCann points out, was a minor branch of the world-wide protestant missionary enterprise and represented 'the mercantile view of Christianity' — bible and contract in close conjunction. Newfoundland experienced a cultural imperialism every bit as forceful and organised as that witnessed in Ireland. At about the same time, with far greater success, the Society transplanted 'England's laws, England's language, England's children and England's church' and, in the process, trampled down indigenous culture and custom. It created a community imbued with imperial patriotism and sober religiosity. Newfoundland is an interesting case study to set against Ireland.

New Zealand, says John Openshaw, saw the attempted inculcation of 'mass loyalty and individual conformity' in the 1920s. The perceived need for strong, unquestioning imperial patriotism following the war shaped both the ideology and practice of primary education. Curriculum and staff had the task of stimulating strong patriotic emotion. It was a time of anxiety. Fear of Asian aggression produced strategic insecurity. Schools' doors were open to the Navy League but closed to the League of Nations. Internal factors, too, played their part in an upsurge of chauvinism. The forceful patriotism of the period, suggests Openshaw, was a form of social control creating loyal and co-operative workers antagonistic to militant socialism, and wedded to the work ethic in a time of economic recession. At one level, therefore, schools had a clear-cut role in promoting national and imperial unity; at another they became locations for instilling commitment to capitalism. Conservative politicians and educationalists used argument, symbol and ritual remorselessly as emotional bulwarks behind which they defended imperial association on the one hand, and resisted rising proletarian consciousness on the other. As in Ireland, in the long run, the efforts of the establishment were far from successful. Values, strongly asserted, suggests Openshaw, created resistance and rejection. By the thirties 'imperial patriotism' had given way to internationalism, despite the sharpening economic recession. Progressivism grew in the ascendant. A new middle-class generation with international sympathies, charged by conservative intolerance, came to possess the administrative and bureaucratic infrastructure of education.

Sharp ideological conflict has scarcely been a feature of schools for the very young of the English upper-middle classes. The private preparatory system has been a 'rest and recuperation' area for the privileged, well behind the lines of English educational battlefields. It was, Donald Leinster-Mackay informs us, essentially a mid- and late-Victorian manifestation. Its *raison d'être* was to be found largely in the expanded public school system of the second half of the nineteenth century. As it grew, so the 'prepatory schools' grew, serving the public schools as 'feeders'. Together, preparatory and public school formed an integrated and closed system for the education of England's upper-middle classes. The establishment and consolidation of the system coincided with the gradual awareness of the empire and its occupational possibilities. Both types of school became places for imperial training. Both proved effective in preparing the sons of England's privileged classes for imperial careers, and in developing and reinforcing their commitment to imperialism. Both used the games field for the inculcation of necessary imperial qualities — courage, endurance and loyalty. Both taught with equal conviction and success 'the housemaster's credo of King and country'.[62]

The clash between Protestant and Catholic values occur in the essays of Coolahan, McCann and Sherington and Conellan. In Ireland, Catholic tradition eventually gained the upper hand; in other parts of the empire it was a different story. In nineteenth-century Australia, Geoffrey Sherington and Mark Conellan tell us, those with origins in Catholic

Ireland and Protestant England (or Scotland) had very different reactions to the imperial connection. Nowhere was this difference more clearly visible than in the formal education system. In the late nineteenth century, following the withdrawal of state aid for denominational schools, the English public school became the inspiration for Australian Protestants. Australian Catholics, however, imbued with a deep distrust of British imperialism and with a strong allegiance to Irish tradition, held themselves aloof initially from the influence of the 'Anglo-Saxon' public school. Yet, as with the Catholics in England,[63] they could not in the long term wholly ignore pressure, from within and without, to conform to English Protestant principle and practice. Such action was a prerequisite of social acceptance. Sherington and Conellan provide two exemplars of the differing traditions – Sydney Church of England Grammar School and Saint Joseph's College, a Marist school in the same city. They see the Great War as the crucible in which historic differences of attitude to empire finally melted down into indistinguishable commitment. In 1914, loyalty to Australia and empire was symbolised by the imperial warrior. Saint Joseph's did not dissent. By the 1916 Easter Rising in Dublin, the college was asserting a 'new found Australian conservatism and its concomitant of imperial loyalty'.[64] It had overcome a long drawn-out crisis of identity only by embracing the certainties of the other side.

Deborah Gaitskell provides a valuable study of the education of black girls in South Africa from the period of missionary-controlled African education to the assumption of government control under the Afrikaner Nationalist's Bantu Education Act of 1953. She explores three issues: the ideology of the imperialist educator, the experience of their girl pupils and the attitudes and assumptions of officialdom. For the black African, the concept of imperialism came gradually to have less and less resonance, largely as a result of the steady adoption of power by the white South African. And, whatever the Christian imperative, both Missionary and Boer envisaged an education of limited opportunity and experience for the black African girl. Her range of possibilities was narrowly circumscribed. Gender expectations combined with imperial preconceptions to determine educational provision in the colony and later the dominion of South Africa.

As Paul Rich rightly observes, the contribution of public school freemasonry to the British Empire has largely been ignored. Yet public-school lodges at home and overseas were part of the empire's power structure. Rich asserts that the parallel growth of schools and masonry was partly the outcome of the new wealth of the enlarged middle classes of the late-nineteenth century. They could afford both school and lodge fees. There was advantage to be had in paying both. Masonic lodges followed the public-school imperialist into the empire from the earliest moments of British expansion. There were lodges at home for expatriates and lodges 'whenever public schools were founded'. Members comprised a closed circle, so secure in their privacy that, contrary to the universal masonic rule of no publicity, news was openly published in school magazines but never in national or regional newspapers or journals. Rich sees the role of masonry as reinforcing imperial rule and ambition: 'since imperialism sought order, public school free masonry was a helpmate in the rationalizing of imperial society, imposing its strict hierarchy and formality as another means of social control, and with its honours offering another means of reward.'[65] Such ritualistic fraternalism, argues Rich, strengthened the self-confidence with which British administrators exerted cultural domination. This interesting and novel assertion, strongly made, will surely arouse interest and stimulate more extended inquiry in the search for verification.

Patrick Dunae describes a unique phenomenon – an institution for turning 'classically educated schoolboys into hardy, independent colonialists'. Colonial College, Hollesley Bay, Suffolk taught public schoolboys the basic skills of the settler's life. But it was far more than an agricultural or horticultural college. Depository of colonial lore, crammed with artifacts and images of colonial life, heavy with imperial symbolism, it was pledged to heighten the sense of empire among its students, adding the ploughshare to the English gentleman's sword of imperial domination. Robert Johnson, its founder, was an ideologue who reinforced the bond between public school and empire and a visionary who worked for Anglo-Saxon unity throughout the world. His students were acolytes trained to serve his cause.

Clive Whitehead calls into question the validity of widely-accepted canons of belief and interpretation. The Orwellian view that British imperialism was 'something clamped down, in *saecula saeculorum* upon the will of prostrate peoples'[66] exasperates him. His is a boldly revisionist chapter. He calls for a more sophisticated assessment of the colonial educational experience than simply to characterise it as a deliberate policy designed to perpetuate European economic and political control, and offers 'an alternative and hopefully more objective interpretation of British colonial education policy'.[67] He is out of sympathy with monocausal left-wing critics of colonial schooling such as Illich, Freire and Moumouni, and favours the multicausal approach of David Fieldhouse. A worthwhile appraisal of British imperial educational policy, he argues forcefully, has to be based on a comprehensive analysis of the multifarious motives for imperial expansion and the complex nature and purpose of colonial rule. This demand leads him to the conclusion that 'in the interwar years', which he selects for inspection, 'British colonial administrators were more the victims of circumstances largely beyond their control than architects of any deliberate strategy of cultural imperialism.'[68] British colonial rule, and colonial rule in general, he suggests, was not planned exploitation but, as Fieldhouse describes it, a complex improvisation often characterised by confused goals arising out of benevolent intentions.

IV

Early in *Education as Cultural Imperialism*, Martin Carnoy wrote uncontentiously: 'In most societies schooling is an important institution for transmitting knowledge and culture from generation to generation and for developing human traits that contribute to economic output, social stability and the production of new knowledge.'[69] Importance is granted to social institutions, he continued, only in so far as they are legitimate, and the legitimisation of formal Western-type schooling in the Third World stems from its perceived role of agent of 'individual and societal liberation'. He was setting up a straw man. He knocked him down with these short, sharp, verbal blows: ' ... this explanation is misleading ... educators, social scientists and historians have misinterpreted the role of western schooling in the Third World and in the industrialized countries themselves ... far from acting as liberator, western formal education came to most countries as part of imperialist domination'.[70] This is now a common thesis among commentators on the Third World, and while it contains much truth, it is not the whole truth. It constitutes a crude syllogism: domination is bad; imperialism is domination; imperialism is bad. As an explanation of imperial educational motive, as Whitehead protests, it is not unlike the Marxist view of imperialism as capitalism — far too simple.[71] To recast a remark of Eldridge on Hobson and Lenin in an educational mould: the all-embracing nature of Carnoy's argument concerning the primacy of imperial education is by no means satisfactory.[72] It smacks too much of what has been called 'a uni-dimensional and uni-directional form of history'.[73] The rhetoric of wholesale condemnation, born of hobby-horses tethered to hostility, once fashionable, is passing out of fashion. Recognition of subtleties, complications and ambiguities are no longer seen as a failure of liberal nerve but as an attempt at serious analysis.[74] W. Ross Johnson is right: 'It is time to evaluate the good along with the bad: it is time to sweep away the many prejudices both for and against British colonialism which have bedevilled the topic for many years.'[75] If an account is to be kept, the ledger should include credits and debits. Fuller and fresh reflection is required regarding the motives of the British educational imperialist. Altruism as well as exploitation had a part to play in the westernisation

of colonial youth. It was not all calloused conscience. It was not simply
naked social Darwinism of the William Graham Sumner variety. Some
imperialists (if not the proverbial emperor) wore clothing, to quote
Edmund Burke, 'furnished from the wardrobe of a moral imagination'.[76]
And colonial educators were sometimes too confused to be as strong-
minded as Carnoy requires. To some extent, and in some cases no doubt,
this reflected the fundamental ambivalence of reasonable men with
unreasonable responsibilities.

The point is this. There is no longer, if there ever was, as Harold Silver
has reminded us, in history or elsewhere, 'a monolithic conservatism, or
Marxism or liberalism'.[77] With a cutting aphorism, he went on, 'Escape into
historical certainty is not difficult but it is increasingly difficult to justify.'[78]
And in a further passage worth recording in full, he asserted,

> The history of education is in fact multiple histories, because education is
> itself no simple and homogeneous concept or category, and because its
> history can be explored in relation to almost endless variables. Whether
> education is conceived as itself an indefinite cluster of experiences or as a
> more narrowly definable process related to a variety of other processes, it
> has no meaning when presented in isolated and discretely institutional
> terms.[79]

It is hoped that this volume will illustrate the complexity of the levels at
which the history of imperial education needs to be written. To quote
Silver again (it could scarcely be put better): 'If it is about pioneers and their
reputations, it is also about ideas and movements. If it is about ideologies, it
is also about the … nature of popular expectations and attitudes. If it is about
policy on a grand scale, it is also about experience. If it is about theories, it is
also about the historian's own … interpretation.'[80] Such a comprehensive
approach raises both the issue of ways in which national experiences can
converge and diverge, and the question as to what extent it is possible and
desirable 'to write the history of education across frontiers' — not simply
political, it might be added, but also academic?[81] Should there be in
educational, historical studies a determined and progressive shift in
analytical emphasis from national to international, experiential,
institutional and structural relationships? Is there a future for a
'comparative social history of education'?[82] Of course this raises still further
and more difficult questions about present and past limitation of
perspective, about disciplinary and sub-disciplinary boundaries (and
sensible and amiable transgression) and about adequate methodologies: 'a
prerequiste of cross-cultural history across frontiers … has to be sustained
dialogue among [all types of] historians, not only about the cross-cultural

meaning and possibilities but also about cross-disciplinary experience'.[83] Too true. There is also the additional and critical prerequisite of the identification of significant foci. Silver offers 'accountability' as one, arguing that *inter alia* historians 'would find themselves exploring not just parallel and juxtaposed traditions or data, but also different perceptions of educational and political relationships'.[84] Another, he adds, might be the history of adolescence which would require a large vision and a many-sided approach including definitions of childhood, variety in patterns of authority, the role of youth movements, and many other complex phenomena.[85] A final concept which lends itself well to cross-cultural historical analysis, he suggests, is 'reform' — at three levels: (I) national patterns of legislative, executive and institutional change; (II) communities, agencies and processes of change and resistance to change, and (III) ideologies and the associated contrary and conflicting bases of interpretation.[86]

These arguments, in my view, are germane both to this and to future studies of imperialism and education. Such studies should be a common meeting ground for several kinds of historian as well as social scientists. After all, as Joan Simon has remarked, historians are learning to take account of society in depth, even if they still have to recognise 'that the educational process lies at the heart of things'. 'Indeed,' she says, 'it might be regarded as the core of history since social achievements are stored in an external, esoteric form and must be mastered by each generation'.[87] If she is correct, then education, with its close association to politics, economics, religion and social structure, lends itself especially well to a new and ambitious commonality of intellectual effort. The study of imperialism and education could provide an early focus, and this volume an early stimulus.

Notes

I should like to thank Sheldon Rothblatt most sincerely for his helpful comments, in the midst of many commitments, on an early draft of this Introduction, and also to thank John MacKenzie, in his more obligatory role of Series Editor, for his equally valuable remarks at a somewhat later stage in its evolution but at a similarly pressing time for him.

I am also very grateful to L. H. Gann for the interest he has taken in this project on socialisation, education and imperialism, and his kind invitation to the Hoover Institution on War, Revolution and Peace at Stanford University where this volume was discussed. Needless to say, I am wholly responsible of course for the final arguments, views and synopses in this Introduction.

1 John M. MacKenzie, *Imperialism and Popular Culture*, Manchester University Press, Manchester, 1986, p. 14
2 See especially Chapters II, III, IV, VII, X and XI.
3 C. C. Eldridge, *Victorian Imperialism*, Hodder and Stoughton, London, 1978, p. 3.

4 George H. Nadel and Perry Curtis, *Imperialism and Colonialism*, Macmillan, London, 1966, p. vii.
5 Nadel and Curtis, *Imperialism and Colonialism*, p. 25.
6 Nadel and Curtis, *Imperialism and Colonialism*, p. 25.
7 A. P. Thornton, *The Imperial Idea and its Enemies*, Macmillan, London (2nd Edition), 1958, p. vii.
8 Harold Silver, *Education as History*, Methuen, London, 1983, p. 23.
9 C. A. Bodelsen, *Studies in Mid-Victorian Imperialism*, Teritz, New York, 1968 (first published, 1924), p. 7.
10 E. C. Mack, *Public Schools and British Opinion, 1780–1860*, Methuen, 1938, and *Public Schools and British Opinion Since 1860*, Columbia University Press, New York, 1941.
11 C. C. Eldridge (ed.), *British Imperialism in the Nineteenth Century*, Macmillan, London, 1984, p. 19.
12 Christine Bolt deals occasionally with education in her chapter on 'Race and the Victorians'.
13 Eldridge, *British Imperialism in the Nineteenth Century*, p. 19.
14 See for example, J. A. Mangan, *The Games Ethic and Imperialism: Aspects of the Diffusion of an Ideal*, and T. O. Ranger, 'African attempts to control education in East and Central Africa, 1900–1939', *Past and Present*, No. 32, 1965, pp. 57–85.
15 Thornton, *The Imperial Idea and its Enemies*, p. XXV.
16 Dennis Judd, *The Victorian Empire: A Pictorial History, 1837–1901*, Praeger, New York, 1970, Preface.
17 Jan Morris also completely ignores education in her pictorial study, *Spectacle of Empire*, Faber and Faber, London, 1982.
18 Brian Simon, however, notes the importance of colonialism to research in the history of education. See Brian Simon, 'Research in the history of education', in W. Taylor (ed.), *Research Perspectives in Education*, APS Publications Inc, New York, 1973, p. 123.
19 See MacKenzie, *Imperialism and Popular Culture*, p. 2.
20 W. H. G. Armytage, *Four Hundred Years of English Education*, Cambridge University Press, 1970 (2nd edition), pp. 191–2.
21 Armytage, *Four Hundred Years of English Education*, p. 231.
22 *The Comparative Education Review*, a journal published in the United States, has interesting material on the history of imperialism and education from time to time. See, for example, the special issue entitled 'Colonialism and education', Vol. XV, No. 2, June 1971.
23 Ronald Hyam, *Britain's Imperial Century, 1815–1914. A Study of Empire and Expansion*, Batsford, London, 1976, p. 57.
24 Simon, 'Research in the history of education', p. 138.
25 Fred I. Greenstein, 'Political socialization', *International Encyclopedia of the Social Services*, Macmillan and the Press, New York, 1968, p. 551.
26 Martin Kaplan, 'The most important questions', *Oxford Educational Review*, Vol. 3, No. 1, 1977, p. 90.
27 This will be published by Manchester University Press and will contain contributions from Allen Warren, Anne Bloomfield, Robert Berard, Tony Stockwell, Robert Cowan, Krishna Kumar, Gerald Studdert-Kennedy, Alan McClelland, T. V. Sathyamurthy, Patricia Rooke, Janice N. Brownfoot and John Barrington.
28 Quoted in Simon, 'Research in the history of education'. p. 138.

29 For a discussion of this relationship, see Mangan, *The Games Ethic and Imperialism* and L. H. Gann and Peter Duignan, *The Rulers of British Africa 1870–1914*, Stamford, Stamford University Press, 1978.

30 See Chapters III, VII, IX and X.

31 R. F. Currey, *The History of St Andrew's College, Grahamstown*, Grahamstown, 1955, p. 56.

32 Jean Barman, *Growing Up British in British Columbia: Boys in Private Schools*, University of British Columbia Press, 1984, p. 173.

33 Esmé Wingfield Stratford, *Victorian Tragedy*, RKP, London, 1930, p. 262.

34 R. O. Collins, 'The Sudan political service: A portrait of the imperialists', *African Affairs*, Vol. 71, No. 284, July 1971, *passim*.

35 See Mangan, *The Games Ethic and Imperialism*.

36 Charles Bryce, 'Public schools and empire', *Macmillan's Magazine*, Vol. 1, No. 2, November 1905, pp. 73–4.

37 Patrick Dunae, *Gentlemen Emigrants: From the British Public Schools to the Canadian Frontier*, Douglas and McIntyre, Vancouver, 1981.

38 Ronald Hyam and Ged Martin, *Reappraisals in British Imperial History*, Macmillan, London, 1975, p. 4.

39 Bernard Porter, *The Lion's Share: A Short History of British Imperialism 1850–1983*, Longman, London, 1975, pp. 199–200.

40 See A. P. Thornton, *For the File on Empire*, Macmillan, London, 1968, pp. 17ff, Thornton, *The Imperial Idea and its Enemies*, pp. 89–96, Hyam, *Britain's Imperial Century*, pp. 160–1, and Eldridge, *British Imperialism in the Nineteenth Century*, p. 186.

41 For a brief and early discussion of Allan Glen's, its famous reforming headmaster, John Guthrie Kerr, and its science ethos, see J. A. Mangan, 'John Guthrie Kerr and the adaptation of an indigenous Scottish tradition', in *Pleasure, Profit and Proselytism: British Culture and Sport 1700–1914*, Cass, forthcoming. The Scottish 'science schools' represent a wholly-neglected tradition of *technical* imperial education.

42 A. J. P. Taylor, *A Personal History*, Athenaeum, New York, 1983, p. 23.

43 Edward Grierson sets us a nice conundrum: 'whether the empire produced the English public school or the public school the empire remains a moot point'. See his *The Death of the Imperial Dream: The British Commonwealth and Empire, 1775–1969*, Doubleday, New York, 1972, p. 232. Grierson deals relatively fully with imperial education but concentrates heavily on the public schools.

44 J. A. Mangan, 'The grit of our forefathers: invented traditions, propaganda and imperialism', in MacKenzie, *Imperialism and Popular Culture*, p. 136.

45 Two studies of interest are M. Kezim Bacus, 'The primary school curriculum in a colonial society', *Journal of Curriculum Studies*, Vol. 6, No. 1, May 1974, pp. 74–7 and Stephen J. Ball, Imperialism, social control and colonial curriculum in Africa', *Journal of Curriculum Studies*, Vol. 15, No. 3, pp. 237–63. An early paper of interest is V. Jones's 'The content of history syllabuses in Northern Nigeria in the early colonial period', *West African Journal of Education*, Vol. 9, October 1965, pp. 145–81.

46 Richard Symonds, *The British and Their Successors*, Faber and Faber, 1966, p. 238.

47 Stafford Kay and Bradley Nystrom, 'Education and colonialism in Africa: an annotated bibliography', *Comparative Education Review*, Vol. 25, No. 2, June 1971, pp. 240–59. This complements an earlier bibliography by Barbara Yates in *Comparative Education Review*, Vol. 3, No. 2, October 1964, pp. 215–28, and *Comparative Education Review*, Vol. 3, No. 2, December 1964, pp. 307–19. A bibliography restricted to Africa south of the Sahara is Howard Drake, *A*

Bibliography of African Education South of the Sahara, Aberdeen University Press, Aberdeen, Anthropological Museum Publication, No. 2, 1942, and one dealing with East Africa, but within a very limited time scale, is James J. Shields, *Selected Bibliography on Education in East Africa: 1941–1961*, Kampala, Makerere University, Kenya, 1962. Finally a more general bibliography dealing with the whole of Africa is Margaret Couch, *Education in Africa: A Select Bibliography*, Part 1: British and Former British Territories. London: Supplement 5 to Educatiion Libraries Bulletin, Institute of Education, University of London, 1962.

48 'Imperialism' and 'colonialism' are considered synonymous terms in this volume.

49 Kay and Nystrom, 'Education and colonialism in Africa: An annotated bibliography', p. 243.

50 Taking us, for example, beyond the pioneering study of Brian Holmes (ed,), *Educational Policy Mission Schools: Case-Studies from the British Empire*, Routledge and Kegan Paul, London, 1968. For a constructive review of the limitation of Holmes's approach, see A. C. F. Beale's review of his book in *British Journal of Educational Studies*, Vol. 26, No. 3, August 1968, pp. 353–4. There are, of course, excellent publications which deal *inter alia* with missionary work and education, especially Stephen Neill, *Colonialism and Christian Missions*, McGraw-Hill, New York, 1966, and Rowland Oliver, *The Missionary Factor in East Africa*, Longmans, London, 1965, and two studies of particular merit which discuss the topic in specific colonies: Sonia F. Graham, *Government and Mission Education in Northern Nigeria, 1900–1919*, Ibadan University Press, Ibadan, 1966, and M. A. Laing, *Missionaries and Education in Bengal, 1793–1837*, 1972.

51 To apply the ideas of Syed Hussein Alatas in his brilliant *The Myth of the Lazy Native*, Cass, London, 1977, to a wider imperial setting.

52 It would be interesting, for example, to update the comparative studies of W. B. Mumford in the 1930's and to extend the analysis of David B. Scanlon in *Traditions in African Education*, Columbia University Press, 1964.

53 Robert Koehl has a useful paper on the evolution of higher education in the colonial empire, 'The uses of the university past and present in Nigerian educational culture'. *Comparative Education Review*, Vol. 25, No. 22, June 1971, pp. 116–31. And, of course, we have been handsomely served by Sir Eric Ashby's renowned studies: *Universities: British, Indian, African: A Study in the Ecology of Higher Education*, Weidenfeld and Nicolson, London, 1966, and *African Universities and Western Tradition*, Oxford University Press, Oxford. 1964.

54 A. Rahman *et al, Imperialism in the Modern Phase*, Vol. 2, People's Publishing House, New Delhi, 1977, pp. iii ff.

55 An exploratory paper of interest on this topic is Kevin M. Lillis, "Africanizing the school literary curriculum in Kenya: A case-study in curricular dependency', *Journal of Curriculum Studies*, Vol. 18, No. 1, pp. 63–84.

56 Philip G. Altbach, 'Education and neocolonialism: a note', *Comparative Education Review*, Vol. 25, No. 2, June 1971, pp. 237–9.

57 Simon, 'Research in the history of education', p. 126.

58 Two studies of modern national leaders and their education, both concerned with Africa, are J. E. Goldthorpe, *An African Elite: Makerere College Students, 1922–1960*, Oxford University Press, Nairobi, 1965, and Lloyd A. Fallers (ed.), *The King's Men: Leadership and Status in Buganda on the Eve of Independence*, Oxford University Press, London, 1964.

59 T. O. Ranger, 'African attempts to control education in East and Central Africa, 1900– 1939', p. 57.

60 See Chapter IV, p.76.

61 See Chapter V, p. 94.
62 Gertrude Himmelfarb, *Victorian Minds*, Alfred A. Knopf, New York, 1968, p. 269.
63 For a discussion of Stonyhurst, the Jesuit English public school and its adjustment to English Protestant society, see J. A. Mangan, *Athleticism in the Victorian and Edwardian Public School*, Cambridge University Press, Cambridge, 1981, pp. 163–4.
64 See Chapter VII, p. 132.
65 See Chapter IX, p. 211.
66 George Orwell, *Shooting an Elephant and Other Essays*, Harcourt, Brace and Ward Inc, New York, p. 4. It is interesting to read in this context the spirited defence of the British imperialist ruler by J. U. J. Asiegbu, *Nigeria and its British Invaders, 1857--1920: A Thematic Documentary*, Nok Publishers International, New York, 1984. See especially the General Introduction, pp. xxix to xxx. Asiegbu compares the incorruptibility of the British period with the corruption of subsequent self-rule. I owe this reference to Professor L. H. Gann.
67 See Chapter XI, p. 211.
68 For a discussion of Carnoy's thesis, see Robert Koehl, 'Cultural imperialism as education: an indictment', and Martin Carnoy, 'Education as cultural imperialism: a reply', pp. 276–85 and pp. 286–9 respectively in *Comparative Education Review*, Vol. 19, No. 2, June 1975. Stephen Ball is of the view that Carnoy 'overestimates the economic, and concomitantly underestimates the political functions of the colonial school' and that his perspective involves 'a profound misreading of the objctives of British colonial education policy'. See note 44 for the reference to Ball's critique.
69 Martin Carnoy, *Education as Cultural Imperialism*, David MacKay, New York, 1974, p. 1.
70 Carnoy, *Education as Cultural Imperialism*, p. 3.
71 See Chapter XI, p. 211.
72 Eldridge, *Victorian Imperialism*, p. 131.
73 David B. Tyack in his Foreword to Silver, *Education in History*, p. xii.
74 See Himmelfarb's comment on intellectual fashions in *Victorian Minds*, p. 220.
75 W. Ross Johnson, *Great Britain, Great Empire: An Evaluation of the British Imperial Experience*, University of Queensland Press, St Lucia, 1981, p. 204.
76 For an article which strikingly underlines this point, see Kenneth Dike Nworah, 'The Liverpool "sect" and British West African policy, 1895–1915', *African Affairs*, Vol. 70, No. 281, October 1971, pp. 349–64.
77 Quoted In Himmelfarb, *Victorian Minds*, p. 27.
78 Silver, *Education as History*, p. 3.
79 *Ibid.*
80 *Ibid.* p. 4.
81 *Ibid.* p. 281.
82 *Ibid.*
83 *Ibid.* p. 284.
84 *Ibid.* p. 288.
85 *Ibid.*
86 For a full description of these three foci, see Silver, *Education as History*, pp. 288–91.
87 Joan Simon, 'The history of education in past and present', *Oxford Review of Education*, Vol. 3, No. 1, 1977, p. 71.

CHAPTER ONE

Imperialism in the study
and teaching of history

Richard Aldrich

This chapter is set in a British[1] context and is divided into three parts. The first section considers the relationship between imperialism and formal historical study in the 1880s and subsequent years; the second revisits that relationship in the 1980s, and finally, in the third, some brief conclusions are drawn. Regrettably, in a piece of this length which takes a broad historical span for the purpose of indicating both change and continuity over time, many key issues can only be indicated rather than developed.

I

The formal educational system of a society, particularly as expressed in its formal curriculum, represents a selection from the activities which certain members of that society — politicians, benefactors, administrators, clerics, teachers, parents, employers, students, pupils — regard as being particularly worthwhile.[2] A hundred years ago, the place of history in the formal curriculum of England was becoming measurably stronger, and recognised as worthwhile, just as in the 1980s it has become measurably weaker.[3] In the 1870s, separate honours degrees in history were established in the universities of Oxford and Cambridge. The *English Historical Review* was founded in 1886. At Manchester from 1890 and at London from 1903, Tout and Pollard respectively helped to develop important historical schools in the newer universities. From the 1870s, history also became an accepted subject of study amongst the upper standards of elementary schools — a grant-earning 'Class' subject, indeed, under the terms of the Code of 1875. In 1900 it was included in the list of subjects expected to be taught in elementary schools 'as a rule'. The secondary school regulations of 1904 made history a compulsory subject at secondary school level.[4] Thus history was to achieve an important, if not always central, role in the formal curricula of the English educational system.

What is history and why should it be studied and taught?[5] The word has been used in several ways to mean: the past, the human past, or the disciplined study of the human past. By the 1880s, the apparatus of such disciplined study — university courses, an academic journal, a 'scientific' rather than a 'literary' approach — were emerging. In 1906 the Historical Association was founded. Its first council, which included eleven university staff, nine from secondary schools and four from training colleges, reflected the status which history had achieved throughout the educational system and provided a forum for collaboration amongst its practitioners.[6]

In the 1680s, John Locke had written that 'As nothing teaches, so nothing delights more than history.'[7] Two hundred years later the new breed of professional historians were less interested in delighting their audiences and readers, and more concerned to find and teach the lessons of history.

At their head stood John Robert Seeley,[8] Regius Professor of History at Cambridge from 1869 until his death in 1895. His lecture course on the British Empire, delivered in 1881-2 and subsequently published as *The Expansion of England* (London, 1883), established imperialism as a central theme of modern British history, and in the public mind. Within two years his book had sold 80,000 copies and it remained in print until 1956. Thus Seeley, in the words of one of his followers, 'threw a powerful searchlight on the development of British empire, and brought home to thousands of readers, who have never before thought of it, the sense that, after all, our Colonies are only England beyond the seas — a greater England but England all the same ...'.[9] Seeley, who had previously been Professor of Latin at University College, London, and who had been appointed to the Cambridge chair by Gladstone, thus helped to popularise and legitimise British imperialism in an intellectual sense, although the term was only used twice in the book, and on both occasions in reference to despotic rule.[10] The irony of all this was not lost upon contemporaries. In 1895 Jacobs, writing in *The Athenaeum*, declared, 'our Imperialism of today is the combined work of Beaconsfield and of Seeley, a curious couple of collaborators'.[11]

What then did Seeley contribute to imperialism, socialisation and education? On imperialism itself, Seeley had little to say that was new as a result of research or analysis. Neither his idea nor his term of 'Greater Britain' was novel. The lesson which he drew from the history of the USA, namely not that colonists would inevitably outgrow the mother country but that in North America a federal state had been created which in spite of vast territories and a civil war was a nation of the first rank, was widely appreciated. But, in predicting the emergence of Russia and the USA as the two superpowers and in arguing that if Britain wished to join them she must become a federal empire, he offered Greater Britain an ideal, which he justified by reference to her history.

Seeley's ideal of empire which influenced statesmen, administrators, the general public, and students in universities and schools, both within Britain and within the empire as well, may be summed up as follows. The British Empire was unlike most previous empires. It represented, particularly in Canada, Australia and New Zealand, an extension of British people into lands which were so thinly populated that little conquest or domination took place. This was Britain's or England's natural destiny, achieved in unplanned fashion, 'in a fit of absence of mind'.[12] Seeley even extended some of this interpretation to India: 'for we are not really conquerors of

India and we cannot rule her as conquerors'.[13] No specific racial superiority was claimed. Rather did he argue that medieval societies needed to be transformed into modern ones — by peace, good government, railways, even sanitation and Christianity — and that being part of the British Empire was a mutually beneficial way of achieving these ends. He recognised that 'great mischiefs' as well as 'vast benefits'[14] might occur in India, and acknowledged that a nationalist movement, as opposed to a mutiny, could not be resisted. He also acknowledged that Canada and the West Indies might prefer to join the USA rather than to stay with Britain.

Seeley's examples were drawn from the 'white' dominions, India and the West Indies, but the principle of mutual benefit was subsequently extended to all areas. Lord Lugard, for example, expounded the principle of the 'Dual Mandate' — that British rule benefited the colonised as much as the colonisers — in respect of central Africa.[15] In 1924 Lord Leverhulme, with complete disregard for historical accuracy, declared that 'organizing ability is the peculiar trait characteristic of the white man' which would make the 'African native ... happier, produce the best, and live under the larger conditions of prosperity when his labour is directed and organized by his white brother who has all these million years' start ahead of him'.[16]

The flaws in Seeley's own analysis are easily seen. He failed sufficiently to examine the legitimate needs and aspirations of colonial populations or to provide practical schemes for promoting mutual self-interest.[17] At the turn of the century, John Burns, John Morley and Lloyd George were amongst the leading Liberal critics of empire as the defeats, incompetence and deaths of 20,000 Afrikaners (mainly women and children) in concentration camps during the second Boer War polarised imperial sentiment. In *Imperialism* (London, 1902) John A. Hobson, the journalist and economist, characterised the British Empire as an expression of exploitation and economic greed. By 1902, moreover, as Judd and Slinn have pointed out, barely twelve per cent of the people of the empire were of European let alone British origin, whilst Hinduism and Islam were the major religions.[18]

Seeley's contribution to the doctrine of imperialism, however, must be coupled, for the purposes of this study at least, with his concept of the historian as the educator, particularly the political educator, of the whole nation. His role in this respect may be compared with that of the historians of the so-called 'Prussian school', notably Droysen, Sybel and Treitschke, who used historical analysis to explain and justify the rise of Prussia into Germany.[19] The opening sentences of *The Expansion* indicate Seeley's personal commitment to the use of history for the purposes of socialisation and of education:

It is a favourite maxim of mine that history, while it should be scientific in its method, should pursue a practical object. That is, it should not merely gratify the reader's curiosity about the past, but modify his view of the present and his forecast of the future. Now if this maxim be sound, the history of England ought to end with something that might be called a moral.[20]

Seeley's history, indeed, was future-oriented. Whilst, however, his condemnation of the 'foppish kind of history which aims at literary display'[21] would be widely shared, statements such as 'We shall all no doubt be wise after the event; we study history that we may be wise before the event'[22] were more controversial. Seeley's emphasis was upon the usefulness of historical study and teaching – for the purpose of informing both the present and the future. A scientific approach to history, the mere collection of facts, he warned, would be of little value 'if they lead to no great truths having at the same time scientific generality and momentous practical bearings'.[23] In his concern to establish history as a social science and as a means of socialisation, Seeley argued that the training, equipment and purposes of historians would need to be radically revised: 'Each university will create a school of historians who will be as strong on the theoretical side as on the side of mere research. They will be sociologists, economists, jurists, as well as chroniclers and antiquarians.'[24] Such schools would be particularly concerned with history as 'the lesson book of politics ... a record of truth not to be altered and not to be ended, written to correct our prejudices'.[25] Modern history would predominate. Let the historians of Holland and Sweden dwell in the sixteenth and seventeenth centuries. Their days of national greatness were past. England's development as 'a maritime, colonising and industrial country'[26] should be at the centre of the historical stage.

In the late-nineteenth and early-twentieth centuries, 'a succession of Seeleys'[27] developed these themes. Prominent among them were Hugh Egerton, appointed in 1905 as the first Beit Professor of Colonial History at Oxford, and A. P. Newton, the first Rhodes Professor of Imperial History at the University of London from 1919. They, together with Sir Charles Lucas, Chairman of the Royal Colonial Institute from 1915, not only promoted the study of imperial history at university level, but also sought, through an imperial studies campaign which included popular lectures, lantern slides and the promotion of Empire Day, to raise the imperial consciousness of the nation as a whole. In January 1916, at the height (or depth) of the First World War, the tenth annual meeting of the Historical Association began with a paper from Lucas on 'The teaching of imperial history', which topic coupled with naval history, dominated the whole meeting.[28]

Lucas's campaign for the teaching of imperial history was based upon his belief that the general public, and particularly many elements of the working classes, had failed sufficiently to appreciate the benefits of empire. This was very serious in wartime when German propaganda might turn the empire into a source of weakness rather than of strength. Thus in 1915 in *The British Empire*, six lectures addressed to the members of the Working Men's College, Lucas sought specifically to counter 'a feeling among some, at any rate, of the working men of England, that the Empire was of no use to them, and that they had no use for the Empire'[29] with two main arguments. The first was the superiority of the British concept of empire over that of Germany. The Germans, he asserted, sought merely 'to remake men in their own image'.[30] The British approach, on the other hand, was 'to combine general supervision and control with toleration, and not toleration only, but encouragement of diverse customs and characteristics'.[31] Secondly, he argued that the success of this policy was shown by the support given by all members of the empire, even the recently-defeated Boers, to the war effort.

Two years later, in an introduction to A. P. Newton's *The Old Empire and the New* (London, 1917), itself based on a course of Rhodes lectures delivered at University College, London in the spring term of 1917, Lucas placed the responsibility for socialising the public further into the imperial ideal firmly upon history teachers in schools and universities:

> The citizens must be reached through the teachers: the teachers must be of the best quality: the universities, especially the younger universities in the great industrial centres must provide and equip the teachers ...
>
> When Imperial Studies are mentioned, history naturally rises first to view, and none can doubt that greater prominence than at present ought to be given to our overseas history in courses of study, examinations and text-books.[32]

After the war Lucas continued to press the message that teachers should educate pupils to accept the nation's and their own imperial destiny and responsibilities. Thus, for example, in 1921 he gave a series of lectures at the Royal Colonial Institute to a study circle of London County Council teachers, lectures subsequently published as *The Partition and Colonization of Africa* (Oxford, 1922). Trusteeship was his theme. Given the historical fact that Africa had become 'a dependency of Europe',[33] Europeans, he argued, should be 'trustees of the black men until in some distant future (if ever) the black men have become able to stand by themselves'.[34]

In his inaugural lecture as Beit Professor, delivered in April 1906, Hugh Egerton echoed Seeley in several respects: the study and teaching of colonial history would make for 'practical edification'[35] in respect of the present and the future; modern history was stressed; the year 1837 at which the Oxford English history course terminated 'marks the starting point of the self governing British Empire of today',[36] and the time had come 'when the history of England should be identified with the history of the English Empire'.[37] Egerton went beyond Seeley, however, in his ideal of empire as 'a collection of allied nations under a common crown rather than a fusion of nationalities into a single type'.[38] Such an ideal also involved a greater awareness of other historical perspectives — an empathetic approach: 'It is for us to teach and learn history in such a way, as that the historical imagination may be cultivated, and we may recognize the point of view of those from whom we may fundamentally differ.'[39] Such a point of view included that of many North Americans who, Egerton informed his audience, thought 'of our land as a played-out island, chiefly inhabited by the unemployed and by decaying industries.'[40]

With the outbreak of war in 1914, however, Egerton, in common with other university dons, put his pen to national service with his contributions to the series of Oxford Pamphlets.[41] C. R. L. Fletcher, fellow of Magdalen and co-author with Rudyard Kipling of the highly patriotic *A School History of England* (Oxford, 1911), took the responsibility of explaining the German Empire to the British public. *The Germans, their Empire, and How They Made It* (No. 6) was an historical account of Prussian policy from the seventeenth century, whilst *The Germans, their Empire and What They Covet* (No. 7) warned of the territorial ambitions aroused by the pan-German school. Sir Ernest Trevelyan in *India and the War* (No. 22) discussed 'the reasons which account for the striking manifestations of Indian loyalty', whilst Egerton contributed *The British Dominions and the War* (No. 21) and *Is the British Empire the Result of Wholesale Robbery?* (No. 23). In supplying a negative answer to this particular question, Egerton argued that overseas expansion was a natural development for powerful states, that much of the British Empire had been acquired before the creation of Germany, that in the acquisition the British had been no more unscrupulous than other colonising powers, and that it was now the responsibility of the current generation to show themselves worthy, in battle, of the empire which their forefathers had committed to their care.

Egerton died in 1927, Lucas in 1931, Arthur Newton, some twenty years their junior, lived on until 1942. His *A Junior History of the British Empire Overseas*, published in 1933, was written at the suggestion, and with the support, of the Education Committee of the Federation of Chambers of

Commerce of the British Empire, and of the Imperial Studies Committee of the Royal Empire Society, from whom teachers might borrow lantern slides and further pictures to supplement the several illustrations in the book itself. One distinctive feature of this work was its emphasis upon the co-prosperity of the empire. In the 1920s and 1930s, economic issues often outweighed political or military considerations, and the value of the empire to the hungry and unemployed of Britain needed to be reaffirmed. Thus emphasis was placed upon the role of Africa as a supplier of raw materials and as a market for manufactured products: 'West Africa gives us the palm oil from which soap and margarine are largely made in British factories by British workmen' whilst 'A demand arises for manufactured goods that must be imported, and so trade flows both ways — raw materials out of Africa and manufactures in. So both sides benefit ...'.[42]

The general contribution of history text-books to the socialisation of British children, both in respect of imperialism and of other values, has been well-charted in recent years and will not be further considered here. In 1970 Valerie Chancellor examined the nineteenth-century schooling process in *History for their Masters*,[43] whilst John MacKenzie showed that the message was not only conveyed through history text-books but that geography, English and religion were also used as vehicles of imperial instruction.[44] F. Glendenning placed the racial attitudes contained in nineteenth- and twentieth-century history text-books in a comparative perspective,[45] whilst a recent study by Kathryn Castle has distinguished British stereotypes of Africans, Chinese and Indians in school text-books and children's periodicals in the period 1890–1914.[46]

Suffice it to say that, by the early years of the twentieth century, although the formal teaching of imperial and colonial history as such was not dominant either at university or school levels in Britain, three basic tenets were widely accepted. Firstly, that there was an empire with which Britain's immediate past, present and future was inextricably bound up, an empire whose bonds had been strengthened and bounds increased by a common experience in the First World War. Secondly, that such an empire could be justified on the grounds of British technological, cultural, financial, constitutional, legal, moral and religious superiority, a superiority which, though not predetermined, was explicable in terms of her history and of her heroes. Thirdly, that the peoples of the empire were largely contented with their increasing prosperity, and appreciative of British order, justice and fair play, and would in the fullness of time achieve dominion status within a federal system to which the term 'commonwealth' would be more appropriate than 'empire'.

II

In the 1980s in Britain the place of imperialism in the study and teaching of history is very different from what it was in Seeley's or even Newton's day. Radical changes have particularly taken place within the last twenty-five years. Ronald Robinson, Beit Professor and thus a successor of Egerton, acknowledged these changes in his introduction to the second edition of *Africa and the Victorians* (London, 1981), first published some twenty years earlier. Robinson there stated that, had he and the late John Gallacher been writing in the 1970s their 'gaze would have been fixed less on imperial decisions at the centre and more on African co-operation and resistance', but warned against simply replacing 'an empire of rulers almost without subjects' by another 'of subjects almost without rulers'.[47]

This section will be divided into two broad areas: the first will examine the general consequences for historical study of the ending of empire, and the second will focus upon the specific implications for history-teaching in schools in Britain today.

In the 1880s, Britain had a colonial empire whose existence impinged upon the histories of many other countries. Such an empire no longer exists. Thus imperialism, as far as Britain is concerned, would appear to have a past but not much of a present or a future. Britain's claims to superiority over other nations and peoples have been severely dented. The commonwealth, a not insignificant residue or achievement of empire, has no close federal structure. Britain herself is often isolated in commonwealth discussions. She hovers uncertainly between the commonwealth, Europe and a 'special relationship' with a former colony — the United States.

Bernard Porter's widely-acclaimed volume, *The Lion's Share* (2nd edition London, 1984), may be seen as rationalising for British opinion in the 1980s the disappearance of empire, much as Seeley's *Expansion* had rationalised its appearance one hundred years before. Porter's argument that imperialism was for Britain a symptom not of strength but of decline. a development which helped to obscure fundamental weaknesses in British society and economy which were becoming apparent by the 1870s, has been corroborated by studies from other historical perspectives.[48] His theory that Britain's freedom to pursue the true interests of her people was severely compromised by the need to maintain and defend the empire appears to have been confirmed once again by the decision to pursue the costly principle of 'fortress Falklands'. Porter, arguing within the broad concept of British decline, concluded that 'The empire which she had accumulated ... was an incident in the course of that decline. It was acquired originally as a result of that decline to stave it off. It was retained largely in spite of that decline and it was surrendered as a final confirmation of that decline...'.[49]

A second historical consequence of the disappearance of the visible British and other European colonial empires has been to focus attention on other types of imperialism, both pre- and post-colonial. International capitalism, multinational companies, communism, foreign-aid programmes, cultural programmes and the major military alliances dominated by the USA and USSR may be counted as examples of post-colonial imperialism.[50] Such a development may allow a more detached view to be taken by historians of recent European imperialism. Indeed, David Fieldhouse has suggested that 'The modern imperial historian, unlike Seeley, has no territorial base, or for that matter loyalties. He places himself in the interstices of his subject, poised above the "area of interaction" like some satellite placed in space, looking, Janus-like, in two or more ways at the same time.'[51] One example of this overarching approach is to be found in R. O. Collins (ed.), *Problems in the History of Colonial Africa, 1860–1960* (Englewood Cliffs, N.J., 1970) which comprises forty-four readings (including one from Fieldhouse headed 'the myth of economic exploitation') from a wide range of authors, grouped around seven key historical 'problems'. Such claims to detachment and objectivity, however, may be interpreted rather as an attempt to soften the full force of the legitimate reinterpretation of European colonisation from the perspective of the colonised.[52]

Greater emphasis upon pre- and post-colonial periods of history, and a reconsideration of the profit and loss account of the colonial period itself, are two of the main themes in the recent historiography of formerly colonised countries, as of Britain. The cultural damage inflicted by imperialist powers who denied or diminished the history, religion, customs and language of those whom they conquered has been identified. Historians like Gopal have emphasised the harm rather than the benefit done by the British to the Indian economy in respect of agriculture, industry and commerce, and hence to Indian society as well.[53] The doctrine of dual mandate or mutual benefit has been countered by Walter Rodney, amongst others, with his work on *How Europe Underdeveloped Africa* (London, 1972). Much of this reinterpretation has taken place within a Marxist-Leninist historical framework.

There is no space here to consider in detail Lenin's theory of imperialism as the highest stage of capitalism — the oppression of nations on a new historical basis. In turning to consider the contemporary situation in British schools, however, instructive comparisons may be made with communist and colonial and post-colonial classrooms.

History lessons in all secondary schools in the USSR 'are conducted according to common programmes and textbooks' and are thoroughly grounded in Marxist-Leninist philosophy. In their study of the first forty years of the twentieth century, ninth-grade pupils pay particular attention to Lenin's teaching on imperialism which is 'considered in the light of the economic, social and political development of foreign countries, including Britain. The programme covers the treatment of working-class and socialist movements, national-liberation struggles of peoples in Asia, Africa and Latin America ...'. In the following year, the culmination of these struggles is considered in a major topic entitled 'National liberation movements and the collapse of the imperialist colonial system'.[54]

More than thirty years ago in the pages of *History*, F. Musgrove reported on his experience of teaching School Certificate history to boys in Uganda. In an article entitled 'History teaching within a clash of cultures', he noted that his pupils had little interest in the history of the British Empire other than to criticise and to rejoice in its defeats. Given such an attitude, Musgrove found his attempts to promote the glory of belonging to the empire and the ideal of commonwealth falling upon deaf ears. 'If a pupil is already critical in his approach to the Empire, he will tend to read in its history only those things which discredit it: he looks for and sees, the way in which it has broken up rather than the way in which it has grown.'[55] In the 1950s the Ugandan boys' heroes were the newly-liberated peoples of India and their leaders who had succeeded in throwing off British rule, not Warren Hastings or Robert Clive.

In India itself Jogindra Banerji, in a 1957 publication of the International Text-Book Institute at Brunswick in West Germany, confirmed this analysis but also described a progression to the neutralist position. As school children, Indians:

> were made to learn Indian history that sought to provide justification for the political relationship prevailing between Britain and India. Paradoxically, the reaction, at later stages of India's national struggle, was to create blind spots in the young people's mind, encourage a black-and-white attitude to history that tended to make Britain the villain of the piece. Today, against the background of friendship between India and Britain the entirely negative attitude of such history teaching has become evident.[56]

In British schools today, history teachers have the role of explaining to their pupils the end of empire. Within such schools, moreover, are many pupils who themselves, or whose parents or grandparents, were born in former colonies. The multicultural empire and its passing has produced, or rather re-emphasised and reproduced, the concept of multicultural Britain. Musgrove wrote of teaching history within a conflict of cultures. Today's history teachers face the daunting but important task of teaching their subject within a conciliation of cultures.

One strategy for achieving this end has been to emphasise Britain's earlier imperial or colonial past — as a part of the Roman empire, or as conquered by Angles, Saxons, Danes and Normans. For example, this longer historical perspective has been employed to good effect at Tulse Hill School in South London which poses the question to its second years of 'Who are the British?' Answers include not only Angles, Saxons, Danes and Normans, but also others from continental Europe, Irish and Jews who came to Britain in the early-modern and modern periods.[57] Similarly, a study of earlier black settlement in Britain provides a useful perspective on post-Second-World-War settlement by people from Afro-Caribbean countries.[58]

Another strategy has been to repeat the regular call for greater attention to be paid in school history courses to the histories and achievements of non-European civilisation and empires. Such a strategy may be justified by the very small proportion of the world's population who live on the European continent, by the increasing interdependence of today's world, and by the need to counter the doctrines, attitudes and assumptions of innate racial superiority and inferiority often fostered, explicitly or implicitly, by some earlier teaching of imperial history.[59]

Further reference to the problems and successes of school history teaching (including imperial history) in contemporary Britain may be found in such publications as David Edgington's *The Role of History in Multicultural Education* (London, 1982) and *History in the Primary and Secondary Years: An HMI View* (London, 1985).

III

Two points may be made in conclusion — in respect of imperialism, socialisation and the contribution of the study and teaching of history to education.

British imperialism rested ultimately upon a belief. By the end of the eighteenth century, as Marshall and Williams have shown, '... educated Englishmen and some wider sections of British society had come to believe both that the workings of non-European societies were comprehensible to them, and that what was being revealed were societies inferior to their own and capable of being changed for the better by outside intervention'.[60]

Socialisation into acceptance of that belief became one of the purposes of the study and teaching of history. A collective historical consciousness or memory, based on a series of selected concerns or episodes, was established and handed down. The origins of empire were projected backwards to the Tudor period. Heroes, and less frequently heroines, were chosen to exemplify certain values and qualities — often exhibited in pursuit or defence of the cause of Greater Britain. Thus in the 1950s an Historical Association pamphlet entitled *Notes on the Teaching of British Imperial History* by C. R. N. Routh, in extolling the worth of imperial history as a vehicle for moral value and the improvement of character, declared that 'Vision, courage, humanity and faith are qualities which shine out for all to see in such men as Raffles, Durham, Livingstone, Rhodes, therefore "Let the Great Story be Told".'[61]

Nevertheless, it is important to notice that Routh's starting point was the neglect of imperial history in schools and universities, coupled with pupils' suspicions of imperialism. Socialisation through history teaching in Britain has not been as closely controlled as in many other countries in which centrally-prescribed syllabuses, text-books and teaching methods have been employed. Whilst the themes of this chapter, and indeed of this book, have led to an emphasis on the highly visible manifestations of imperialism, socialisation and education, important counter-currents have also flowed throughout the last two hundred years. Opposition and indifference to imperialism has shown itself in Britain in all classes of society and on a variety of grounds — social, political, moral and economic. Such opposition and indifference has also been reflected in the study and teaching of history.

Notes

1 Although regrettably the use of the term 'British' in respect of the historical treatment of this topic is not consistent, and is often equated with 'English'.

2 On this point, see D. Lawton, *Class, Culture and the Curriculum*, London, 1975, pp. 85–6.

3 See R. Aldrich, 'Interesting and useful', *Teaching History*, 47, 1987, pp. 11–14 and A. Taylor Milne, 'History at the universities: then and now', *History*, 59 (195), 1974, pp. 33–46, particularly with reference to Scotland.

4 P. Gordon and D. Lawton, *Curriculum Change in the Nineteenth and Twentieth Centuries*, London, 1978, pp. 15–23.

5 See A. Rogers, 'Why teach history? The answer of fifty years', *Educational Review* 14, 1961–2, pp. 10–20 and 152–62. For a recent international discussion, see *Informations, Mitteilungen, Communications*, 7 (2), 1986, pp. 90–102 (the Journal of the International Society for History Didactics).

6 *The Historical Association, 1906–1956*, London, 1955, p. 8.

7 J. L. Axtell (ed.). *The Educational Writings of John Locke*, Cambridge, 1968, p. 292.

8 On Seeley, see Deborah Wormell, *Sir John Seeley and the Uses of History*, Cambridge, 1980, which has an extensive bibliography.

9 H. E. Egerton, *A Short History of British Colonial Policy*, London 1897, p. 6.

10 For the context, see R. Koebner and H. D. Schmidt, *Imperialism: The Story and Significance of a Political Word, 1840-1960*, Cambridge, 1964, pp. 173–4.

11 Quoted by Peter Burroughs, 'John Robert Seeley and British imperial history', *Journal of Imperial and Commonwealth History*, I (2), 1973, p. 207 (hereafter *JICH*).

12 Sir John Seeley, *The Expansion of England*, London, 1883, p. 8.

13 *Ibid*. p. 234.

14 *Ibid*. p. 305.

15 F. D. Lugard, *The Dual Mandate in British Tropical Africa*, London, 1922.

16 Quoted in A. Temu and B. Swai, *Historians and Africanist History: A Critique*, London, 1981, p. 153.

17 Though he supported the Imperial Federation League. See Koebner and Schmidt, *Imperialism*, pp. 177–95.

18 D. Judd and P. Slinn, *The Evolution of the Modern Commonwealth, 1902–80*, London, 1982, p. 4.

19 For an appreciation of the Prussian school, see H. Flaig, 'The historian as pedagogue of the nation', *History*, 59 (195), 1974, pp. 18–32.

20 Seeley, *Expansion of England*, p. 1.

21 *Ibid*. p. 166.

22 *Ibid*. p. 169.

23 *Ibid*. p. 3.

24 J. R. Seeley, 'The teaching of history' in G. S. Hall (ed.), *Methods of Teaching History*, Boston, Mass. 2nd edition 1902, p. 201.

25 *Ibid*. p. 202.

26 Seeley, *Expansion of England*, p. 80.

27 C. P. Lucas, *The British Empire*, London, 1915, p. 233. For a discussion of Seeley's successors, see two articles by J. G. Greenlee, '"A succession of Seeleys": The "Old School" re-examined', *JICH*, IV (3), 1976, pp. 266–82 and 'Imperial studies and the unity of empire', *JICH*, VII (3), 1979, pp. 321-35.

28 For an account of this meeting, see Keith Robbins, 'History, the Historical Association and the "national past"', *History*, 66 (218), 1981, pp. 413–25. The Vere Harmsworth Professorship in Naval History was established at Cambridge in 1919, and converted into Imperial and Naval History in 1933.

29 Lucas, *The British Empire*, p. 1.

30 *Ibid*. p. 197.

31 *Ibid*.

32 A. P. Newton, *The Old Empire and the New*, London, 1917, pp. vi–vii.

33 C. P. Lucas, *The Partition and Colonization of Africa*, Oxford, 1922, p. 196.

34 *Ibid*. p.207.

35 H. E. Egerton, *The Claims of the Study of Colonial History upon the Attention of the University of Oxford*, Oxford, 1906, p. 8.

36 *Ibid*. p. 11.

37 *Ibid*. p. 21.

38 *Ibid*. p. 22.

39 *Ibid*. p. 32.

40 *Ibid*. p. 23.

41 The five Oxford pamphlets referred to in this paragraph were all published in London in 1914. For a full discussion of Oxford's involvement with imperialism, see Richard Symonds, *Oxford and Empire: The Last Lost Cause?*, London, 1986.

42 A. P. Newton, *A Junior History of the British Empire Overseas*, London, 1933, pp. 241–3.

43 Valerie Chancellor, *History for their Masters: Opinion in the English History Textbook 1800–1914*, Bath, 1970. The Historical Association's collection of text-books is now housed in the School of Education at the University of Durham. A catalogue of the

pre-1915 material was published as an appendix to the *History of Education Society Bulletin*, 33, 1984, whilst a separate handlist covering the period 1915–39, compiled by J. S. Thompson, was published by the Historical Association in 1985. Both lists have useful introductions by Gordon Batho.

44 John MacKenzie, *Propaganda and Empire*, Manchester, 1984, especially Ch. 7, 'Imperialism and the school textbook'.

45 F. Glendenning, 'School history textbooks and racial attitudes, 1804–1911', *Journal of Educational Administration and History*, 5 (2), 1973, pp. 33–44. F. Glendenning, 'The evolution of history teaching in British and French schools in the 19th and 20th centuries, with special reference to attitudes to race and colonialism in history textbooks' (unpublished Ph.D. thesis, University of Keele, 1975).

46 K. Castle, 'An examination of the attitudes towards non-Europeans in British school history textbooks and children's periodicals, 1890–1914, with special reference to the Indian, the African and the Chinese' (unpublished Ph.D. thesis, CNAA, 1986).

47 R. Robinson, J. Gallacher and A. Denny, *Africa and the Victorians: The Official Mind of Imperialism*, 2nd edition, London, 1981, pp. xxii–xxiii.

48 See, for example, M. J. Wiener, *English Culture and the Decline of the Industrial Spirit*, Cambridge, 1981.

49 B. Porter, *The Lion's Share: A Short History of British Imperialism, 1850–1983*, 2nd edition, London, 1984, p. 364.

50 For a discussion of the paradoxes of imperialism after empire, see Ronald Robinson, 'Imperial theory and the question of imperialism after empire', *JICH*, XII (2), 1984, pp. 42–54.

51 David Fieldhouse, 'Can Humpty-Dumpty be put together again? Imperial history in the 1980s', *JICH*, XII (2), 1984, pp. 18–19.

52 On this point, see A. Temu and B. Swai, *Historians and Africanist History: A Critique*, London, 1981, especially pp. 115–20, 'The fallacy of objectivism'.

53 S. Gopal, *Modern India*, London, 1967.

54 A. G. Kiloskov, 'Teaching history in the Soviet secondary general education school', *Teaching History*, 37, 1983, pp. 12–13.

55 F. Musgrove, 'History teaching within a conflict of cultures', *History*, XL (140), 1955, p. 301.

56 J. K. Banerji, *Laying the Foundation of 'One World'*, Brunswick, West Germany, 1957, p. 3.

57 Tulse Hill School history syllabus. See also Nigel File, 'History at Tulse Hill School, London', *Teaching History*, 32, 1982, p. 14.

58 See Nigel File and Chris Power, *Black Settlers in Britain, 1555–1958*, London, 1981.

59 See Ian Grosvenor, 'History and the multi-cultural curriculum: a case study', *Teaching History*, 32, 1982, pp. 18–19, and the support materials produced by the Metropolitan Borough of Sandwell. Although A. Dyer, *History in a Multi-Cultural Society*, London, 1982, has suggested that the multi-cultural make-up of Britain makes British history more, not less, important.

60 P. J. Marshall and Glyndwr Williams, *The Great Map of Mankind: British Perceptions of the World in the Age of Enlightenment*, London, 1982, p. 303.

61 C. R. N. Routh, *Notes on the Teaching of British Imperial History*, London, undated, 1952?, p. 5.

Further reading

Edgington D., *The Role of History in Multicultural Education*, London, 1982.

Fieldhouse D., 'Can Humpty-Dumpty be put together again? Imperial history in the 1980s', *JICH*, XII (2), 1984.

Judd D. and Slinn P., *The Evolution of the Modern Commonwealth, 1902–80*, London, 1982.

Koebner R. and Schmidt H. D., *Imperialism: The Story and Significance of a Political Word, 1840–1960*, Cambridge, 1964.

MacKenzie J., *Propaganda and Empire*, Manchester, 1984.

Porter B., *The Lion's Share: A Short History of British Imperialism, 1850–1983*, 2nd edition, London, 1984.

Robinson R., 'Imperial theory and the question of imperialism after empire', *JICH*, XII (2), 1984.

Seeley J., *The Expansion of England*, London, 1883.

Symonds R., *Oxford and Empire: The Last Lost Cause?*, London, 1986.

Wormell D., *Sir John Seeley and the Uses of History*, Cambridge, 1980.

CHAPTER TWO

English elementary education and the growth of the imperial ideal: 1880–1914

Pamela Horn

I

It was against a background of territorial expansion in the 1880s and 1890s that the propagandists of imperialism turned their attention to elementary education. Their aim was to give the nation's children a sense of patriotic mission and a level of physical fitness which would enable them to sustain Britain's position in the world, with all that that entailed. For, as one enthusiast, the 12th Earl of Meath, pointed out, the task was too great to be left to a small band of dedicated pioneers. Instead it had become the duty of all:

> In former ages the burdens of Empire or of the State fell on the shoulders of a few; now the humblest child to be found on the benches of a primary school will in a few years be called on to influence the destinies not only of fifty-four millions of white, but of three hundred and fifty millions of coloured men and women, his fellow subjects, scattered throughout the five continents of the world.[1]

To carry out these responsibilities they needed diligence, obedience, thrift, self-denial, endurance and 'indomitable pluck'.[2] It was here that the elementary school would play its part by inculcating these virtues through the medium of its curriculum and the mode of its organisation.

The view of education as an instrument for social and moral reform was, of course, not a new one. Nor was Meath alone in applying it to the cult of Empire. In 1899 Edmond Holmes, HMI, adopted this approach when he wrote of the village school as having a 'national, not to say imperial' role to perform. 'Its business is to turn out youthful citizens rather than hedgers and ditchers; ... preparing children for the battle of life (a battle which will ... be fought in *all* parts of the British Empire).'[3]

The moulding of young minds in favour of the imperial ideal was to be achieved in part by the slanting of school syllabuses so as to link them with the idea of colonial expansion. As early as 1878 the Education Department directed HMIs to excite interest 'in the Colonial and Foreign Possessions of the British Crown'. This was carried a stage further in the Elementary School Code of 1882, when geography for Standard VI pupils was to include information on the British colonies and dependencies.[4] Three years later came the Department's new 'Instructions' to inspectors encouraging them to draw attention, in the higher standards, to the 'English Colonies and their productions, government, and resources, and to those climatic and other conditions which render our distant possessions suitable fields for emigration, and for honourable enterprise'.

The process was strengthened in the Code of 1890 by the introduction of an 'alternative' syllabus for the upper standards of geography that placed especial emphasis upon the imperial link. It also included, for the first time, the 'acquisition and growth of the colonies and foreign possessions of Great Britain' as part of the history syllabus.[5]

In the upsurge of patriotism which accompanied the outbreak of the Boer War in 1899 these tendencies were powerfully reinforced. In some schools, maps of South Africa were prominently displayed with the 'position of friend and foe' appropriately marked.[6] Military metaphors even adorned the comments of HMIs. 'If the curriculum be taken to represent the strategy of the Educational army', wrote Chief Inspector J. A. Willis, 'the syllabus or scheme of work will correspond to its tactics, while the method of instruction is the handling of the battalion, or nowadays the company-unit.'[7]

Pupils' reminiscences confirm the enthusiasm for the imperial cause which grew in the war years. At Arlington, Sussex, Gaius Carley recalled the closeness with which events on the battlefield were followed. 'We loved to read about the soldiers fighting in South Africa ... The Relief of Ladysmith, Mafeking and Kimberley were great days for us, a half-holiday.'[8] Likewise to Walter Southgate in Bethnal Green, the war became a part of everyday childhood activities. 'We played games like "English versus Boers", wore celluloid buttons in our lapels portraying our favourite generals like Buller, White, Baden Powell and Lord Roberts.'[9]

Indicative of the popular mood is the fact that military drill, first included as an 'alternative' activity in the Elementary School Code of 1871, found renewed acceptance at this time. In some Devon schools servicemen were engaged as drill sergeants and at Thurlestone the boys were supplied with toy guns, white sailor suits, and two airguns, under the supervision of the local RNVR coastguard, 'in the hope of making them good marksmen'.[10]

The Board of Education shared in the general enthusiasm, with officials stressing the value of drill for boys.[11] Teacher training colleges, too, incorporated it in their own curricula, and by 1900 many male students had become keen members of a volunteer corps. At Cheltenham all physical instruction was given 'through the agency' of the volunteer corps, which also owned the college gymnasium. Later this was replaced by formal drill instruction, but in 1908 a miniature rifle range was opened, to the evident approval of the editor of the students' magazine.[12] Saltley training college also had a 'good rifle corps connected with the college'.[13] In this way trainees were prepared physically and mentally for the duties they were later expected to perform in the elementary schools.

However, combined with the Boer War's patriotic influence was its importance in pinpointing the poor physique of many potential recruits, especially from the large urban centres. This aroused anxiety about the nation's overall health and in 1902, in an effort to meet the demands for greater fitness, the Board of Education issued a 'Model Course of Physical Training for use in the Upper Departments of Public Elementary Schools'. It was drawn up after consultation with the War Office, itself a move which aroused suspicion in some quarters, and was based largely on army training methods.[14] As such it was little suited to the daily routine of the average elementary school. With the 'Model Course' the Board also issued a letter from the War Office urging school managers to compel teachers to attend drill instruction — something which the NUT, in particular, resented. So whilst The Times of 24 February 1903, could praise the initiative as laying 'the foundations of a military spirit in the nation', others were less sanguine. The former elementary school teacher and NUT activist, T. J. Macnamara, MP condemned the move as an attempt to exploit current health worries 'by making the elementary schools and the Board of Education a sort of antechamber to the War Office'. The opposition was sufficiently strong for amended physical training syllabuses to be drawn up in 1904 and 1909. But an examination of these reveals a continued heavy reliance on army methods.[15]

The Boer War, then, focused attention on the need to improve the physique of elementary scholars and, in official circles at least, linked this with military drill. It also encouraged the Board of Education to consider the ethical values of the school curriculum. In 1900, for the first time, history became a subject to be studied 'as a rule' in elementary schools; hitherto it had been adopted in less than a quarter of the departments eligible to take it.[16] Five years later, in its 'Suggestions for the Consideration of Teachers and Others Concerned in the Work of Public Elementary Schools', the Board made clear why it considered history and geography so important:

> from … geography lessons the scholars know that Great Britain is only one country among many others. It is, therefore, important that from the history lessons they should learn something about their nationality which distinguishes them from the people of other countries. They cannot understand this … unless they are taught how the British nation grew up, and how the mother country in her turn has founded daughter countries beyond the seas.[17]

A year later a new 'Code of Regulations for Public Elementary Schools' introduced 'moral instruction' into the curriculum. Among the desirable qualities it was to foster were courage, self-denial, and 'love of one's country'.[18]

Publishers, especially those concerned with history and geography textbooks, responded to these initiatives by producing works stressing what has been called the 'Holy Trinity' of 'Citizenship', 'Empire', and 'Patriotism'.[19] 'I don't think there can be any doubt that the only safe thing for all of us who love our country is to learn soldiering at once, and to be prepared to fight at any moment', declared the authors of *A School History of England* (1911) in typical mood.[20] This was especially important since the great expansion of the British Empire which had occurred during the 'last ninety-six years' had 'not come about without a great deal of jealousy from the other European powers; and this jealousy was never more real or more dangerous than it is to-day'.

To George T. Warner, in *A Brief Survey of British History* (1899), the achievements of the imperial past were both a cause for pride and a pointer to the efforts needed to maintain and extend them in the future:

When we look at a map of the world, and see how wide is the red that marks the British empire, we may well feel proud ... Our race possesses the colonial spirit which French, Germans, and Spaniards do not possess: the daring that takes men into distant lands, the doggedness that keeps them steadfast in want and difficulties, the masterful spirit that gives them power over Eastern races, the sense of justice that saves them from abusing this power and attaches those they rule with so ... strong an attachment.[21]

In a later textbook, published in 1911 and written with a co-author, Warner referred to Britain's overseas possessions as constituting 'the vastest and most beneficent empire yet known to history'.[22]

Regrettably in some books these inherently racist views were expressed in language more offensive than that employed by Warner. *A School History of England* contemptuously observed that the prosperity of the West Indies, 'once our richest possession', had largely declined since slavery was abolished in 1833.

The population is mainly black, descended from slaves imported in previous centuries, or of mixed black and white race; lazy, vicious and incapable of any serious improvement, or of work except under compulsion. In such a climate a few bananas will sustain the life of a negro quite sufficiently; why should he work to get more than this? He is quite happy and quite useless, and spends any extra wages he may earn upon finery.[23]

The damaging effect of such propaganda upon young minds is distressing to contemplate, especially as this particular work remained in print until 1930, despite adverse comments on its strident racialism made by some contemporary reviewers.[24]

Even G. A. Henty, famed as a writer of boys' adventure stories and usually more restrained in his racial comments than many authors of school books, dismissed the native inhabitants of Australia and New Zealand as 'thinly-scattered bodies of savages', in a history text produced at the end of Queen Victoria's reign.[25] But one of his major concerns was to highlight the value of the colonies as potential homes for 'tens of thousands of British emigrants', and the need for imperial unity.[26] Other elementary school texts also linked emigration with imperialism and with Britain's economic advance. One source optimistically described Australia as the 'future home of 100,000,000 Britons'. Another suggested that colonisation was 'a necessary condition of human advancement, and judicious emigration, especially ... to another part of the Empire, [was] one of the best remedies for over-population, and consequent depression of trade'.[27]

Geography texts occasionally used some of the same techniques. One reader described Africa as the 'Dark Continent' because of the barbarous conditions under which its inhabitants lived. It suggested that the future lay largely in European hands, since the natives were incapable of developing it themselves. 'Africa has treasures of many kinds, and the time has come when its resources must be opened up for the common good of humanity.[28]

Far rarer were works which adopted the measured tones of *Jack's Historical Readers*, published between 1901 and 1905 and written mainly by elementary schoolteachers. Their more questioning approach was typified by the pronouncement that military victories were only 'won at the cost of much suffering and misery, and of great loss of life and money'.[29] In Volume 5 of the series credit was given to the valour of opponents in some of the colonial skirmishes, while in discussing the Boer War, the author paid tribute to those Afrikaaners who had been 'wiser and more generous than President Kruger and his followers. ... The Uitlanders, on their side, were not altogether blameless. They made no allowance for the great wrench it would be for a ruling body to give up its power at a moment's notice.'[30]

Teachers, for their part, often embraced imperialist sentiments with enthusiasm. At Salford, Robert Roberts remembered that 'fed on Seeley's imperialistic work *The Expansion of England*, and often great readers of Kipling, [they] spelled out patriotism ... with a fervour that with some edged on the religious'.[31] At certain boys' schools, the masters joined local yeomanry or territorial army regiments and were periodically absent from their desks so that they might take part in military manoeuvres.[32]

Alongside these preoccupations there developed an almost mystical reverence for the flag. 'I should like to think that every boy and girl in this country realises that the Union Jack is the flag of the British Empire — whose children they are — the emblem of its greatness', wrote Field-Marshal Earl Roberts in 1911. ' ... without such knowledge it is not possible for boys and girls to understand what the flag ought to be to them — an incentive to so conduct themselves that ... they may prove themselves worthy of being members of the great Empire which the Union Jack represents'.[33]

Twenty years before, the Earl of Meath, as a newly elected Alderman of the London County Council, had been shocked to discover the ignorance of the capital's elementary pupils about the flag. To remedy this, in 1892 he offered £50 to enable school board officials to purchase a flag for each school. According to him, the proposal met with initial hostility from the 'advanced Radicals' who condemned it as 'a ritual in keeping with that semi-barbaric worship of national fetiches (sic) known as "Jingoism", ... ' Board records confirm that some trade unionists, in particular, opposed the initiative. The South Woolwich Branch of the Gas Workers' Union, for example, referred to the desirability of suppressing 'such tales of the triumphs of the British flag, as have made the name of Englishman a pretty general byword for rapacity, tyranny and oppression throughout the world'. Instead efforts should be made 'to sink the vaunt of racial superiority, and encourage in the young mind the nobler ideals of a reign of universal brotherhood and peace'.[34]

After several months' deliberation the board decided to accept Meath's £50 and to supply, from its own funds, a flag 'to any department for which application is made by the Managers'. In addition, members agreed to consider how to incorporate passages of 'high literary merit' in school readers so as to 'set forth deeds of heroism' and 'help in the formulation of character and in strengthening the sense of civic duty'.[25]

Textbooks also took up the theme of the Union flag. The *King Edward History Reader* pointed out that although it was 'merely a strip of blue silk or stuff with one white and two red crosses upon it', yet 'thousands of our brave sailors and soldiers have shed their blood ... to save it from falling into the hands of the enemy. ... When we cease to love it, or can no longer defend it, then the great and glorious British Empire will totter and fall to pieces,'[36] In *Highroads of History*, published by Thos. Nelson from 1907, Book V(a) opened with a eulogy on the flag. 'No Briton can help being proud of the Union Jack. It flies over the greatest empire the world has ever known; and wherever it flies, there are to be found at least justice and fair dealing for every man ... Every British boy and girl will desire not merely to keep the flag unsullied, but to blazon it still further with the record of noble deeds nobly done.' This volume was still used in at least one Buckinghamshire elementary school in the late 1920s, and exercised a considerable influence upon its young readers.[37]

II

These efforts by officialdom and the textbook publishers to promote the imperialist cause were supplemented by private initiatives. Thus the Conservative MP, Sir C. E. Howard Vincent, produced a special school map which, according to his biographers, by 1912 was to be found 'in village schoolrooms all over England'.[38] Apart from marking all British possessions in red, it detailed 'General Imperial Facts', such as the size of the Empire, its population, its annual trade and revenue, and its combined merchant marine and naval strength. Pupils learnt that the Empire was 'fifty-five times the size of France, fifty-four times the size of Germany', and 'three and a half times the size of the United States of America'. They were exhorted to recall that 'the Union Jack guards the Gates of the Seas and that Britain holds in her armed hand the Coal Supplies and Coaling Stations of the Oceans. If these are closed to any other Nation, the ships of war and sea trade of that country become powerless.'[39] So popular did the map become that by 1902 it had run into eleven editions.

A smiliar contribution was made by the Navy League, founded in 1894 to give 'to the peoples of this Empire definite knowledge of the necessity for a supreme Fleet'.[40] In 1898 it, too, produced a map 'Illustrating British Naval History' and stressing the size and importance of the Empire. An advertisement claimed that it was completed up to June 1898, 'but owing to recent conquests several alterations in the colouring of countries will be made in the next edition'.[41] It was dedicated to the 'Children of the British Empire' and was widely circulated in the schools (as well as appearing on hoardings in the London railway termini).

Sometimes, as in late Victorian and Edwardian Bristol, Navy League textbooks were also distributed to the schools, and essay competitions organised.[42] The Bristol initiative went ahead despite the reservations of some school board members, who disliked the League approach of substituting 'for the history of peoples and the useful and peaceful arts, stories of wars and the personal history of kings'. One critic sourly commented that he had 'hoped the time had come when we had had enough of war, and when the spirit of Jingoism was abating'.[43] In reality, public opinion was moving in the opposite direction to that he desired, whilst the Navy League itself gradually developed a 'hidden' agenda. Instead of concentrating on past battles, it began to discuss possible future conflicts. As

Caroline Playne has noted, during these pre-1914 years, youth was familiarised with the idea of fighting for the imperial ideal. 'Subtly the desire for war was introduced ... in order to consolidate the strength of the Empire.'[44]

The Conservative statesman and MP, Walter Long, likewise stressed the contribution individual boys and girls could make to imperial greatness when he told pupils at Redcliffe Boys' School, Bristol, in 1901 that as 'British boys' they would have 'in their turn to take [a] share of the Empire's responsibilities'. Each must be ready to 'strengthen the links of the Empire, and to leave some little mark for good on the history of the country'.[45]

But perhaps the greatest enthusiast for the linked causes of imperialism and youth was the 12th Earl of Meath. As we have seen, in the early 1890s he had become involved in promoting patriotic principles within the London board schools. Soon his ambitions spread far wider. According to an admirer, he desired that 'from their earliest years the children of the Empire should grow up with the thought of its claim upon their remembrance and their service'.[46] To this end he became involved with a range of youth organisations, including the Lads' Drill Association, which he formed in 1899 to promote the 'Systematic Physical and Military Training of all British Lads', and 'their instruction in the use of the rifle'. By 1905 he could boast the Prince of Wales as its Patron and the Duke of Connaught as its President.[42] In the following year it affiliated to the National Service League, itself spearheaded by the Boer War hero, Earl Roberts, and the campaign for military training in schools became a plank in that organisation's platform, too. Although his efforts were ultimately unsuccessful, Meath bombarded the Board of Education with memoranda, wrote letters to the press, asked questions in parliament, and published relevant booklets of speeches.[48] He was joined by others, including the Rt. Hon. H.O. Arnold-Forster, Conservative Secretary for War.[49]

Fresh hope was given to the propagandists in 1907 when the new Liberal Secretary for War, R. B. Haldane, introduced a cadet clause into his Territorial and Reserve Forces Bill. Although he apparently had the recruitment of public schoolboys primarily in mind, some MPs, like Sir Henry Craik, a vice-president of the Lads' Drill Association, argued that a cadet corps 'should be open to the schools of every grade throughout the country'.[50] In the end the proposal was decisively defeated by the 'pacifists and socialists in the Commons who objected to the heresy of compulsory military training for boys while at school'.[51]

The Lads' Drill Association and its linked causes formed only one part of Meath's strategy. He also set up a Duty and Discipline Movement whose main message was that lack of discipline among school children threatened the future of the Empire. It, too, issued propagandist essays between 1911 and 1912.[52]

But it was another initiative, the Empire Day movement, which most unambiguously expressed the Earl's imperial ideals in regard to elementary education. He adopted the idea in the late 1890s, following the example of Canada, where the provinces of Ontario, Quebec and Nova Scotia had by 1898 established 'Empire Day' as a date to be observed in their schools.[53] In 1901 the national parliament followed their lead by making 24 May, the anniversary of Queen Victoria's birthday, a Bank Holiday throughout Canada, to remind the children of their history and heritage.[54] Initially Meath's attempts to promote a similar movement in Britain met with lukewarm interest and it was not until 1916, during the First World War, that the government gave formal recognition to it. Earlier attempts to gain official blessing had foundered on the powerful anti-jingoist sentiment within the Commons.

Nevertheless, by dint of hard work, in 1904 Meath was able to organise the first mass observation of Empire Day in Britain itself, with a number of local education authorities and elementary schools persuaded to support his efforts. From modest beginnings the movement spread until on 24 May 1905, he could claim that 5,540 elementary schools and six teachers' training colleges had celebrated Empire Day in this country. Two years later, at a time when there were 20,541 elementary schools in England and Wales alone, these totals had risen to 12,544 and eleven respectively, with the movement continuing to grow thereafter.[55] Among the later recruits were the schools of the London Education Committee — the largest LEA in the country — which joined in on 24 May 1907. By 1919, support was such that 27,323 'Schools, Training Colleges and Institutions in the United Kingdom' were celebrating Empire Day. By then only the education authorities of the two Welsh counties of Anglesey and Merioneth, and the three boroughs of Colne, Darwen and West Ham had failed to give official sanction to the celebrations.[56]

At first the spatial impact of the movement was highly variable. In 1906, when 8,684 elementary schools participated, its strongest representation lay in the southern counties, from Kent to Somerset. This included the middle-class suburbs of London and many southern coastal resorts and cathedral cities. It was an area broadly Conservative in politics and where naval and military establishments were heavily concentrated. By contrast, relatively little impression was made in the agricultural belt from East Anglia to the Cotswolds, or in the industrial North-East. In Wales, only two counties, Glamorgan and Montgomery, recorded celebrations in 1906, and in

Scotland a mere sixty-one schools joined in, twenty-seven of them in Edinburgh.[57]

In an Open Letter, first published in 1905 and reissued in succeeding years, Meath stressed that Empire Day promoters wished to inculcate the ideals of good citizenship.[58] These included imperial and national patriotism, loyalty to the monarch, and obedience to authority. He associated them with the Japanese concept of *bushido*, a social and moral code taught in Japanese schools since 1867 and derived from that nation's warrior past. It stressed the importance of loyalty, patriotism, and self-sacrifice.[59] In a speech on Empire Day 1905, the Earl not only praised the Japanese example but suggested that the 'gallant little people of the Rising Sun' were 'daily furnishing us with object lessons' which should be absorbed.

A provisional Empire Day programme was also drawn up. It included the hoisting and saluting of the Union flag, and the singing of the National Anthem. Most schools joining in the celebrations seem broadly to have followed that pattern. At Salford, Robert Roberts remembered classrooms festooned with the flags of the dominions and pupils gazing with pride as teachers pointed to wall maps with their patches of red showing that 'this, and this, and this' belonged to Britain.[60] At Steventon, Berkshire, Miss Margaret Tyrrell recalled the celebrations as a climax to references made during the year by the headmaster to King, Country and Empire. 'I ... wallowed in the singing of patriotic songs.'[61]

Sometimes militaristic overtones were added to the general patriotic mixture. At St Silas's Boys' School, Bristol, celebrations in 1909 included trooping the colour, as well as singing hymns and saluting the Union flag.[62]

Occasionally plays and pageants were also incorporated, although these became more popular after 1914. Nevertheless in 1909 a pageant of 'Britannia and her Possessions' was organised in Liverpool, with 480 children taking part, plus 10,000 others forming a living Union flag with the aid of red, white and blue caps and jerseys. At Oxford in the same year a 'cinematograph entertainment, "Our Navy"' was shown to over a thousand children in the town hall. At the end they were addressed by the rector of Exeter College, who exhorted the boys to learn to shoot straight so as 'to be able to take part in the defence of their country'; the girls were to encourage their brothers and friends 'to take as much interest in handling a rifle as in playing football and cricket'.[63] His remarks were loudly applauded.

Meath's quasi-religious attachment to the Empire even extended to the issuing of an Empire Day catechism, which the children were to learn off by heart. On his own initiative he visited elementary schools, seeking to persuade head teachers of its value in geography lessons.[64] Questions were included on the dimensions of the Empire compared to other countries, but much stress was laid on the importance of instilling the correct moral sentiments. In all, thirty-four questions and answers were included in the catechism. Their general thrust was to encourage the adoption of the passive virtues of endurance and obedience by the lower orders, in contrast to the 'active' qualities of initiative and leadership expected from their social superiors.

Later Meath claimed that many young men who 'rushed to the Colours during the bloody years from 1914' had learned at school 'the watchwords of the movement' and had been influenced thereby to answer 'their country's call so readily'.[65] He may have been correct. What was less in doubt was that many children found the stories of heroism and national glory which were the staple of Empire Day celebrations a welcome change from ordinary school routine. 'They taught us we were the best nation in the world and must live up to it', declared one Bristol pupil, born in 1899. 'We mustn't cause any trouble or bring disgrace on the country, because if we did anything wrong we should disgrace not just ourselves but the nation.'[66]

Not all scholars, however, were so impressionable. A girl who attended a North Warwickshire village school recalled the wearing of a special white dress for the morning ceremonial and the granting of a half-holiday in the afternoon as her clearest memories of Empire Day, rather than the imperial message itself.[67] Still less susceptible were pupils from a radical or socialist background, whose families were hostile to the values of imperialism and militarism. In London, parents who were trade unionists or members of socialist organisations sometimes condemned the introduction of Empire Day celebrations into the capital's schools, and informed the LCC Education Committee of their objections. As late as 1913, protesters included the London Society of Compositors, the London branch of the National Society of Operative Printers and Assistants, the London and Provincial Union of Licensed Vehicle Workers, the National Union of Clerks, the Paddington and Kensington Labour Council and the Poplar Labour League. Some merely expressed opposition; others suggested the substitution of a Peace Day.[68] Walter Southgate's father, a strong critic of the imperialist tendencies of the day, commented sourly on the way the LCC was prepared to spend thousands of pounds of ratepayers' money in buying flagstaffs, so that 'scholars could salute the Union Jack on Empire Day'. Yet they refused to provide needy children with a free meal. Mr Southgate called it 'Patriotism up the pole'.[69] But the Education Committee ignored these views, which were seemingly held by a minority of parents anyway.

Only occasionally did the complaints win official backing, as at Derby in 1909, when the Education Committee narrowly refused to recognise Empire Day because it was the 'thin end of militarism'. However, determined parents could always take matters into their own hands by keeping children away from the morning ceremonial.[70]

III

Concern over Britain's initial failures in the Boer War and the subsequent pressure for military victory undoubtedly strengthened patriotic sentiment in the early twentieth century. It created a current of imperialistic thought more definite, and more assured, than the ebullient jingoism which raged between 1899 and 1902.[71] But the War also influenced another area of public policy — that of the nation's health. As we have seen, the poor physical condition of many would-be recruits led the Board of Education to issue special physical training manuals for use in schools. It also led to other initiatives, including the appointment of an Inter-departmental Committee on Physical Deterioration, whose task was to investigate the nation's overall physical efficiency. Its report, published in 1904, in many ways proved reassuring. It concluded that the poor physical shape which had led to the rejection of 8,000 out of 11,000 would-be volunteers in Manchester applied only to the congested central areas of the major towns. Elsewhere standards of health were probably advancing. But in the black spots, anxiety was justified, with a number of children suffering from malnutrition. To counter this, the Committee recommended steps be taken to ensure youngsters attending school received adequate nourishment. Attention was also drawn to the lack of competence of many working-class mothers in such matters as household management, hygiene, and nutrition. This was seen as contributing to the poor health of their offspring, and almost all those giving evidence before the Committee blamed it upon the girls' elementary schooling, with its over-emphasis on the three R's at the expense of more practical skills.[72]

With this evidence, the imperialist argument took a new turn. It now stressed the importance of giving food and medical treatment to deprived elementary pupils, and instruction in domestic duties to the girls who were the future wives and mothers of the working classes. That included instruction in domestic economy, cookery and infant welfare. As the Liberal MP, T. J. Macnamara, stressed in 1905, a coherent plan for school feeding and continuous medical supervision was essential. 'All this sounds terribly like rank Socialism', he admitted, ' ... but I am not in the least dismayed. Because I know it also to be first-class Imperialism. ... I know

Empire cannot be built on rickety and flat-chested citizens.'[73]

Lord Rosebery presented the Social Darwinist argument still more starkly when he declared that 'the true policy of Imperialism' related 'not to territory alone, but to race as well. The Imperialism that, grasping after territory, ignores the conditions of an Imperial race, is a blind, a futile, and a doomed Imperialism.'[74]

Even Lord Roberts, who saw social reform and defence as the two most pressing problems, put social reform first if the hearts and minds of future soldiers were to be won to the imperialist cause. Without this, he argued, the conditions under which millions of people lived were so bad that they would not 'care a straw under what rule they may be called upon to dwell ... I can quite understand their want of patriotic feeling'.[75]

So the social imperialists joined with Radicals and socialists, who wanted reform for its own sake, to applaud the Education (Provision of Meals) Act of 1906 and the creation of a compulsory school medical service in 1907. Unfortunately the former initiative, a permissive measure only, had even in 1911–12 been adopted by only 131 out of the 322 local education authorities in England and Wales. Not until 1914 could the Board of Education compel authorities to undertake the feeding of necessitous school children.[76]

More widespread was the giving of a 'domestic' bias to the curriculum for elementary schoolgirls. As early as 1905 the Board of Education had asserted that girls must receive a thorough training in domestic duties and be taught 'to set a high value on the housewife's position'. The Elementary School Code of 1906 included new regulations for the teaching of these subjects in the future.[77]

A preoccupation with 'national efficiency' and child welfare were two bi-products, therefore, of the cult of imperialism in late Victorian and Edwardian Britain. But there is little doubt that the prime objective of imperialists was to instil in the rising generation pride in an achievement which had painted so much of the world map red. To this end, the elementary school curriculum was adjusted to emphasise the desired message and a range of youth organisations was promoted which inculcated a love of country and of Empire, and a willingness to sacrifice self for the common good.

Notes

1 The Rt Hon the Earl of Meath, 'Duty and discipline in the training of children', Essay No. 6 in *Essays on Duty and Discipline*, London, 1911, p. 59.
2 *Ibid.* p. 60.
3 *Report of the Board of Education for 1899–1900*, Parl. Papers, XIX, pp. 254–6.

4 *Elementary School Code for 1882*, Parl. Papers, 1882, XXIII, p. 135 and *Instructions to Inspectors on the Administration of the New Code*, London, HMSO, 1878, p. 21.

5 *New Code of 1890*, Parl. Papers, 1890, XXVIII, pp.147 and 151.

6 *Report of the Board of Education for 1900–1901*, Parl. Papers, 1901, XIX, p. 59.

7 *General Reports of HM Inspectors on Elementary Schools and Training Colleges for 1901 and 1902*, Parl. Papers, 1903, XXI, p. 115. Hereafter cited as *General Reports for 1901–2*.

8 F. W. Steer (ed.), *The Memoirs of Gaius Carley*, Chichester, 1964, p. 4.

9 Walter Southgate, *That's the Way it Was. A Working Class Autobiography 1890–1950*, Oxted, 1982, p. 32. St Silas's Boys' School Log Book, 1894–1905, entry for 25 May 1900, at Bristol Record Office.

10 Roger R. Sellman, *Devon Village Schools in the Nineteenth Century*, Newton Abbot, 1967, p. 139.

11 *Revised Instructions Issued to Her Majesty's Inspectors and Applicable to the Code of 1899*, London, HMSO, 1899, p. 19.

12 *The Chelt*, November 1908, p. 1; *Report of the Board of Education for 1900–1901*, p. 207 and for *1899–1900*, p. 341; *General Reports for 1901–2*, p. 175.

13 *Report of the Board of Education for 1900-1901*, p. 207.

14 Peter C. McIntosh, *Physical Education in England Since 1800*, London, 1952, pp. 139–40. *Board of Education: Model Course of Physical Training for Use in the Upper Departments of Public Elementary Schools, 1902*, London, HMSO, 1902.

15 Peter C. McIntosh, *Physical Education*, pp. 140–1, 149.

16 Professor H. L. Withers, *Memorandum on the Teaching of History in the Schools of the London School Board*, London, 1901, p. 2. At the Greater London Record Office, SBL. 1419.

17 *Suggestions for the Consideration of Teachers and Others Concerned in the Work of Public Elementary Schools*, London, HMSO, 1905, p. 61.

18 *Code of Regulations for Public Elementary Schools*, London, HMSO, 1906, p. 3.

19 John O. Springhall, 'Lord Meath, youth, and empire', *Journal of Contemporary History*, 5, 1970, p. 103.

21 C. R. L. Fletcher and Rudyard Kipling, *A School History of England*, Oxford, 1911, pp. 244–5.

21 George T. Warner, *A Brief Survey of British History*, London, 1899, pp. 248–9.

22 George T. Warner and C. H. K. Marten, *Groundwork of British History* Part II, London, 1929 ed., p. 716. This book, first published in 1911, was still in print, in revised form, up to the Second World War. Between 1923 and 1929 alone it was reprinted six times.

23 C. R. L. Fletcher and Rudyard Kipling, *A School History*, pp. 239–40.

24 John M. MacKenzie, *Propaganda and Empire: The Manipulation of British Public Opinion, 1880–1906*, Manchester, 1984, p. 183.

25 G. A. Henty, *The Sovereign Reader: Scenes from the Life and Reign of Queen Victoria to the End of the Nineteenth Century*, London, n.d. [1901], p. 256.

26 *Ibid.* p. 260.

27 *The Queen's Jubilee Atlas of the British Empire*, London and Liverpool, 1887, p. 1. *Howard Vincent Map of the Empire*, 11th ed., London, 1902, not paginated.

28 *Chambers's Geographical Readers of the Continents: Asia and Africa*, London and Edinburgh, 1904, p. 140.

29 Charles F. Vernon, *The Jack Historical Readers: Second Book From the Norman Conquest to the Battle of Bosworth Field*, London, n.d. [1901], p. 156.

30 A.W. Dakers, *The Jack Historical Readers: Fifth Book, Hanoverian England: From the Death of Queen Anne to the Present Time*, London, n.d. [c. 1904–5, pp. 105 and 199.

31 Robert Roberts, *The Classic Slum*, Manchester, 1971, p. 112.
32 St Clement's Boys' School Log Book, Oxford, 12 September, 1910 and St Frideswide's Boys' National School Log Book, Oxford, 28 April and 6 May, 1910, T/SL.24 and T/SL.32 respectively, at Oxford Local History Library.
33 Field-Marshal Earl Roberts, 'An appeal to British boys and girls, what does it mean to be a member of the British Empire?', Essay No. 40 in *Essays on Duty and Discipline*, p. 455.
34 London School Board Minutes, meetings on 23 February, 22 June and 26 October 1893, pp. 207, 694 and 1164, at Greater London Library: Reginald, 12th Earl of Meath, *Memories of the Nineteenth Century*, London, 1923, pp. 328 and 332.
35 LSBM meeting on 18 May 1983, p. 1469. By October 1893, the Board had accepted a tender to supply flags at 5s. 6d. each.
36 *Pitman's King Edward History Reader*, London, n.d. [1904], p. 115.
37 Jack Horn, 'History and patriotism' in *History Workshop Newsletter*, 4, Spring, 1986, pp. 41 and 45; *The Royal School Series: Highroads of History* Book V, (a), London, 1915 ed., pp. 7–8.
38 S. H. Jeyes and F. D. How, *The Life of Sir Howard Vincent*, London, 1912, p. 259.
39 *Howard Vincent Map of the Empire*, 11th ed.
40 Caroline E. Playne, *The Pre-War Mind in Britain*, London, 1928, p. 140, *Report of the Navy League for 1908*, London, 1908, p. 4.
41 *The Navy League Journal*, October 1898, p. 155. Letter from the Sea Cadets to the author, 22 April 1986.
42 Minutes of Bristol School Board, meetings on 29 July 1901 and 28 April 1902, at Bristol Record Office. *Western Daily Press*, 30 July 1901, p. 7, and 29 April 1902, p. 7.
43 *Western Daily Press*, 29 April 1902, p. 7.
44 Caroline E. Playne, *The Pre-War Mind*, p. 143, discussing a view put forward in 1906 by Jacques Bardoux.
45 *Western Daily Express*, 17 December, 1901, p. 7.
46 John O. Springhall, 'Lord Meath', p. 97.
47 'Introduction' by the Earl of Meath, Chairman of Lads' Drill Association to Field-Marshal Earl Roberts, *Defence of the Empire*, London, 1905, frontispiece.
48 John O. Springhall, 'Lord Meath', p. 101.
49 PRO, letter from the Marquess of Londonderry to the Rt Hon H. O. Arnold-Foster, 1 July 1905, ED.24/408.
50 *Hansard* (Commons) 4th ser. CLXXVI, 243, 245 and 250, 17 June 1907.
51 John O. Springhall, 'Lord Meath', p. 101.
52 *Ibid.* p. 104.
53 *United Empire*, V, New Series, 1914, p. 521 and VI, New Series, 1915, p. 154.
54 *The Empire Day Movement Report*, 1932, p. 35. *The Times*, 24 May 1921.
55 Open letters from the Earl of Meath on 'Empire Day', issued in 1905, 1906 and 1907, copies of which are in the Bodleian Library, 2297.e.5.
56 *The Empire Day Movement Report*, 1919, pp. 8–9, in Royal Commonwealth Society Library. I am indebted to the Librarian for his help.
57 'Empire Day' movement: List of Places where 24 May 1906 was kept as Empire, Victoria, Commonwealth Day, in the Bodleian Library, 2297.e.5.
58 Open letter from the Earl of Meath for 1906, p. 2.
59 *Ibid.* p. 9.
60 Robert Roberts, *The Classic Slum*, pp. 112—13.
61 Letter from Miss M. E. Tyrrell of Marcham, Abingdon to the author, 18 August 1986.

62 St Silas's Boys' School Log Book, 1905–17, entry for 24 May 1909, at Bristol Record Office.

63 *Oxford Times*, 29 May 1909 *Federal Magazine*, 15 July 1909, p. 77.

64 London County Council: Education Committee Minutes and Proceedings, meeting on 20 May 1908, p. 1636, at Greater London Library. Henceforward referred to as LCC Education Committee Minutes.

65 *The Times*, 24 May 1921, p. 11 (interview with the Earl of Meath).

66 Stephen Humphries, '"Hurrah for England": Schooling and the Working Class in Bristol, 1870–1914', *Southern History*, 1, 1979, p.184.

67 Reminiscences of my mother concerning Austrey School, Warwickshire, before 1914.

68 LCC Education Committee Minutes, meeting on 11 June 1913, p. 1050.

69 Walter Southgate, *That's the Way it Was*, p. 56.

70 LCC Education Committee Minutes, meeting on 3 July 1907, p. 2116, for example. John O. Springhall, 'Lord Meath', p. 110.

71 Caroline E. Playne, *The Pre-War Mind*, p. 199.

72 Carol Dyhouse, *Girls Growing up in Late Victorian and Edwardian England*, London, 1981, p. 92. *Report of the Interdepartmental Committee on Physical Deterioration*, Parl. Papers 1904, XXXII, p. 348, para. 69.

73 T. J. Macnamara, MP, 'In corpore sano', *Contemporary Review*, February 1905, pp. 245 and 248.

74 Bernard Semmel, *Imperialism and Social Reform*, London, 1960, p. 63.

75 *Lord Roberts' Message to the Nation*, London, 1912, p. 43.

76 Bentley B. Gilbert, *The Evolution of National Insurance in Great Britain*, London, 1966, pp. 113 and 116.

77 Carol Dyhouse, *Girls Growing Up*, p. 94.

Further reading

Chancellor, Valerie E., *History for their Masters*, Bath, 1970.

Dyhouse, Carol, *Girls Growing Up in Late Victorian and Edwardian England*, London, 1981. *Essays on Duty and Discipline*, London, 1911.

Gilbert, Bentley B., *The Evolution of National Insurance in Great Britain*, London, 1966.

Humphries, Stephen, *Hooligans or Rebels?*, Oxford, 1983 ed.

MacKenzie, John M., *Propaganda and Empire*, Manchester, 1984.

Semmel, Bernard, *Imperialism and Social Reform*, London, 1960.

Springhall, John O., 'Lord Meath, youth and empire' in *Journal of Contemporary History*, 5, 1970.

C

CHAPTER THREE

The nineteenth-century English preparatory school: cradle and crèche of Empire?

Donald Leinster-Mackay

For each perfect gift of thine
To our race is freely given,
Graces human and divine,
Flowers of earth and buds of heaven

Verse from Victorian Hymn: *For the Beauty of the Earth,*
Folliot Sandford Pierpoint, 1835—1917

It is one of the ironies of the history of the English public school that Haileybury, founded to provide recruits for service in India four years after the East India College closed in 1858,[1] should have as one of its most famous old boys, if not *the* most famous old boy,[2] Earl Attlee. As Prime Minister in 1947, Attlee presided over (*pace* Lord Mountbatten) the granting of independence to India and Pakistan. Earl Attlee was to Haileybury what Sir Winston Churchill was to Harrow: the school's most favoured twentieth-century son. Winston Churchill was also a pupil at Brunswick House dame preparatory school, so too, Clement Attlee was a prep-school boy at the less fashionable school of Northaw Place at Potters Bar.[3] This point is stressed because so often it is overlooked that, before boys attend public school, they first learn life-skills at their prep school.

Young Clem Attlee's headmaster at Northaw Place — an average-size prep school for the 1890s of thirty-five boys — was typically a cleric, the Rev F. J. Hall, whose main interests were cricket and the Bible, in that order. In another way, too, Hall's was a typical prep school for the 1890s. As an ex-mathematics master at Haileybury, the Rev Hall maintained a strong link between Northaw and Haileybury so that in the days long before the foundation in 1922 of Haileybury Junior School (alias Clewer Manor), Northaw, was a feeder school for Haileybury College.

The foregoing preamble has been very necessary since it is the purpose of this chapter to consider this symbiotic relationship between prep schools and public schools, and in particular to examine the several functions of the English preparatory school during the palmy days of the British Empire and the methods by which these functions were fulfilled.

The English public school and the English preparatory school were both Victorian phenomena. T. W. Bamford analysed the rise of the public schools in the book of that title in which he demonstrated that, although some of the major schools such as Winchester and Eton had histories stretching back to the fourteenth and fifteenth centuries and even further back, as did some of the 'revived endowed grammar schools' such as St Peter's, York and King's School, Canterbury (both seventh century), they were nevertheless essentially Victorian institutions.[5] It was only after the earlier reforms of Samuel Butler of Shrewsbury (1798-1836) and Thomas Arnold of Rugby (1828–42) *et al.* that the English public school emerged as an institution capable of meeting the rising aspirations of a newly-emergent middle class who sought for their sons gentlemanly polish.

As Bamford has carefully noted, before this revival of the public school, with its greatly enlarged clientele, the schools experienced fluctuating numbers of pupils and an attendant lack of institutional security.[6] Similarly, the English preparatory school was in essence a Victorian phenomenon, the *raison d'être* of which was to be found largely in the English public school itself.[7] Although some of the earliest prep schools had histories going back to the early nineteenth century, as in the cases of Twyford (c. 1809)[8] and Temple Grove (c. 1810),[9] and even back to the seventeenth century, as in the case of Cheam School (1645),[10] they nevertheless did not emerge as private 'feeder' schools to the public schools until about the 1860s, at the time of the Clarendon and Taunton Commission Reports. Of necessity, the revived English public schools had to establish a previously-unknown hegemony before the private preparatory schools could become their acknowledged feeders, preparing boys primarily for public-school entry. Before the 1860s, therefore, 'preparatory' schools such as Cheam and Temple Grove were more accurately rival 'private classical schools'.[11]

The articulated public-school system of the twentieth century, of which the prep schools form an integral part, grew out of two types of school with totally different origins. Public schools were largely institutions associated with philanthropy (in the case of collegiate and endowed schools) and with public or religious interests (in the case of proprietary schools), whilst the private preparatory schools were invariably private venture schools with a 'legitimate' private-profit motive.[12] The two types of school gradually coalesced during the second half of the nineteenth century to form, by the end of the century, an integrated system of education for English middle- and upper-class boys.[13]

This gradual process of integration occurred during the fifty or so years between about 1864 and 1914. The four stages of this process in the longer term have been indicated elsewhere.[14]

The rise of the English prep school *qua* prep school was, to a very large extent, dependent on the rise of the English public school. By the late 1860s, both institutions were developing gradually as an integrated system for the education of England's upper- and middle-classes. This system was, to some extent, strengthened by the endowed schools legislation of 1869-74, following the Taunton Commission or Schools Inquiry Commission Report of 1867–68, since a major outcome of that report and subsequent legislation was the reform of many schools' governing bodies, as the

Endowed Schools Commissioners, and later the Charity Schools Commissioners, set about their allotted task.

This reform of many of the endowed public schools and the emergence of private preparatory schools coincided too with the gradual increase in awareness of the British Empire amongst the British middle classes. The Indian Mutiny of 1857 and the subsequent abolition of the East India Company did much to raise the general level of consciousness about the empire. Certainly by 1870 the level of consciousness had been raised in certain sections of that population. For example, John Ruskin, who in 1870 had just been appointed Slade Professor of Fine Art at Oxford, devoted his inaugural lecture to the subject of 'Imperial duty'. Such was the charismatic nature of Ruskin as a lecturer that Oxford undergraduates filled the University Museum to hear him and, when that was found to be too small, they proceeded to cram the larger Sheldonian Theatre, the venue having been rapidly changed to accommodate a larger audience. Ruskin's lectures and addresses were not of the nature to go unnoticed; they were stirring and cogent in their message and, as Morris has observed, 'audiences of every kind hung upon his phrases'.[15] Ruskin placed the British Empire firmly in the nation's consciousness or, more accurately, in the consciousness of some of its future society leaders. But it was not just the rhetoric of Ruskin's imperialist imperative that turned the nation towards a new imperial consciousness. Benjamin Disraeli bedazzled the nation with his flamboyant imperialistic policies. His death in 1881 allowed another dandy to assume the new imperialist mantle: Joseph Chamberlain. As Secretary of State for the Colonies in the third Salisbury government, Chamberlain presided over the imperialist extravaganza known as the Diamond Jubilee.

But if the Diamond Jubilee of 1897 was the apogee of empire, the 1890s were also the heyday of both public and preparatory schools. It was, for example, the period when the arch-imperialist, J. E. C. Welldon, later Bishop of Calcutta, was headmaster of Harrow School (1885-98) and when the emerging preparatory schools formed their professional association of headmasters, the inaugural meeting for which was occasioned very symbolically by the need to discuss the appropriate size of cricket balls and cricket pitches for young boys between the ages of eight and thirteen. But more of that later. Suffice it to say at this stage that the education of males for the upper- and middle-classes in the 1890s could be discerned generally to consist of three clearly-defined stages: preparatory school; public school and, for a great many, a private tutor or 'crammer' before going either to university, the Civil Service (Home and Indian) or commissioned service in the Army. For the young Winston Churchill, for example, his experiences at Brunswick House from 1884 to 1888[16] and later at Captain James' 'crammer' in Cromwell Road, London,[17] were just as formative and necessary as his more publicised days at Harrow. It is the burden of this chapter to show that the preparatory schools were just as orientated towards the British Empire as either the public school or the examination-orientated private tutor.

Recognition of the part played by the preparatory schools in the late nineteenth century enterprise of ruling the empire is to be found in Philip Mason's *The Men Who Ruled India*, when he observed that:

> Plato taught that the guardians of the State should not know their parents; the English did not go as far as that, but when they were eight years old the children from whom rulers were to be chosen were taken away from home for three-quarters of every year, taught not to mention their mother or their own Christian names, brought up in the traditions of the Sparta which Plato admired. And the children grew up to be true guardians; no other people in history can equal this record of disinterested guardianship.[18]

That conditions were Spartan and harsh in the early prep schools such as Twyford and Temple Grove is not to be gainsaid, but at the same time this was to be expected since the first half of the nineteenth century was a period of general harshness and asperity before the onset of the animal comforts of life, such as room-illumination by gas and more comfortable travel. But traditionally life at school, especially boarding school, had been harsh and discipline strict, and remained so in the nineteenth century. Flogging or birching in school was commonplace and there are many references to cruelty and corporal punishment in autobiographies, but perhaps the worst example of this concerns the case of John Lawrence (1811-79), the future Governor-General of India, who it was alleged was 'flogged every day of (his) life at [a Mr Gough's] school except one, and then [he] was flogged twice'.[19] Similarly, Henry Labouchere's skin was permanently discoloured because of the constant floggings he received at a school in Brighton in 1825.[20] The relatively tender years of prep-school boys did not spare them the rod, so that, for example, Dr Leopold Bernays (1847-60) of Elstree, a feeder school for Harrow, had almost as notorious a record as Dr John Keate of Eton for being liberal with the cane. It has been alleged that Bernays used to froth at the mouth when caning boys, which must have alarmed his victims.[21] But one old boy, despite not liking Bernays, nevertheless wrote of his old headmaster: 'I maintain that with all the hard and severe discipline of those days (and severe it was) still we ought to be grateful to those who turned out courteous, brave high minded gentlemen from the school at Elstree Hill.'[22] These were sterling qualities for boys being moulded eventually for a place in imperial service. The Spartan conditions of prep-school life, of frequent beatings, indiscriminate bullying, plain and sometimes inadequate food, helped to condition young boys to self-dependence and 'manliness'.

Notwithstanding the attack by W. E. W. Collins in *Blackwood's Edinburgh Magazine* in 1894 on the contemporary preparatory school, suggesting that it 'should be a nursery for hardening young cuttings, not a hot-house to force exotic plants',[23] some prep schools in the 1890s were still chill, Spartan institutions. At Temple Grove, for example, according to the late Meston Batchelor, 'In the dormitories snow frequently piled upon the blankets and ice formed on the water jugs: the lavatories ... would have been condemned in a slum tenement.' Batchelor was writing about the period between 1880 and 1907.[24]

It was not only the physical conditions at Temple Grove that were harsh: the daily régime was also a long and wearisome one for very young boys. We know this from a letter sent by Martin White Benson, the eldest son of Archbishop Benson of Canterbury to his father,[25] outlining thus the typical day at Temple Grove in the early 1870s:

6.30 am	Get up
7.00 am	Go to get boots
7.15 am	Work till 8.30 am
8.30 am	Prayers and breakfast
9.30-10.45 am	Work
10.45-11.15 am	Drill
11.15 am	Work
12.30 pm	Play
1.00 pm	Dinner (meat and pudding, beer or porter)
4.00-6.00 pm	Work
6.00 pm	Tea (with bread and butter)
7.00-8.00 pm	Work
8.00 pm	Prayers
8.30 pm	Bed (after a very simple snack)[26]

The great value, however, of the preparatory schools for the public schools was the process of socialisation which prep-school boys experienced before entry to their public schools. As their very name indicates, preparatory schools functioned to give small boys a foretaste of their life after the age of thirteen. The prep schools thus mirrored the public schools, not only in their concentration on the study of the classics (at least in the nineteenth century) but also in the small classes for such study.

Like the public schools, many of the preparatory schools had their own chapels. At Aysgarth School, for example, the chapel is extremely handsome, having a most splendid barrel ceiling, and a pulpit that once stood in Easby Abbey. In prep-school chapels, such as that at Aysgarth, were preached sermons echoing sentiments similarly expressed by Thomas Arnold, Edward Thring and Henry Montagu Butler. H. M. Butler, for example, may have called Harrovians patriotically to a higher sense of duty as he did on 21 October 1866 in a sermon on the subject 'England expects every man to do his duty'[27] but it was the Rev F. de W. Lushington, assistant master at Elstree School, who delivered sermons, not only on the great truths of Christianity but also laced these sermons with references to the British Empire in the service of which, no doubt, many of his boys' parents were then active. A few examples of these imperial *obiter dicta* must suffice. In a sermon entitled 'The same, but not the same' preached on the Fifth Sunday after Easter 1898, Lushington observed:

> Most of you have read in the papers of the great victory recently gained by our troops in Egypt over the Dervishes at the battle of Atbara; and in the illustrated papers you must have seen pictures showing the long British line advancing, quietly and steadily advancing though exposed all the time to a heavy fire from the Arabs behind the Zariba.[28]

Lushington may have been trying to engage the boys' interest by referring to the Dervishes, with whom most of them would have been familiar through the large number of boys' adventure tales for which the empire formed a natural setting, but he was also planting the notion of British Empire firmly in their minds.

Lushington, no doubt, in a sermon entitled, 'The Queen — why so great[?]', quickly engaged the attention of the boys when he said: 'Some of you have relations in distant lands [? "He must be talking about Pater and Mater!"]; today you must feel united to them in the unity of the common prayer ... To-day, instead of thinking ourselves as individuals we think of ourselves as members of a great empire.'[29]

Later Lushington alluded very obliquely to Kipling's 'white man's burden' and the 'great white Queen' when he asked the boys to remember 'that just as all that is good in the influence of the Queen comes from her trust in God, and because His wisdom has guided her and His arm strengthened her so you too can only get the power to influence others for good from God'.[30]

Such religious imprecations were reinforced, as already suggested, by schoolboy stories of adventure, fair play and sportsmanship. Some of these were written by a headmaster of Eagle House Preparatory School, the Rev

A. N. Malan (1874-1905) who, during the 1880s and 1890s, was a writer of short stories and a regular contributor to *Boys' Own Paper (BOP)* where he amused the young Clive Barnard with his stories about Dr Porchester's Academy for Young Gentlemen.[31] Other contributors to *BOP* wrote of bravery by young Englishmen guarding an Empire on which the sun never set. In much the same way, the Rev Lushington introduced the defence of Lucknow[32] into one of his sermons as part of the subconscious socialisation of his prep-school boys. Lushington was an ingenious preacher since, in the same sermon, 'Ezekiel's Vision — strength out of weakness', he managed to encapsulate with the defence of Lucknow the then recent death of Edward Benson, Archbishop of Canterbury, in William Ewart Gladstone's parish church at Hawarden.[33]

Another form of reinforcement of the imperial ethos amongst preparatory-school boys was the study of history (including empire history). A history competition was instituted for preparatory schools in 1885 called the Harrow History Prize.[34] Eric Blair (alias George Orwell) and Cyril Connolly, both of St Cyprian's School, Eastbourne, won the Harrow History Prize in different years.[35] As we shall see in Chapter 7, a typical history text-book of the time, published by the Oxford University Press and written by the distinguished, if unconventional, historian, C. R. L. Fletcher, and the keen imperialist Rudyard Kipling was *A School History of England* (1911). It was probably used by *junior* classes in preparatory schools. The preface to this school history consisted of one sentence: 'This book is written for all boys and girls who are interested in the story of Great Britain and her Empire.' The joint authors, when commenting on the many British colonies in Africa, observed: 'the natives everywhere welcome the mercy and justice of our rule, and they are no longer liable, as they were before we came, to be carried off as slaves by Arab slave dealers'. At an early age, the British ruling classes were being made aware of 'the white man's burden'. Needless to say, there appeared in it a map of the world with the possessions of the British Empire clearly marked.

Socialisation of the preparatory-school boy for his future public school took other forms. Many preparatory schools adopted a form of prefect system, thus giving great responsibility to boys of twelve to thirteen, an ideal early training for future African or Indian District Commissioners. But, of all forms of preparatory school socialisations, perhaps the most significant was that of organised games which, in the wake of public-school fervour for such games and sports from the 1860s onwards, was widespread also in preparatory schools. This very important point will be taken up later in the chapter.

Meanwhile, it can be seen by reference to such contemporary works as

The Public Schools and Empire (1913),[36] *Eclipse or Empire?* (1916)[37] and *The English Tradition of Education* (1929),[38] all three written by public-school headmasters, that the preparatory schools were an integral part of the public-schools system. That was now taken for granted. Being thus tied to the public schools, they were also hitched to the notion of empire. James Morris epitomised this brilliantly in his *Farewell the Trumpets*. He wrote:

> That small kilted boy... when he returns to his preparatory school at the end of the holidays, will not often be allowed to forget that he is born to an imperial heritage. Every day's curriculum reminds him. School prayers, for a start, will doubtless include a prayer for the Queen-Empress and her subjects across the world, may well include a sermon about imperial responsibilities or missionary needs, and is very likely to end with some devotional hymn of empire. Refulgent upon the classroom wall will hang the map of the world, on Mercator's projection preferably, for no other shows to such advantage the lavish slabs of red which mark the authority of the British — and perhaps a shipping chart, demonstrating by its distribution of boat-shaped blobs how overwhelming is the British maritime power — and possibly some inspiring steel engraving too, Caton Woodville's famous picture of the Khartoum memorial service, or one of Lady Butler's celebrated reconstructions of British gallantry in the field.

He continued:

> Luncheon nevertheless, in school hall, and perhaps there is some old boy at high table, home from the war, swaggering in red and gleaming brass, and reminiscing airily to the envious masters all about. To the cricket field next, nursery of England's style, where Newbolt's verses echo always, if not among the players — at least among the umpires —
>
>> There's a breathless hush in the Close tonight —
>> Ten to make and the match to win —
>> A bumping pitch and a blinding light,
>> An hour to play and the last man in.
>> And it's not for the sake of a ribboned coat,
>> Or the selfish hope of a season's fame,
>> But his Captain's hand on his shoulder smote —
>> Play up! play up! and play the game!
>
> And when our little friend goes to bed after prep that night, to a good read under the blankets, there G. A. Henty awaits him no doubt, with his tales of British adventure, or Rider Haggard's vision of Africa or perhaps just the Boys' Own Paper ... in which the pluck of British youth is for ever matched, and for ever victorious, against wickedness, savagery and foreignness.[39]

H.S. Shelton was of the opinion that the main reason for the close connection between public and preparatory schools was the evolution of the scholarship system.[40] Eton and Winchester, by dint of their ancient foundation scholarships, were first in the scholarship field. But Harrow School, as early as 1840, offered the Gregory Scholarships of £100, tenable for four years, in order to attract able boys to the school. The Rev H. Montagu Butler helped Harrow to achieve this aim by instituting, in 1865, further entrance scholarships. It is worth noting in this context that Montague J. Rendall (1860–1950), the arch-imperialist,[41] was the first boy from Elstree to win an entrance scholarship to Harrow.

Such developments in the provision of scholarships for entry to the leading public schools served as an incentive for drawing even more closely together prep schools with public schools, some schools developing almost a special relationship. Summer Fields, for example, through its winning scholarships under the Rev Dr C. E. Williams, was closely linked with Eton, as Harold Macmillan noted in 1964.[42]

But if many close links were established between preparatory and public schools through competitive scholarship examinations, it should be recognised that the bulk of boys leaving preparatory school for public school did so via an entrance rather than a scholarship examination. The entrance examinations, conducted over decades before finally being formalised by the institution of the common-entrance examination in 1903, sought to establish a candidate's basic literacy and classical competency. This continuing process of examination over a period of time helped to cement associations between prep and public school,[43] and this in turn helped to confirm the process of socialisation for public school which should be seen as the principal *raison d'être* for the preparatory schools.

A second major function of the preparatory school from early times to the twentieth century was the preparation of boys for entry into the Royal Navy. As many as 230 IAPS schools and thirteen non-IAPS prep schools prepared boys for the Royal Navy in 1924.[44] This often overlooked function of the preparatory schools linked them with the British Empire *sui generis* in so far as the Royal Navy in the nineteenth century was the nation's bulwark against possible foreign interference. The Royal Navy provided a secure framework and global communications between the several parts of the empire and as such was a linchpin in the imperial system. The preparatory schools were thus truly the cradles of empire in so far as *they* educated future naval officers in their early years.

The ties between private preparatory schools and the Royal Navy were strengthened in 1838 by the introduction of an entrance examination. Although the examination was at first very easy, the institution of any examination entailed the possible failure of some to gain entry. It was then that such schools came into their own. In anticipation of this, Windlesham House was founded in 1837 by Lt Charles Malden, RN. This was the school that was recognised in 1900 as the first of the English preparatory schools.[45] Inaccurate as was that assessment,[46] it was nevertheless of great significance that Windlesham House should be founded by a retired naval officer.

Shortly after the opening of Windlesham House, a second preparatory school which gained a reputation for preparing boys for the Royal Navy which was second to none opened its doors in 1841. This was Stubbington House Preparatory School, founded by the Rev William Foster. Admiral Lord Charles Beresford (1846–1919), who as a captain took part in the bombardment of Alexandria in 1882, was a pupil at Stubbington House before entering the navy at the age of thirteen in 1859.

Several biographies and autobiographies have described the school days of old Stubbingtonians, including *The Life of Major General Wauchope*, a record of the life of a Black Watch officer killed at the Battle of Magersfontein during the Second Boer War.[47] Wauchope's biography is a signal witness to the fact that Stubbington House, if a pre-eminent 'naval' preparatory school, also gave early education to other pioneers and soldiers of empire.

By the 1880s, many other preparatory schools were preparing boys for the naval-entrance examination. Amongst those that achieved a considerable measure of recognition because of their very satisfactory success rate was Eastman's Royal Naval Academy which became a preparatory school *per se* in the twentieth century.

Cordwalles School was another preparatory school of long-standing[48] which, before it became St Piran's in 1919, had strong connections with the naval training ship *HMS Britannia*. Between 1890 and 1910 eleven boys passed from Cordwalles to Royal Navy training who later became Rear Admirals. Rear Admiral H. C. Allen, for example, took part in the capture of the Taku Forts in China at the time of the Boxer Rebellion in 1900 when he was still a midshipman.[49]

Yet another function of preparatory schools was for them to serve as crèches for the children of those engaged in the maintenance or defence of empire. On the stage of world politics, the ninety-nine years from Waterloo in 1815 to the beginning of World War I in 1914 could be seen, compared with the seventeenth and eighteenth centuries, as a period of unprecedented peace, broken mainly by the martial interlude of the Crimean War. But this would be a mistaken view. According to W. L. Burn, commenting on the early part of the nineteenth century:

British troops had been in action against Gurkhas, Pindaries, Mahrattas, Sikhs, Afghans, Burmese, Chinese, Kaffirs, Ashantis and Boers. Ships of the Royal Navy had bombarded Algiers, routed the Turks at Navarino, operated against Mehemit Ali, underwritten Latin American independence, blockaded Buenos Aires and the Piraeus, captured slavers and waged war on pirates from the Caribbean to the China Sea. Assam, Sind and the Punjaub and a great part of Burma had fallen to British arms.[50]

It was, however, the second half of the nineteenth century which saw a pronounced upsurge in imperialist activity, including the acquisitive activity of Cecil Rhodes, whose ambitions were given rein in the scramble for Africa in the 1880s and 1890s, during which time Britain took the lion's share of Africa. By the end of the century, Britain had acquired an empire of more than 13,000,000 square miles containing a population of between 400 and 420 million. To win and maintain such a vast empire had made, and continued to make, huge demands on British manpower. Moreover, territories that had been either taken by conquest or annexed needed to be administered and it was in this enterprise that the English public and preparatory schools made their greatest national contribution. The prolonged absence from the mother-country of her menfolk, either serving with the regiment in far-off India or administering as District Officer a vast tract of African land, often necessitated the expatriation of their wives too. For this very cogent reason there was a need to put children into boarding-schools. The need was met by preparatory schools serving a national purpose: they became the crèches of empire. In other words, whilst father and mother were abroad, the preparatory schools became the national crèches or surrogate homes for their younger progeny.

So far this chapter has acknowledged the intense socialisation process provided by preparatory schools for future public-school pupils. It has acknowledged the close ties between the two types of school, made even closer by early-established scholarships and a common-entrance-examination system from 1903 onwards. It has acknowledged, too, the very special contribution of the preparatory school to the creation and maintenance of empire through its early education of future naval officers and the special function of prep schools as crèches of empire. It remains now to examine more closely an aspect of the socialisation that fully cemented preparatory schools and public schools: the intensive playing of organised games, denounced by some as 'the cult of athleticism'.

It is of the greatest significance that the preparatory schools came to associate together professionally through a shared interest in establishing special rules for preparatory-school cricket. As the resolution passed by some fifty preparatory-school headmasters on 30 March 1892 indicated,[51] it was felt that small boys should not have to play cricket in the same way as their elder brothers; allowance ought to be made for their diminutive size. As Mr A. J. C. Dowding, a former headmaster of St Ninian's Preparatory School, Moffat, observed in 1900 of his own Scottish experience: 'The distance between the wickets was *twenty one* yards, which I regard as the outside limit that a young boy can comfortably command without risk of overbowling himself. We used the undersized ball, which Mr Wisden specially introduced to meet the wishes of Preparatory schools, which some of us had expressed to him.'[52] Dowding was a young man in the 1860s when he first entered preparatory schoolmastering, at which time when there were but few preparatory schools *per se* and certainly no tradition of organised games. But the next 'thirty years which saw the rise of Preparatory Schools'[53] also witnessed the rise of organised games, not only in public schools but also in their junior counterparts. Although the small size of individual preparatory schools initially had the effect of inhibiting the playing of competitive games, this situation gradually changed as the schools increased in pupil numbers. Consequently, it was only by the late-Victorian period that preparatory schools could be seen as incipient exemplars of Muscular Christianity.

One of the earliest examples of enthusiasm for cricket was at Elstree School, where the new headmaster, the Rev Lancelot Sanderson (1869–1900), within a short time of taking office enlarged the school cricket field. Between 1874 and 1900 Elstree boys made seventy-seven appearances at the Lord's Eton v. Harrow match. In 1885, a particularly good year for Elstree representation, seven out of the eleven Harrow players were originally from Elstree. For example, Archie Maclaren, the Captain of Lancashire County Cricket Club and the England team in five Test series against Australia, was an ex-Elstree boy.[54] One of the reasons for this early reputation as a cricketing school was that Sanderson enlisted cricket blues on his staff and employed two bowling professionals from Lord's to coach the boys.

Preparatory schools were taking their cricket seriously in the 1870s and 1880s, perhaps sometimes to an excessive degree. At St Andrew's School, Eastbourne, the bluff Yorkshireman and headmaster (1890–1933), the Rev E. L. Browne, ('E. L. B.') carried cricket to the very limits, making cricket in his school a quasi-religion. His school magazine was filled with endless reports of school matches and estimates of individual players' form. The first edition of the school magazine in 1900 carried the following 'poem' composed by 'E. L. B.' which, while written in jest, clearly indicated his zest for games and his contempt for those who did not share his enthusiasm:

The Feminine Boy

If cursed by a son who declined to play cricket
(Supposing him sound and sufficient in thews),
I'd larrup him well with a third of a wicket,
Selecting safe parts of his body to bruise.
In his mind such an urchin King Solomon had
When he said, 'Spare the stump, and you bungle the lad!'

For what in the world is the use of a creature
All flabbily bent on avoiding the pitch?
Who wanders about, with a sob in each feature,
Devising a headache, inventing a stitch?
There surely would be a quick end to my joy
If possessed of that monster — the feminine boy!

The feminine boy who declines upon croquet,
Or halma, or spillikins (horrible sport!),
Or any amusement that's female and pokey.
And flatly objects to behave as he ought!
I know him of old. He is lazy and fat,
And sadly in need of the thick of a bat!

Instead of this Thing, fit for punishment drastic,
Give, Fortune, a son who is nimble and keen;
A bright-hearted sample of human elastic,
As fast as an antelope, supple and clean;
Far other than he in whose dimples there lodge
Significant signs of inordinate stodge.

Ay, give me the lad who is eager and chubby,
A Stoddart[55] in little, a hero in bud;
Who'd think it a positive crime to grow stubby,
And dreams half the night he's a Steel[56] or a Studd![57]
There's the youth for my fancy, all youngsters above,
The boy for my handshake, the lad for my love![58]

E. L. B., not unlike the British comedian Jimmy Edwards in appearance, was utterly besotted with the power of cricket. Even the school chapel where he preached was not immune from this pervasive pseudo-religion. On at least one occasion, Brown explained the mystery of the Holy Trinity to his boys in terms of 'Three Stumps; one wicket'.

Cricket was played at St Andrew's throughout the summer with regular morning practice in the nets with 'E. L. B.' in command at the bowler's end dressed in a large white apron from whence he produced an endless series of cricket balls.[59] *Every* boy in the school entered in competitions for throwing the cricket ball. E. L. B. often took his boys to the Saffrons, the county cricket ground, where the Indian Ranjitsinhji was a celebrity player.

The aim of all this emphasis on cricket was its character-building value. Basing much faith on two current and interdependent educational theories — faculty psychology and the transfer of training, both applied equally faithfully in the classroom to the learning of Latin and Greek, public and preparatory schoolmasters saw in games, especially cricket, the means to the development of another side of boys' faculties not touched on by the classroom. Games were seen as a means for the effective development of boys, fitting them to deal in later life with social problems — at home or abroad! As Dowding observed in 1900:

> It is the spirit that loves these games and in turn is fostered by them, that has made England a dominant nation — to be covetous of honour, slow to admit defeat, appreciative of discipline, self-reliant, ready of resource, quick to catch an opportunity, prompt to accept responsibility, and above all, to be willing to sink the personal in the public interest, is to be English-like, and we pride ourselves on the foreigner's inability to understand the mad Englishman who finishes his game of bowls within sight of an Armada, or who while his rivals are hurriedly raising earthworks and sinking rifle pits, levels himself a cricket ground.[60]

Apart from cricket, preparatory schools in the late nineteenth and early twentieth centuries played several other sports, including both soccer and rugger, athletics, paper-chasing, running, golf, cycling and swimming, all of which aimed at producing manliness and character in those participating. Certain schools earned reputations in certain sports. Fonthill School (1820) developed a strong soccer tradition through the efforts of one assistant master, W. W. Radcliffe of the Wanderers' Club, which won the FA Cup in the early years of its history, and of another, the Rev R. V. Sealy, an England soccer player.[61] Elstree, too, quickly won a reputation for association football, largely through the coaching efforts of two of its assistant masters: C. P. Wilson (1883–98) and Arthur Dunn (1885–91), both of whom were soccer internationals.

Another major exponent of the games cult amongst preparatory-school headmasters was Mr E. P. Frederick of Wells House School, Malvern (1903-28). Frederick had taught mathematics at Loretto from 1882 to 1892 under that redoubtable philathlete, H. H. Almond, whom he admired greatly. One of Frederick's first reforms on arrival at Wells House School was to replace association by rugby football because he reckoned it was a better preparation for games at public school. One of Wells House's first inter-school rugby fixtures was with the Dragon School. Inspired by Almond, Frederick worked hard to ensure Wells House's high reputation for rugby amongst preparatory schools. Within five years, his first XV excelled itself by scoring 252-0 against its opponents. Whilst Wells House School shone at rugby, Parkside Preparatory School, Cobham, excelled at hockey and Aysgarth exemplified a leading golfing school.[62]

From the 1920s onwards, the notion of manliness derived from team games, especially cricket and football, gave way to a more individualistic ethos, of which educational emphasis Professor T. P. Nunn of the London Institute of Education was the exemplar. This revamped philosophy of individualism to be seen as a forceful reaction against the then dominant influence of idealism in British education[63] contributed to the emergence of an alternative tradition to manliness, *esprit de corps* and team games.

One sporting activity which did not rely on *esprit de corps* but on individual skills was rifle-shooting. School teams competed against each other and a Preparatory Schools Rifle Association (PSRA) was founded in 1905,[64] but this new sporting activity was essentially based on the efforts of discrete individuals and individual scores. The origins of this sport have perhaps even closer ties with the British Empire than say football or cricket, whose influence on imperial development could at best be said only to be indirect. Rifle-shooting on the other hand was closely linked with the aspirations of General Lord Roberts, the most successful of Queen Victoria's generals, to introduce universal military training for the British male populace.[65]

The origins of school rifle-shooting went back perhaps to the 1850s after the traumas of the Crimean War and Indian Mutiny when many schools' volunteer corps were established to give boys some preliminary military training.[66] Naturally in public schools, amongst more senior boys, the volunteer corps took off well, although Uppingham under Edward Thring's influence remained a notable exception to the rule, well after his death in the late 1880s. But even amongst preparatory schools and their diminutive pupils volunteer corps were established, one of the earliest established being that at Mostyn House in 1860.[67]

The Second Boer War was another major influence in the formation of the PSRA. In 1904 an article on rifle-shooting appeared in the *Preparatory Schools Review (PSR)*.[68] Mr A. G. Grenfell (Mostyn House), the Rev E. L. Browne (St Andrew's, Eastbourne), the Rev Herbert Bull (Wellington House, Westgate-on-Sea) and Mr Robert Vickers (Scaitcliffe) showed an early interest and, with the help of Captain Soltau-Symons, the Adjutant of Eton College Corps, the PSRA was formed, the main function of which was to organise an annual shooting competition amongst preparatory schools.

A less militaristic alternative to the vounteer rifle corps in both public and preparatory schools were the scout groups. The scout movement was established by Robert Baden Powell, an old Carthusian and hero of Mafeking who had been educated in his early years at Rose Hill Preparatory School. Colonel Ulich de Burgh, the Deputy Chief Commissioner of the scout movement played a not inconsiderable part in the creation of scout troops in preparatory schools from 1908 onwards. Three schools in particular — Windlesham House, West Downs and Colwall — went so far as to make the scout troops and cub packs a major part of the school organisation. The scout movement, the volunteer corps and the rifle-shooting clubs represented a closer and more direct affinity with the interests of empire. At least two of these later developments — rifle-shooting clubs and the scout movement — had some links with the emergent individualistic ethos after the First World War. By 1924, for example, Stanley S. Harris, Headmaster of St Ronan's Hawkehurst, Kent, could write about the 'false values' that had been placed upon school games causing him never to appoint Blues to his staff.[69] Such a critical attitude contrasted sharply with the earlier situation at Dunchurch Hall Preparatory School where the headmaster was a former Oxford cricket Blue, and of his six assistant masters, two had played rugby for England, one had captained Kent at cricket, one was a famous Corinthian and soccer international, and one had played hockey for England.[70] As Eric Parker[71] once observed: 'Get a Blue, and you will see your money back again.'[72] This somewhat cynical comment has perhaps less to do with this book than has a comment by E. S. Dudding, Headmaster of Wolborough Hill School (1892-8) who once observed: 'The boy who learns to play for his side at school will do good work for his country as a man.'[73] Preparatory school games not only prepared a boy for public school at home but also for public service abroad.

Notes

1 The main school building and the quadrangle were built in 1806 for the East India College. After the Indian Mutiny of 1857 and the demise of the East India Company, the school was closed but reopened as the refounded Haileybury College in 1862.

2 Doubts exist because Rudyard Kipling was a pupil at Westward Ho! which later became the Imperial Service College. Haileybury and Imperial Service College amalgamated in 1942. Bronze busts of both Earl Attlee and Rudyard Kipling are to be found in the Haileybury Library.

3 Kenneth Harris, *Attlee*, Weidenfeld and Nicolson, 1982, pp. 7-8. Northaw Place was opened in 1881.

4 T. W. Bamford, *The Rise of the Public Schools*, Nelson, 1967.

5 Some nineteenth-century public schools in any case, having been founded after 1837, were unquestionably Victorian.

6 *Ibid*. pp. 1-16.

7 Preparatory schools catered also for entry into the Royal Navy as midshipmen. See below, pp. 65-6.

8 See C. T. Wickham (ed.), *The Story of Twyford School*, Winchester, Wykeham Press, 1909. See also R. G. Wickham, *Shades of the Prison House*, Foxbury Press, 1986.

9 See Meston Batchelor, *Cradle of Empire, A Preparatory School Through Nine Centuries*, Phillimore Press, 1981.

10 See Edward Peel, *Cheam School from 1645*, Thornhill Press, 1974.

11 See Nicholas Hans, *New Trends in Education in the Eighteenth Century*, Routledge and Kegan Paul, 1951, pp. 117-35.

12 Such motivation was 'legitimate' in the sense that, in order to ensure a reasonable level of living in retirement, a private preparatory school principal had to make sufficient profit to allow for this sombre but inevitable fact.

13 Michael Sadler, for example, boldly asserted that preparatory schools were 'Secondary' schools at a time when 'Secondary' still held a class connotation. Further, Sadler declared the public and preparatory schools were one articulated system.

14 See Donald Leinster-Mackay, *The Rise of the English Prep School*, Falmer Press, 1984, p. 18.

15 See James Morris, *Heaven's Command*, 1973, Penguin, 1984, p. 379.

16 Donald Leinster-Mackay, *English Prep School*, pp. 97-8.

17 Winston Churchill, *My Early Life*, Fontana Books, 1930, 1959, pp. 36-7.

18 Philip Mason, *The Men Who Ruled India*, Jonathan Cape, 1985, pp. xiv-xv.

19 See G. G. Coulton, *A Victorian Schoolmaster: Henry Hart of Sedbergh*, Bell & Sons, 1923, p. 8.

20 See Hesketh Pearson, *Labby — The Life of Henry Labouchere*, Hamish Hamilton, 1936, pp. 17-18. Henry Labouchere was the nephew of the 1st Baron Taunton, Chairman of the Schools Inquiry Commission.

21 See Mary E. Richardson, *The Life of a Great Sportsman*, Vinton & Co, 1919, p. 56.

22 Ian C. M. Sanderson, *A History of Elstree School and Three Generations of the Sanderson Family*, privately printed, 1978, pp. 5-6.

23 Blackwood's Edinburgh Magazine, March 1894, Vol. 155, p. 387.

24 'Temple Grove from 1880', *Temple Grove Magazine*, 1968, p. 4.

25 See David Newsome, *Godliness and Good Learning*, J. Murray, 1961, pp. 148-94.

26 *Ibid*. p. 165. See also Meston Batchelor, *Cradle of Empire*, Phillimore, 1981, p. 24.

27 Rev H. Montagu Butler, *Sermon presented in the Chapel of Harrow School*, Macmillan, 1869, pp. 157-62.

28 Rev F. de W. Lushington, *Sermons to Young Boys, delivered at Elstree School*, John Murray, 1898, p. 42.

29 *Ibid*. Sermon preached on 20 June 1897, p. 51.

30 *Ibid*. Sermon preached on 'The Queen — why so great', p. 54.

31 See H. Clive Barnard, *Were those the Days? A Victorian Education*, Pergamon Press, 1970, p. 66.

32 Lushington, *Sermons to Young Boys*, pp. 77-8.

33 *Ibid*. pp. 81-2. There is a plaque in Hawarden's parish church commemorating this dramatic event.

34 Named after an assistant master at Harrow School, it is now called the Townsend-Warner History Prize.

35 See Peter Stansky and William Abrahams, *The Unknown Orwell*, Granada, 1982, pp. 72-3. See also Sonia Orwell and Ian Angus, *The Collected Essays, Journalism and Letters of George Orwell*, Vol. IV, Penguin Books, 1968, 1971, 'Such, such were the joys', p. 386.

36 H. B. Gray, *The Public Schools and Empire*, Williams & Norgate, 1913, pp. 58-66. H. B. Gray was Headmaster of Bradfield College.

37 H. B. Gray and Samuel Turner, *Eclipse or Empire?* Nisbet & Co., 1916, pp. 49-51. H. B. Gray was the senior author. For those who harbour any doubts about this, please turn to the title page!

38 Cyril Norwood, *The English Tradition of Education*, John Murray, 1929, pp. 70-1 and 133-5.

39 James Morris, *Farewell the Trumpets: An Imperial Retreat*, 1978, Penguin Books, 1982, pp. 49-50.

40 H. S. Shelton, *Thoughts of a Schoolmaster*, Hutchinson, 1932, p. 84.

41 See J. A. Mangan, *The Games Ethic and Imperialism*, Viking, 1986, pp. 28-33. See also J. D'E. Firth, *Rendall of Winchester*, Oxford University Press, 1954, pp. 12 and 189-219.

42 Richard Usborne (ed.), *A Century of Summer Fields*, Methuen, 1964, the Foreword. See also p. 19.

43 See D. P. Leinster-Mackay, *English Prep School*, pp. 113-17.

44 See C. H. Deane and A. P. W. Deane (eds.), *The Public Schools Year Book*, H. F. W. Deane & Sons, Year Book Press, 1924, pp. 795-813.

45 Board of Education, *Special Reports on Educational Subjects*, Vol. 6. *Preparatory Schools for Boys: Their Place in English Secondary Education*, HMSO, 1900, Kyoto Rinstu Book Company, 1974, p. 1.

46 See Donald Leinster-Mackay, *English Prep School*, pp. 23-35.

47 Sir George Douglas, *The Life of Major General Wauchope*, Hodder and Stoughton, 1904.

48 Cordwalles's history is obscure going back possibly to the eighteenth century. See Donald Leinster-Mackay, *English Prep School*, pp. 24 and 27. See also David R. Briggs, *The Millstone Race*, Short Run Press Ltd. The school is now called St Piran's and is situated in Maidenhead.

49 *Ibid.*

50 W. L. Burn, *Age of Equipoise*, Unwin Books, 1968, p. 56.

51 The resolution passed was that 'This meeting is of the opinion that it is not advisable for boys under fifteen to use a full-sized ball with the wickets pitched at twenty-two yards.'

52 The 1900 Board of Education *Special Report*, Vol. 6, 'Games in preparatory schools', p. 354.

53 *Ibid.* p. 344.

54 I. C. M. Sanderson, *A History of Elstree School*, privately printed, p. 23.

55 Andrew E. Stoddart (1864-1915) was a Middlesex county player who scored 485 in one innings in 1886. He was in the front rank of English amateur cricketers and visited Australia in the England team in 1887, 1891, 1894 and 1897.

56 Alan G. Steel (1858-1914) captained the Cambridge XI in 1883. A slow bowler, he was in the Gentleman's Eleven v. the Players and was a powerful bat in an early Australian Test Series.

57 Sir Kynaston Studd (1858-1944) of Eton and Trinity College, Cambridge, captained Cambridge in 1884. He later became President of the Regent Street Polytechnic and was subsequently both Sheriff of London (1922) and Lord Mayor (1928).

58 Paul Spillane, *St Andrew's School*, Hobbs of Southampton, 1977, pp. 25-6.

59 *Ibid.* p. 27.

60 Board of Education *Special Report 1900*, No. 6. A. J. C. Dowding, 'Games in preparatory schools', pp. 344-5.

61 M. A. F. Cooper (ed.), *Fonthill 1920*, privately printed, 1970, p. 19.

62 See *Aysgarth School Magazine*, 1, 3, December 1909, for reference to the eight greens at this Yorkshire school.

63 See Peter Gordon and John White, *Philosophers of Educational Reformers, The Influence of Idealism on British educational thought and practice*, RKP, 1979, pp. 177, 201 and 207-16.

64 See G. W. Place, *Preparatory Schools Rifle Association, History and Competition Results 1905-1985*, Preparatory Schools Rifle Association, 1986, pp. 1-5.

65 *Ibid.* p. 2.

66 P. C. McIntosh *et al.*, *Landmarks in the History of Physical Education*, Routledge & Kegan Paul, 1957, p. 188-9.

67 At this time Mostyn House was more an all-age private school, not becoming a prep school until the 1890s. But see G. W. Place, *Preparatory Schools Rifle Association*, p. 1.

68 *P.S.R.*, Vol. 4, No. 29, December 1904, p. 174.

69 Stanley S. Harris, *The Master and His Boys*, Warren & Son, 1924, 1925, p. 69.

70 Desmond Young, *Try Anything Twice*, Hamish Hamilton, 1963, p. 18.

71 The *nom de plume* of the writer Frederick Moore Searle (1870-1955).

72 Eric Parker, 'Private schools: ancient and modern', *Longman's Magazine*, Vol. 29, November 1896-April 1897, p. 448.

73 Richard Watts, *A History of Wolborough Hill School 1877-1977*, Newton Abbot, 1977, p. 8.

CHAPTER FOUR

Imperialism and the Irish national school system

John Coolahan

THE BRITISH LION AND THE IRISH MONKEY

Monkey (Mr. Mitchell). "One of us MUST be 'Put Down.'"

Punch. & Y

Ireland was England's oldest colony, and from an early stage English rulers expressed concern about the linguistic and cultural differences between England and her very close colonial neighbour. With the Tudor conquest, a series of enactments relating to education began, aimed at using schools as an agency to reduce the cultural distinctions between Ireland and England. The Act of Henry VIII of 1537 conveyed the policy clearly and sought to promote 'a conformity, concordance and familiarity in language, tongue, in manners, order and apparel',[1] between the Irish and their English rulers. However neither such legislation promoting schools nor later penal legislation opposing native Irish schools made significant inroads in reducing the cultural 'diversitie' between the two races.

Following the Act of Union of 1800 a more organised effort was made to promote cultural assimilation and political socialisation policy, with the school as a main agency in the process. The report of a Royal Commission in 1812 recommended that the Government should appoint a Board of Commissioners who would be allocated parliamentary grants to establish and administer a state-supported system of elementary schools. The Board would have extensive powers of supervision and control, as is indicated by the quotation: 'To decide in the last resort on the Appointment, Conduct, and Dismissal of Masters, to prescribe the Course and Mode of Education, to provide for the Expence of furnishing Books, and to have a general Control over the Whole of the proposed Establishments for the Instruction of the lower classes.'[2]

The national school plan

Guided by the principles enunciated by the Commission in 1812, and by a growing policial consensus, Lord Stanley, Chief Secretary for Ireland, announced in parliament in September 1831 the government's intention of establishing a national school system under a Board of government-appointed Commissioners.

In his letter of appointment to the Duke of Leinster, as chairman, Stanley set out the guiding principles for the new system. The guidelines which affect the theme of this paper were as follows. One of the main objects of the national system (Stanley's phrase) was to unite in one system children of all denominations by offering a combined literary education while allowing for separate religious instruction, appropriate to the various denominations. It was the government's intention that the Board 'should exercise a complete control' over the various schools conducted in association with it. The Board was 'to exercise the most entire control over all the books to be used in the schools, whether in the combined moral and literary or separate religious instruction'. Teachers were to have testimonials of good conduct and of general fitness from the Board and were also subject to fines, suspension and removal from service by the Board. The Board was to be responsible for teacher-training. The Board was also empowered to edit and print school text-books and to make these available at not lower than half-price.[3]

The phrases 'exercise a complete control' and 'exercise entire control' were symptomatic of the concern of the legislature that the national education system would be directed along policy lines of cultural assimilation and political socialisation approved by the government. The controls exercised over the courses of study, text-books used, teacher-training and teacher conduct would go a long way towards ensuring that the official policy prevailed. The mixed-denominational principle of the national school system drew a great deal of criticism and opposition from the various church authorities and eventually, while remaining a mixed system *de jure*, it was in practice shaped predominantly along denominational lines at local level.[4] Despite the controversies which surrounded it, the new state-aided system grew impressively, so that by 1870 there were 6,800 national schools with about a million pupils enrolled.[5] While religious-controlled schools, such as the schools of the Christian Brothers and the Church Education Society, continued to operate distinct from the national school Board, the national schools became by far the most prominent form of schooling and, by 1870, had almost completely replaced the hedge schools. The controls exercised over teachers, curriculum and text-books were to be the key elements in shaping the system along desired socialisation lines.

Teachers and teacher-training

The Board produced its regulations for teachers at a very early stage. The type of person sought is revealed in the following character profile which was retained unchanged throughout the century: 'National teachers should be persons of Christian sentiment, of calm temper and discretion; they should be imbued with a spirit of peace, of obedience to the law, and of loyalty to their Sovereign ...'[6]

These were qualities which earlier official reports had found wanting among the traditional hedge schoolmasters. It was not surprising that the Commissioners would seek to foster them among the new breed of teachers and among the older brigade who agreed to be employed under the new system. Teachers were forbidden to attend any meetings held for political purposes or to take part in elections other than by voting. Teachers were also to avoid fairs and markets and to abstain from controversy. While local school managers had the right to hire and dismiss teachers, the Board retained the right to sanction appointments and to remove recognition from teachers as being eligible to receive payment under the national Board.[7] An efficient network of school inspection was in operation which kept the Board informed about the implementation of its regulations and programmes by teachers and on the efficiency of the teachers' work.

Withdrawal of recognition from teachers did occur from time to time, on the grounds of political disloyalty and spreading subversion. The main occasions on which such occurrences took place, accompanied by public controversy, were on the occasions of nationalist insurrections. One instance of this was the outbreak of the Fenian Rebellion in 1867. Lord Naas admitted in parliament that twenty-nine schoolmasters had joined the rebels. The Commissioners imposed strict penalties including dismissal of teachers suspected even of being in sympathy with Fenianism. Teachers were also dismissed for marching in processions in commemoration of the Manchester Martyrs.[8] Another notable instance of alleged teacher disloyalty was on the occasion of the Easter Rising of 1916, sometimes termed 'the teachers' rebellion'. It was alleged that the rising was fomented 'by the careful instilling of revolutionary principles in the teaching of many of our primary schools'.[9] In response to public controversy, the Commissioners set an enquiry in train in 1916 which only confirmed a few instances of ascertainable disloyal teaching and which concluded by stating: 'No evidence has been adduced which would warrant the conclusion that seditious teaching in the national schools exists to any appreciable extent.'[10]

The Commissioners were never able to exert the control over teacher-training which they originally envisaged. They established a teacher-training college and twenty-seven district model schools for teacher-training. These institutions were totally under the Board's management and were conducted on the mixed-education principle. As such, they were opposed by the Catholic Church authorities, particularly from 1850. They placed an outright ban on attendance at them in 1863. The Church of Ireland also sought state support for separate, denominational teacher-training institutions. The conflict on control of teacher-training proved to be a long drawn-out one. It was only resolved in 1883 when the government eventually yielded and agreed to make state funds available for denominational teacher-training, albeit on less favourable terms than for the board's own training college.

A key factor in the conflict related to the importance placed by all parties on the formative influence which the ethos of the training college would have on the trainee teachers. The change in earlier government policy heralded a weakening of its policy on mixed denominationalism. While there is no evidence that active disloyalty or nationalism was cultivated within the denominational colleges, it is likely that, from the late nineteenth century onwards, they provided a more nationally-orientated ethos for students who may have been influenced by the variety of cultural nationalist movements then flourishing.

The Irish language

The Irish language, for a variety of political, social and economic reasons, had already gone into decline as a generally-used vernacular prior to the establishment of the national school system.[11] In 1825 it was estimated in the report of the Royal Commission that not less than 500,000 used Irish as their sole language, while at least a million more were estimated 'to use Irish as the natural vehicle of their thoughts'.[12] According to the first reliable census on the use of Irish, about twenty-three per cent of the six and a half million population were able to speak Irish in 1851, while five per cent used it as their sole language.[13]

Quite clearly, it was no part of the national Board's remit to promote the learning of the Irish language and the curriculum laid down by the Board made no mention of the Irish language. It was generally understood that the government's aim was to promote the imperial language and culture. Promotion of the English language was favoured by the Roman Catholic hierarchy also as being consonant with its pastoral and missionary concerns. The population generally recognised English as the language of commerce and of social mobility. For those bound for emigration ships, the fate of increasing numbers as the century progressed, English was the language of communication and job opportunities in their adopted countries. Thus, the drive for literacy and numeracy, the promotion of the three Rs under the National Board, was understood by all concerned as being through the medium of English.

One of those who raised his voice against the contemporary neglect of the Irish language was Thomas Davis, a prominent leader of the Young Ireland movement. This movement, inspired by the ideology of cultural nationalism, emerged in the early 1840s and sought to turn back the tide of anglicisation. It informed people about, and urged them to cultivate, their cultural heritage, in terms of language, history, songs, antiquities and customs. As regards the Irish language, Davis asserted that: 'A nation without a language of its own is only half a nation. A nation should guard its language more than its territories — 'tis a surer barrier, and more important frontier, than fortress or river.'

He held that 'the Irish language should be cherished, taught, and esteemed, and that it can be preserved and gradually extended'.[15] He accepted that it was not realistic to expect Irish to be introduced into the schools in the eastern and English-speaking regions but he stated:

Simply requiring that teachers of the national schools in these Irish-speaking districts to know Irish, and supplying them with Irish translations of the school books would guard the language where it now exists, and prevent it from being swept away by the English tongue, as the red Americans have been by the English race from New York to New Orleans.[16]

A series of events in quick succession impeded the momentum which the ideas of the Young Ireland movement might have fostered. The failure of the Repeal of the Union Movement led by Daniel O'Connell, the outbreak of the Great Famine in 1845, the untimely death of Davis in 1846 and the abortive Young Ireland Rebellion in 1848 all left a legacy of gloom and dashed much of the optimism of the early 1840s.

However, a real educational dilemma continued to exist for pupils in Irish-speaking districts when the language and medium of instruction in the national schools were solely English. The attention of the Commissioners was forcefully and intelligently drawn to the appalling difficulties this caused for such children in the annual reports submitted by a head inspector, Patrick Keenan, in 1855, 1857 and 1858. Having visited schools in Irish-speaking districts, he saw at first hand the educational inadvisability of proceeding in the manner prescribed by the Board. He argued: '... the Irish-speaking people ought to be taught the Irish language grammatically, and school books in Irish should be prepared for that purpose ... English should be taught to all Irish-speaking children through the medium of Irish'.[17]

The Board ignored these requests and made no effort to resolve the problems. The problems, if anything, became more acute following the introduction of the payment-by-results policy in 1872. Now a teacher's income partly depended on the annual examination results of individual pupils. But the examinations were conducted in and through a language which was foreign to the same children. There is a considerable literature testifying to the anachronisms which arose, affecting pupils, teachers and school managers in the Irish-speaking districts. The payment by results system, while concentrating on the core three R subjects, also permitted examination in two 'extra subjects' by senior pupils who had satisfied the examiners in the core subjects. Included were languages such as Greek, Latin and French. A number of agencies pressed the Commissioners to designate Irish also as an extra subject. These included the Irish National Teachers' Organisation, the Historical and Archaeological Association of Ireland and the Society for the Preservation of the Irish Language. These representations, as well as support from some Irish MPs, led to a breakthrough in the Board's attitude to Irish. In a split decision, the Board was prepared 'to grant results fees for proficiency in the Irish language on the same conditions as are applicable to Greek, Latin and French'.[18] This was the first dent in the Board's sustained neglect of the Irish language. It was not, however, to be the last. A further concession was made in 1883 which allowed teachers in Irish-speaking districts, if acquainted with the Irish language, to use it 'as an aid to the elucidation and acquisition of the English language'.[19] These rather grudging and minimal concessions were not to prove sufficient to new forces emerging in Irish society.

The rise of cultural nationalist movements with an active revivalist aim, as distinct from the preservationist aim of older societies, was to create increasing pressure on the National Board to make greater provision for the Irish language. The new societies, such as the Gaelic Athletic Association (1884), the Irish National Literary Society (1892) and the Gaelic League (1893), were actively seeking to create a greater climate of awareness and appreciation of a distinctive Irish cultural tradition and to encourage an active revival in a range of Irish cultural pursuits. The policy of the National Board of Education of cultural assimilation and integration came under increasingly strong attack. As regards the language, the Gaelic League was the most important and vociferous protagonist. In 1900–01 alone, the League issued twenty-seven pamphlets with such titles as 'Irish in the schools', 'Ireland's battle for her language', 'The future of Irish in the national schools' and 'The nationalisation of Irish education', which give a flavour of their scope and content. The League was influenced by the progress being made in Wales in the promotion of Welsh within the school system there.

The Gaelic League pressed strongly for the introduction of a bilingual programme of instruction for Irish-speaking districts. Its hopes of success were raised by a speech in February 1900 when Dr Starkie, the Resident Commissioner of the National Board, stated in the course of a public address:

I fancy few practical educationalists will deny that the National Board were guilty of a disastrous blunder in thrusting upon a Gaelic-speaking race a system of education produced after a foreign model and utterly alien to their sympathies and antecedents. Such an attempt was unsound both philosophically and practically ... and I think there can be little doubt that the Board were guilty of narrow pedantry in neglecting as worthless the whole previous spiritual life of the pupil and the multitude of associations, imaginations, and sentiments that formed the content of his consciousness.[20]

The tenor of this speech seemed to betoken a wind of change in policy. However, expectations were dashed and when the new programme for national schools was issued in September 1900 there was no change in the status of Irish. There was great indignation at this and mass meetings of protest took place. Balfour, in parliament, declared that he would not object to the application to the Irish-speaking districts of Ireland of the rules which applied to the Welsh-speaking districts of Wales.[21] The minutes of the Commissioners' meetings indicate a strong hostility among some members to any promotion of the Irish language.[22]

The Gaelic League, which itself had grown from forty-three branches in 1897 to 600 by 1904 with a total membership of 50,000, kept up the pressure for a bilingual programme.[23] It also engaged in a wide-scale educational programme, organising classes in the Irish language, history, dances, music, folklore and so on. In 1901 Irish was permitted to be taught during the school day, provided it did not injuriously affect the general programme. With an already overcrowded programme this concession amounted to less than it seemed. Eventually in 1904 the National Board of Education authorised a bilingual programme for schools in Irish-speaking districts. This was a significant breakthrough and the number of schools following the bilingual programme increased from thirty-six in 1906 to 239 in 1921.[24] The Board was not prepared to sanction the programme unless teachers in the relevant schools had a good literary and oral knowledge of Irish. However, while a part-time teacher of Irish had been permitted in one of the denominational training colleges, the Board took no initiative in facilitating the supply or training of teachers for the bilingual programme. The Gaelic League moved to fill the gap and began establishing summer colleges for teachers mostly situated in Irish-speaking districts. The Board agreed to recognise these colleges and their qualifications and paid grants of £5 for each participant on the courses. By 1920, twenty-three Irish colleges were receiving recognition. As further evidence of changed circumstances, the Board in 1906 agreed to appoint six organisers to help in the development of the study and teaching of the language. It was also prepared to accept Irish as an alternative to book-keeping in the entrance examination to the training colleges.

The Gaelic League was an adept organiser of public opinion and used methods of mass meetings, public-letter campaigns, motions in parliament and resolutions from public bodies to support its campaign. The National

Board gave the impression of grudgingly giving concessions which had to be wrung out of it. The Board found itself in the position of always falling short of the demands made on it. Because of the apparent opposition of the Board, small advances were often hailed as victories by the language revivalists. It is likely that some members of the Board who were opposed to Irish genuinely viewed the teaching of the language as a waste of time and its revival as a retrograde step. However, there were also deeper residual attitudes which saw the political implications involved in such a revival. It was viewed as part of a de-anglicisation policy which, if encouraged or fostered, would have deleterious effects on the Union. This view was publicly aired by Professor Mahaffy of Trinity College, Dublin when he saw the growth of cultural nationalism as essentially political and felt that it contained within it the seeds of the breaking of the Union. He stated:

> It is the mass of those who dislike or who hate England and the English, and who favour any movement which will lead directly or indirectly to a severance between Ireland and Great Britain (who are in favour of Irish) ... (they) know the separation is only a matter of time, provided they can nourish separation in sentiment and revive the hitherto decreasing sense of contrast in race by establishing contrast in language.[25]

Mahaffy was perceptive in this appraisal. What was afoot was a movement which was to lead to the undoing of the Union, and just as the cultural-assimilation policy of the national school system had aimed at buttressing the political reality of the Union, the efforts to change the linguistic and cultural policy of the Board within the schools, allied to a strong and popular extra-mural educational and cultural campaign, was to be a key feature in eroding the Union. The defensive attitude of the Board with regard to the teaching of Irish, coupled with the popular, if erroneous, belief that it was the policy of the Board which was mainly responsible for the decline of Irish in the nineteenth century, created a climate of hope that, when education came under a native government, full redress for earlier hostility and neglect would be made. The national school system was a significant contributory factor to the already established pattern of decline of Irish as a vernacular language. It was simplistic to hope, however, that once the policy of the National Board was altered and replaced by official support and approval for the teaching of the language, its revival as a main language of communication would be assured.

National school text-books

In the early years of the national school system, the Board got to work speedily in preparing its scheme of reading books and by 1834 a scheme of five reading books, as well as other text-books, had been prepared. The reading books were to form the core of the curricular content and were intentionally used for socialisation purposes. The Board's books long enjoyed a monopoly of usage within the schools. Millions of them were published and distributed at subsidised rates. The books enjoyed an international reputation, despite the difficulty of vocabulary, the dull factual content of much of the material and the poor illustrations which they contained. It is their approach to material of a specifically Irish character and interest which is of relevance to the theme of this paper.

The very fact that the Irish school readers proved so popular in other English-speaking countries provided a clue about their contents. They were devoid of material focusing on Ireland, its heritage, landscape and traditions. Throughout the editions of the early decades of the system, they reflected a strong imperialistic outlook. England and the empire were glorified and references to Ireland emphasised its place within the imperial scheme of things and minimised national differences. One of the verses in the early readers which left a long folk memory was that in which children were encouraged to chant: 'I thank the goodness and the grace/Which on my youth has smiled,/To make me in these Christian days/A happy English child.' Another poem which was widely promoted urged children to rejoice about 'The homes of England', 'Where first the child's glad spirit loves/Its country and its God'. A further poem concluded 'Britain thou art my home, my rest,/my own land, I love thee best.'

The place of Ireland within the empire was stressed in extracts such as this from the *Fourth Reading Book*: 'The island of Great Britain, which is composed of England, Scotland and Wales, and the island of Ireland, form ... the British Empire in Europe.'[26]

The *Third Reading Book* stated 'Great Britain and Ireland formed the most powerful kingdom in the world.'[27] In a variety of lessons, Ireland's geographic and linguistic ties with England were emphasised, as in this extract from the *Second Reading Book*: 'On the East of Ireland is England, where the Queen lives, many people who live in Ireland were born in England, and we speak the same language and are called one nation.'[28] The existence of a separate linguistic and cultural identity was constantly ignored in favour of sentiments expressive of close ties of cultural affinity, as in the following extract: 'The people of these islands have one and the same language (all at least who are educated), one and the same Queen — the same laws; and though they differ in their religious worship, they all serve the same God, and call themselves by the name of Christ.'[27]

As if to soften the sense of hurt and bitterness which folk history had kept alive among an oppressed people, the text went on to palliate, if somewhat unconvincingly, 'All this is enough to make them brethren, in spite of many disagreements and faults which history tells of them in their intercourse with each other (English and Irish), when the strong oppressed the weak, and the weak hated the strong; but a better knowledge of their duty will give history better things to record.'[30]

Even lessons dealing with manufactures or occupations concentrated on English experiences and ignored Irish instances with which the pupils could have identified more closely. The same was true of extracts dealing with nature and botanical material. The instances and references were never related to Irish environmental context or habitats. The reading books were punctuated with lessons reflective of purely English considerations and content. When biographical sketches were included as exemplars for emulation or admiration by pupils, they focused on English representatives such as William Hutton, James Ferguson, Catherine of Liverpool, Benjamin West and John Pounds.[31]

Thomas Davis and the Young Ireland movement were early and eloquent critics of the emphasis in the school text-books. While favouring several aspects of the Board's educational endeavours, Davis wrote in 1844 about the Board:

> Founded by the Whigs, who were more imperial than the Tories, the men put on it (the board) were chosen for their want of Irish feeling or character — dry, ungenial men, ignorant of our history, in love with English literature and character, imperialists to the core. Naturally therefore, its books, though models of general information and literary finish, are empty of Irish statistics, history and hopes.

He did not fault the Board for endeavouring to be religiously neutral but went on to state: 'But we do blame them for turning Irish history out of doors, and we must emphatically censure them for the painful skill with which they have cut from every work in their schools the recognition of the literature, antiquities and state of Ireland.'[32]

The Nation newspaper, which focused on cultivating a cultural awareness of an Irish heritage, put the matter pungently when it remarked about the Board's books, 'Very useful and respectable in their proper place they certainly are, but that place is not Ireland.'[33]

Despite such criticisms, the Board undertook no revisions of the books in the early decades, either to change the emphasis in the lessons or to update their content in line with changing socio-economic and industrial circumstances. However, in August 1860, in a parliamentary speech on the national school system, Chief Secretary Cardwell indicated that there could be 'a more national tone in the school books'.[34] Eventually, in

September 1861, the Board adopted the following resolution: 'That the school books of the Board shall be reviewed, so as that without interference with their general character, or departure from the fundamental principles of the system of National Education they may be made in accordance with the present state of knowledge, and still more acceptable than they are now to the people of Ireland.'[35] The books were revised by 1865 but no dramatic change in emphasis had occurred.

Just as the Board had to tread very warily in the area of religious references, the difficulty of providing a history text-book which would be acceptable was indeed a daunting task. Arising from criticism of the lack of Irish historical material for schools, the Commissioners resolved in 1860 that 'steps would be taken as soon as possible, towards the compilation of an historical work, which should contain no matter that could give just cause of offence either on religious or political grounds to persons of any denomination in Ireland'.[36]

However, to fulfil such a prescription in the prevailing religio-political climate was a labour of Sisyphus, as the Commissioners came to acknowledge: 'A compilation of a work on history is felt to be a task of a very delicate and difficult nature; and in consequence of this circumstance the Commissioners have not, as yet, been able to make satisfactory arrangements for bringing out the historical manual alluded to in the foregoing communications.'[37] The Board never succeeded in doing so.

A major review of the operation of the National Education System was undertaken by the Royal Commission of Inquiry (1868–1870), popularly know as the Powis Commission. Criticism of the non-national character of the Board's text-books was voiced by a number of witnesses. One critic stated: 'You might have introduced them into a school in Canada or into a school in Africa, as appropriately as into a school in Ireland.'[38] Cardinal Cullen, in the course of a trenchant attack on the books, stated: 'The value of the books notwithstanding this exclusion of Irishmen and selection of strangers, is very trifling.'[39] Mr Coward, one of the Board's own inspectors, reported: 'The absence of any mention of Irish history in books intended to teach the inhabitants of Ireland was regarded as an attempt to destroy the feeling of nationality, and was the only feature which provoked much resentment.'[40]

Among the recommendations of the Powis Commission was one which stated that the Board should cease to publish school text-books but this policy was not adopted. The Board continued to publish text-books but gradually adopted a more liberal approach to the sanctioning of text-books produced by other publishers. One of the on-going problems of the Board's books, namely the difficulty of vocabulary usage, was highlighted by the introduction of the payment-by-results policy in 1872. Teachers were successful in their objections that the books were pitched at too high a level for the average pupils.[41] As well as simplifying the text-books, the Commissioners took the opportunity of the revision of 1873 to go some way to answer the oft-repeated criticisms of the non-national content. While it was too difficult to produce a history text-book *per se*, the Board now incorporated a greater level of material which focused in a non-controversial way on aspects of Ireland and Irish life, and involved a corresponding decrease in the purely 'English' material. In the senior books, lessons on places of beauty such as the Lakes of Killarney and the Giant's Causeway were included. A series of lessons related to the coastal scenery of Ireland. Nature lessons took note of botanical species readily identifiable on the Irish landscape. In the advanced *Sixth Book*, a number of lessons were included on the Christian antiquities of Ireland. The influence of Sir Robert Kane, the author of *The Industrial Resources of Ireland*, among the Commissioners is observable from a number of lessons on Ireland's natural resources. While the revised readers were better illustrated than the earlier editions, much of the writing was formal, stilted and academic, reflective of the scholarly sources of the various cultural and antiquarian societies from which they were derived. The lessons were not couched to appeal to children's imaginative or affective powers.

The last era of influence by the Board's text-books related to the period of the radical change in curricular policy heralded by the Revised Programme for National Schools in 1900. Inspired by child-centred ideology, a new curriculum was implemented which led to the abandonment of the payment-by-results policy and the adoption of a much wider programme geared more to the interests and capabilities of young children. The new reading books accompanying the programme were, in vocabulary, content and illustration, geared much more towards the stages of development and imaginative awareness of primary-school pupils.

The turn of the tide

The context for the change in curricular policy in 1900 was dramatically different from that prevailing at the establishment of the system seventy years earlier, in 1831. Apart from the influence of the child-centred educational ideology, there was now a very vibrant and influential cultural nationalist movement which aimed at turning back the tide of anglicisation and which identified the Board and the educational system as a barrier to that process. Much of the erosion, in the sense of national identity, which had taken place was attributed to, and projected on, the Board and the school system. In the heightened climate of concern at the time there was a widespread belief that the educational system had been effectively used as a tool of British imperialism.

Indeed, statements by influential personnel associated with the educational system added credence to this belief. Sir Horace Plunkett, President of the recently-established Department of Agriculture and Technical Instruction, wrote:

> The national factor in Ireland has been studiously eliminated from national education, and Ireland is perhaps the only country in Europe where it is part of the settled policy of those who had the guidance of education to ignore the literature, arts and traditions of the people. It was a fatal policy, for it obviously tended to stamp their native country in the eyes of Irishmen with the badge of inferiority and to extinguish the sense of healthy self-respect which comes from the consciousness of high national ancestry and traditions.[42]

He went on to refer to the pressure for change and to the vital necessity for a more national ethos in education: 'A passionate conviction is gaining ground that if Irish traditions, literature, language, art, music and culture are allowed to disappear it will mean the disappearance of the race; and that education in Ireland must be nationalised if our social, intellectual, or even our economic position is to be permanently improved.'[43]

Plunkett could be classified as a southern unionist in political allegiance, as was Dr Starkie who held the key position on the National Board. However, Starkie put forward a similar appraisal when he stated in 1902 about the curricular policy which had been pursued by the Board: 'The thread of continuity with the past ... was ruthlessly snapped. The familiar associations of cairn and ruin, and the heritage of legend, with all its wealth of poetry and mysticism were treated with disdain; the Irish language was the badge of serfdom, even Irish history was proscribed.'[44] With such individuals taking that approach, it was not surprising to find committed nationalists taking a similar line and pressing for changes.

The achievement of the bilingual education policy in 1904, greater scope for Irish as a school subject and state support for summer-college courses for teachers in Irish have already been mentioned. There was also sustained pressure in these years for the inclusion of Irish history on school courses. A range of pamphlets pressed the case with titles such as 'Native history in the national schools', 'The value of history', 'The study of Irish history' and 'The history of Ireland'. Then in 1908, for the first time ever, the National Board sanctioned history as a school subject for national schools, which was hailed as another victory by nationalist opinion. Though no specific programmes were laid down for history, the notes for teachers warned of the 'extremely controversial aspect of so many historical questions' and of the need for 'great moderation and good judgement, and above all, full and accurate knowledge'. That old traditions die hard was evidenced in the further note: 'From the standpoint of the general student whose objective is the history and growth of civilisation, a detailed knowledge of English history appears unquestionably to be more valuable than Irish.'[45] It would seem that this evaluation was rejected by most of the teachers in the classrooms of Irish national schools.

From the 1870s onwards, there was a gradual erosion of the policies which had been fully implemented during the first four decades of the national school system. The content of the readers after 1873 dropped some of the more objectionable imperialist material and included a greater proportion of lessons relating to Ireland, albeit that this latter was still insufficient for nationalist wishes. In 1879 Irish was allowed as an 'extra subject' for payment by results and from 1883 it could be used in schools where it would help 'in the acquisition of English'. From 1901 Irish could be taught as an ordinary school subject, provided the general work of the school was not hampered by its adoption. In 1904 the bilingual programme was authorised. Then in 1908, history was accepted as a subject and it was left to the discretion of the teacher to devise a course and select a text-book for official sanction.

Thus, it could be maintained that the original post-union policy had failed and was now being turned on its head as part of a developing movement which sought either home rule or full separation from Britain. However, many nationalists felt that the system had been only too successful in creating a *déraciné* people with a crisis about cultural identity. It was held that the school system, by neglecting if not showing active hostility to the Irish language and by disdaining the history and general culture of the Irish people, had given a sense of alienation and uprootedness to the people, distorting their self-image and sapping their morale. There is no doubt that there was truth in these allegations. However, some of the nationalist rhetoric exaggerated and did not tell the whole truth. Much of the harshest criticism was more relevant to the early, rather than the later, history of the Board. Padraig Pearse, a schoolmaster himself and the revolutionary leader of the 1916 Rebellion, wrote a trenchant criticism of the education system in an emotively-titled pamphlet called 'The Murder Machine'. In it he stated, 'The English thing that is called education in Ireland is founded on a denial of the Irish nation.'[46] He went on to assert: 'It is because the English education system in Ireland has deliberately eliminated the national factor that it has so terrifically succeeded. For it has succeeded — succeeded in making slaves of us. And it has succeeded so well that we no longer realise that we are slaves.'[47]

Propaganda, of course, in certain political contexts serves important purposes. There was an element of propaganda in Pearse's critique. There is a danger when people believe their own propaganda. There was also an element of this involved in nationalist writings of the time. Apart from a degree of exaggeration in relation to the policy of the National Board, there was a deeper weakness in nationalist analysis. This was the attribution to the school system of greater influences than it can effect as a social institution operating on its own. To succeed effectively, the school must operate in conjunction with other cultural trends in society. In this context there were many factors other than the schools which hastened the decline of Irish and associated cultural values, though no doubt it was an important element in that decline.

Just as Ireland had been Britain's first colony, the Irish independence movement was to break the first link in the chain of the British Empire. The Union was smashed by a new political settlement involving the partition of Ireland. As regards the Irish Free State, the new leaders, committed cultural nationalists, immediately set about undoing what they held was the work of the Union — the efforts at cultural assimilation of the Irish people. The role attributed to the schools in this process inspired and encouraged them to follow the same pathway, but in the reverse direction. The concentration of the education policy of the new state was on the Gaelicisation of the Irish people through the schools. The policy of the new administration was announced to the Commissioners of National Education, on the occasion of their dissolution, by the new régime on 31 January 1922. They were told: 'In the administration of Irish education, it is the intention of the new government to work with all its might for the strengthening of the national fibre by giving the language, history, music and tradition of Ireland their natural place in the life of Irish schools.'[48] The wheel had come full circle.

Notes

1 *Act of Parliament*, 28 Henry VIII, C.15, 1537.
2 *Fourteenth Report of the Commissioners of the Board of Education in Ireland*, H of C, V, 21, 1812–13.
3 *Copy of the Letter from the Chief Secretary for Ireland to the Duke of Leinster on the Formation of a Board of Commissioners for Education in Ireland*, H of C, XXIX, 196, 1831–2.
4 Donald H. Akenson, *The Irish Education Experiment: The National System of Education in the Nineteenth Century*, London, 1970, p. 224.
5 *Thirty-Seventh Report of the Commissioners for National Education in Ireland*, H of C XXIII, c. 599, 1871, p. 9 (henceforth Report of CNEI).
6 *Rules and Regulations of the Commissioners of National Education*, 1855 ed., p. 10.

7 *Ibid.*

8 *Minutes of the Commissioners of National Education in Ireland*, Ms 5549, p. 466 and Ms 5500, p. 457, in National Library of Ireland (henceforth MCNEI, in NLI).

9 MCNEI, 27 July 1916, p. 20, in NLI (printed).

10 Report of CNEI for 1915–16, H of C, XI (c. 8495), 1917–18, p. 719.

11 Maureen Wall, 'The decline of the Irish language', in Brian O. Cuiv (ed.), *A View of the Irish Language*, Dublin, 1969, pp. 81–90.

12 *First Report of Commissioners of Irish Education Inquiry*, I, 1825, 400, p. 82.

13 *Census of Ireland, 1851, Pt. 1. General Report*, H of C, XXXI 2134, 1856, p. xlvii.

14 Thomas Davis, 'Our national language' in *Essays of Thomas Davis: Centenary Edition*, New York, 1974, p. 98 (hereafter *Essays*).

15 *Ibid.* p. 105.

16 *Ibid.* p. 106.

17 *Report of CNEI for 1855*, H of C, XVII Pt. II, Appendix G, p. 76.

18 MCNEI, Ms. 5557, p. 356, NLI and Ms. 8466, NLI.

19 Akenson, *The Irish Education Experiment*, p. 382.

20 Report in *Daily Independent*, 20 February 1900.

21 *Freeman's Journal*, 21 July 1900.

22 MCNEI, Ms 5547, p. 124 and MCNEI for 1901, p. 105.

23 Breandan S. MacAodha, 'Was this a social revolution?', in S. O. Tuama (ed.), *The Gaelic League Idea*, Dublin, 1942, p. 21.

24 *Report of the Department of Education, for the School Year 1924–25*, Dublin, 1926, p. 30.

25 J. P. Mahaffy, 'The recent fuss about the Irish language', *Nineteenth Century*, XXXXV, 1899, p. 218.

26 *Fourth Reading Book of the Commissioners of National Education*, 1861 ed., p. 52.

27 *Third Reading Book*, 1843 ed., p. 159.

28 *Second Reading Book*, 1858 ed., p. 135.

29 *Fourth Reading Book*, 1861 ed., p. 52.

30 *Ibid.*

31 See John Patrick Walsh, 'A comparative analysis of the Reading Books of the Commissioners of National Education and of the Christian Brothers 1831–1900 (unpublished M.A. Thesis, University College, Dublin, 1983), pp. 91–2.

32 Thomas Davis, 'Popular education' in *Essays*, p. 204.

33 Quoted by J. P. Walsh, 'An analysis of the Reading Books...', p. 245.

34 E. R. Norman, *The Catholic Church and Ireland in the Age of Rebellion, 1859–1873*, London, 1965, p. 72.

35 MCNEI, Ms 5549, 27 September 1861.

36 Quoted by J. P. Walsh, 'An analysis of the Reading Books ...', p. 250.

37 *Copies of all Minutes of the Board of National Education passed since 1857, respecting the Revision, Alteration or Increase of the Classbooks*. H of C, XLVI, 509, 1864, p. 417.

38 *Royal Commission of Inquiry into Primary Education* (Powis), H of C 1870, XXVIII, c. 611, Pt. III, q. 15572.

39 *Ibid.* H of C 1870, XXVIII, c. 611, Pt IV, p. 1227–30.

40 *Ibid.* H of C 1870, XXVIII, c. 61, Pt. II, p. 156.

41 John Coolahan, 'The payment by results policy in Irish education' (unpublished M.Ed. thesis, Trinity College, Dublin, 1975), p. 111.

42 Horace Plunkett, *Ireland in the New Century*, London, 1905, p. 152.

43 *Ibid.* p. 153.

44 W. J. Starkie, *Recent Reforms in Irish Education*, Dublin, 1902, p. 10.

45 *Notes for Teachers for the Programme of Instruction*, Dublin, 1913 ed., p. 17.

46 P. H. Pearse, *Political Writings and Speeches*, Dublin, 1952 ed., p. 16.

47 *Ibid*. p. 40.

48 Reported in *The School Weekly*, 11 February 1922, p. 127. For an account of the policies pursued by the new Irish State, see John Coolahan, *Irish Education: Its History and Structure*, Dublin, 1981.

CHAPTER FIVE

The Newfoundland School Society
1823–55: missionary enterprise
or cultural imperialism?

Phillip McCann

The Society for Educating the Poor of Newfoundland, or the Newfoundland School Society — the name by which, despite subsequent changes of title, it was always known — was founded in London in 1823 to provide schools and teachers for the children of the island's fishermen.[1] It was the first organisation to be set up in Britain with the specific aim of educating the poor in one of Britain's colonial possessions. Originating with a group of merchants trading to Newfoundland, led by the Evangelical Samuel Codner, the Society rapidly gained the moral and material support of the British Government; not only did it receive relatively large grants of money ten years before such grants were made to educational bodies in Britain, but the Prime Minister, Lord Liverpool, appointed himself the society's first Vice-Patron and the Colonial Secretary, Lord Bathurst, and the Colonial Under-Secretary, Wilmot Horton, became office-holders.

The unusual nature of the Society's origin and aims raises several important questions. Why, at this particular juncture, did Newfoundland merchants take up the cause of educating the fishermen? What interest did the British government have in subsidising schools in a far-away island? Why did members of the Evangelical wing of the Church of England play the leading role in the activities of the Society? What was its impact on the educational, social and cultural life of Newfoundland? These questions can best be answered by an examination of the early history of the Society; though its activities in Newfoundland lasted until 1923, its most influential period was between 1823, the date of its foundation, and 1855, the year in which Newfoundland was granted Responsible (i.e. cabinet) Government. During this period Newfoundland completed its transformation from a summer fishing station to a fully-fledged colony, the world-wide Protestant missionary movement came into full flower, and the peculiarly Evangelical ideology of 'Christian colonisation', which was to influence missionaries in general and the Society's teachers in particular, was elaborated.

The Newfoundland School Society, according to tradition, had a romantic origin. In the autumn of 1820, Samuel Codner, a Devon merchant trading to Newfoundland, was returning home in the *Mercury* after the summer fishing season. Three hundred miles west of Ireland a storm arose which threw the vessel on her beam ends, broadside to the waves. Disaster seemed imminent, and Codner vowed that if by some miracle his life were saved he would devote the rest of his days to spreading the message of the Kingdom of God. The storm abated before the ship foundered and Codner reached England in safety.[2] The following year, advised to visit Margate for his health, he attended the inaugural meeting of the Isle of Thanet Bible Society and heard the Prime Minister, Lord Liverpool, deliver a weighty speech on the duty of Britons to circulate the Bible not only among all classes and all sects in the Kingdom but throughout Great Britain's 'extensive colonies and foreign possessions'. Codner, an ardent Evangelical, realised how negligent he had been in fulfilling his vow of the previous year. Though he had been active in educational activities and the distribution of Bibles in Newfoundland for many years, he now decided that an enterprise on a larger scale was necessary.[3]

He was impelled to action by the critical state of Newfoundland society. Since the seventeenth century the British government had maintained Newfoundland as a summer station for the West of England fishing fleets, with only a few thousand settlers remaining for the winter. By the end of the eighteenth century, twenty thousand British fishermen were employed in the annual summer fishery, the trade realised more than £600,000 per annum, and Newfoundland ranked second only to the West Indies as a source of wealth to the Crown.[4] Despite laws aimed at the prevention of settlement (and thus the rise of an indigenous and rival fishery), favourable conditions of trade arising from the Napoleonic Wars encouraged immigration — almost entirely from south-west England and south-east Ireland — and by the mid-1820s the population had reached 55,000 and an indigenous shore fishery established.[5]

But there were few civil institutions and justice was largely administered by the British navy through the agency of Surrogate Courts, and a reform movement grew up which demanded improvement of conditions and self-government. The situation was worsened by the slump in trade during the seven years following the victory over Napoleon in 1815. Many merchants went bankrupt, and planters (small boat owners) and fishermen faced debt and sequestration of their property. Fires ravaged St. John's, adding homelessness to the distress, and starving inhabitants attacked merchants' stores and foodships in several localities. Merchants were demanding protection and concern was expressed in the House of Commons. By 1822 popular opposition to Surrogate Courts had reached endemic proportions and the reformers were pressing for immediate changes.[6]

This turbulent situation had, by 1821, convinced both Governor Hamilton and Lord Bathurst that 'some alteration of the laws' by which Newfoundland was governed was necessary.[7] It was precisely at this point that Codner (who had no connection with the reform movement) put forward his proposal to form a society to establish schools in Newfoundland. By early 1823 he had assembled a provisional committee, issued a prospectus and, with the confidence born of his evangelical faith, secured an interview with the Prime Minister himself. The latter approved of the objects of the Society, appointed himself Vice-Patron and empowered Codner to acquaint the Colonial Secretary with the situation.[8] There was little difficulty in interesting the Colonial Office, for the officials were used to working with missionaries and the evangelical sympathies of Lord Bathurst, the Colonial Secretary, and the Under-Secretary James Stephen (a nephew of Wilberforce) were well known.[9] Bathurst, in fact, became President of the Society. Codner then called the inaugural meeting, which met on 30 June 1823, and made three requests to the government: grants of land 'executed in due form of law' on which to build schools, school houses and playgrounds; free passages in HM ships of war or transports for all schoolmasters and schoolmistresses; and instructions from the British Government to the local government in the island to 'give all the aid and support within their power' to the Society's schools.[10]

These requests were granted immediately; a year later, following pressure from Newfoundland merchants, the British government authorised the Governor of Newfoundland to grant the society £500 towards the building of schools and £100 per annum for the salary of a schoolmaster.[11] These were unique concessions, all the more remarkable in that they were granted to an organisation which Governor Hamilton irascibly declared was led by 'inimical dissenters from the present Episcopal establishment', whose first committee and list of Vice-Presidents did, in fact, contain a majority of known Evangelicals, and which in its early years received moral and financial backing from the Wesleyan Methodists.[12]

By this time the British Government, bowing to the pressure for reform, had enacted a series of measures — legal, social and economic, including the abolition of Surrogate Courts — which gave Newfoundland a proto-Colonial status and opened the way to the development of civil and institutional life.[13] The Society's aims were complementary. It envisaged the provision of 'wholesome moral institutions ... especially schools' as the best means of making the population intelligent, industrious, moral, religious and happy, and thus able 'to understand and rightly to appreciate, their connection with and interest in the moral, as well as national greatness of their mother country'. Education, proclaimed John Wells, chairman of the Society's inaugural meeting, would enable its recipients better to appreciate political institutions and would promote among the lower orders obedience to the laws and friendly feelings towards the higher ranks of society. Inculcation of such 'sound principles', it was emphasised, would help to safeguard the property of fishing masters and merchants in an island whose historic, strategic and commercial importance was in striking contrast to the lack of moral culture of its inhabitants.[14]

The Newfoundland School Society was thus established under

merchant auspices with the object not only of providing the children of fishermen with access to literacy but also of socialising them for life in a merchant-dominated economy. The merchant controlled the economy through the credit or truck system. From him, in the spring, the fisherman collected food, clothing and tackle, which was set against the proceeds of the summer fishing season. If the catch were good, the fisherman was in credit with the merchant; if poor, he was in debt. The merchant, who set his own prices, acted (in J. D. Rogers's words) 'as bank, mint and clearing house ... money-lender, export agent and import agent'.[15]

The first school of the Newfoundland School Society opened in St John's, the capital, on 20 September 1824, in a store-room next to a bakery. Four teachers had been engaged, Mr and Mrs Jeynes, Mr William Fleet and a 'female monitor', and they were well trained by the standards of the time at the National Society's Central School in Baldwin Gardens, London. Arriving in St John's at the end of August, after a passage across the Atlantic in HM *John and Isaac*, they spent the next month visiting houses in St John's, encouraging parents to send their children to school. On the first day they welcomed seventy-five children, almost equally divided between boys and girls.[16] Within two years the school had been transferred to 'a commodious stone building' on Duckworth Street, one of the streets which run parallel to the harbour; the school could accommodate 450, though usually only half that number were present. In addition to the three 'R's, the children learnt 'sewing, knitting and net making, together with other useful and industrious habits'.[17] In order to overcome the shortage of trained teachers, the Society would set up a central school under the direction of mature teachers from England and gradually open branch schools in smaller surrounding communities, staffing them with monitors they had trained themselves. In this way the Society, during its early years, made uninterrupted progress. By 1830 it had opened twenty-eight day schools with an enrolment of 1,513 children, eighteen Sunday Schools and ten adult schools. Classes for adults were an important feature of the Society's work, combining the teaching of literacy with instruction in the Gospel. In the school at Carbonear, it was reported that eighteen scholars made 'considerable progress in learning to read the Scriptures'. At St John's, the school was open for the instruction of men and women who worked on the wharves, and at Harbour Grace reading, writing and arithmetic were taught from 6.30 to 8.30 p.m., Mondays, Wednesdays and Fridays.[18]

The Society's first public advertisement had stated that its schools were undenominational, that the Authorised Version of the Bible would be read without note or comment, that instruction in the catechism and formularies of the Established Church would be given after the usual school hours and that the object of the Society was 'moral and religious instruction of the poor children of Newfoundland'. Parents wishing to send their children to the school had to obtain written recommendations from a clergyman or 'two respectable inhabitants'.[19] The schools were thus ostensibly non-denominational, on the lines of their Lancasterian counterparts in Britain, but the teachers were trained by the National Society, practised Dr. Andrew Bell's version of the monitorial system ('as nearly as circumstances may permit'), and all had to be members of the Church of England.[20] In practice, they were selected for their 'serious' attitude to religion and for their 'sound piety'[21] — code words for adherence to the Evangelical faith. Thus, though the Society's schools, in the period under review, always took in a small number of children of Catholics and Dissenters,[22] they were recognisably the institutions of Anglican Evangelicals, a fact quickly noted and deplored by the Church of England ministry in the island.[23]

A reading of the sermons given before the annual meeting of the Society by Evangelical clergymen would hardly have calmed the fears of orthodox Anglicans. These sermons were impassioned expositions of the Evangelical view on the relationship of religion to education. Stopping just short of the position that no education at all was preferable to education without religion, these clergy made clear that vital Christianity ought to form the main content and essential purpose of all instruction for the poor. 'The principles of [the Society's] education must be considered as unaccommodating and unchangeable', the Revd Henry Budd stated bluntly; 'the Scriptures of immortal truth are the subject of its instruction ...'.[24] Without this essential element, secular education could be not only useless but positively dangerous. 'Science, if it stop short of God', warned the Revd G. T. Noel, 'may prove the baleful tree of evil and not of good.'[25] For the Revd R. W. Sibthorp, in his sermon of 1828, the salvation of souls exceeded in importance the making of good members of society or the teaching of reading and writing, which in any case tended to lift the lower orders out of their 'proper stations'.[26] A decade later one George Finch, at the annual meeting of the Society, echoed these sentiments with an angry denunciation of the 'absurd and wicked principle' that secular education alone could improve the moral condition of man.[27]

These precepts clearly had an influence on the teachers in the field. Though the three 'R's formed the basis of their teaching, as Bible Christians they added an overwhelming amount of Scriptural knowledge to the curriculum. In Western Bay, for instance, the senior scholars learned 'three chapters in the Old Testament, the first nine Psalms, nearly the whole of Dr Watt's hymns, besides many portions of Scripture which they were expected daily to repeat'. From other schools came similar reports of the rote-learning of the Scriptures and religious texts, though 'writing and arithmetic', added one teacher without irony, 'are not neglected'.[28] In fact, so full are the letters and journals of the teachers with accounts of the Scriptural content of the curriculum and their success in indoctrinating children with religious formularies, that serious consideration must be given to Ford K. Brown's contention that the fundamental aim of Evangelicals in the pedagogical sphere was conversion rather than education.[29]

The Revd Baptist Noel, in 1831, had devoted a sermon to the proposition that the operations of the Society 'tend to convert the unconverted among those to whom they extend', and 'by leading to their conversion, it gives glory to God through Christ'.[30] A few years later a teacher reported that though the Society may not see 'any immediate conversion result from our labours', there was enough encouragement for them to continue.[31] During the 1830s, in fact, missionary-type work figured increasingly among the Society's activities. Support for the Society in the 1820s, as signatures on its prospectuses and petitions show, came from a wide spectrum of people outside the Evangelical party.[32] In the 1830s, and particularly after the Evangelical Revd Daniel Wilson (later Bishop of Calcutta) had, in 1831, rescued the Society from a financial crisis by a Britain-wide campaign among 'friends, public and private',[33] its Evangelical orientation was confirmed and reinforced, and references to direct religious activity by the teachers began to appear in the Reports.

In 1834 the Society admitted that Spaniard's Bay was, in effect, a missionary station, and the teacher there 'virtually a missionary'. The 1837 Report defined the teachers' duties as three: first, that of schoolmasters; secondly, that of friendly visitors; thirdly, that of Catechists or lay readers. Distribution of Bibles and tracts, especially to the crews of sailing vessels (the conditions on which were considered to be a great source of evil) was also a major feature of the teachers' activities; by 1844 the Society had distributed no fewer than 20,000 Bibles, half a million religious tracts and books 'breathing the doctrinal and unctional spirit of the blessed Reformation', and thousands of prayer books and homilies.[34] In the early 1840s Aubrey Spencer, first Anglican Bishop of Newfoundland and a strong Evangelical, further increased the Society's missionary orientation by ordaining several of the teachers as 'deacon schoolmasters' and opening a number of 'chapelry school-houses', which combined the functions of school and church.[35] These developments prompted the Revd Francis Close of Cheltenham to declare in 1839 that he felt the Society was essentially a missionary body — 'I might say a Missionary Society to the heathen, but they are your own countrymen'.[36]

The Newfoundland School Society was, in fact, a minor but important branch of the world-wide missionary enterprise to which the energies of Protestants were devoted in the middle and later years of the nineteenth century. The upsurge of missionary activity had begun in the last decades of the eighteenth century, coincident with the economic upheaval of the Industrial Revolution, the corresponding growth of the 'second British Empire of trade' and the rise of the anti-slavery movement. The Industrial Revolution had changed the nature of overseas expansion, transforming Asia and much of the rest of the world from suppliers of raw materials and luxury goods to consumers of the products of the machine age; the opening of the 'heathen' areas of the world to commerce stimulated an awareness of the material and spiritual destitution of the so-called native races among the pietistic and evangelical Christians of Western European countries. These developments fostered what might be called the mercantile view of Christianity, adumbrated as early as 1797 by the Evangelical guru Charles Grant, in which virtue and advantage combined. On the one hand the expansion of the Empire facilitated the dissemination of the Gospel of Christ; on the other the spread of Christian civilisation increased the demand for the products of British industry.[37]

As the Empire expanded, Britain became increasingly conscious of its civilising and improving influence. 'Wherever our Empire is acknowledged', Huskisson, as Secretary for the Colonies, told Parliament in 1828, 'we have carried thither our language, our laws and our institutions ...'[38] The growing might of the British Empire dazzled the imagination of both colonists and Christians; it had grown, exulted the *Colonial Magazine* in 1840, to seventy-one possessions extending over 1,120,000 square miles, with a population of 105 million people and an annual return to the mother country of £23 million.[39] This 'vast territorial power' had been 'granted' to Britain by 'the Creator and Governor of the Universe' not for mere temporal aggrandisement but to further commerce, civil government and the 'hallowed purpose of planting the glorious standard of the Cross among the benighted heathens and idolaters'.[40]

The concept of purpose or Providence in the development of the colonial empire was the central tenet of 'Christian colonisation', the peculiar ideology of mid-Victorian evangelisation, in which history proceeded according to God's laws towards the fulfilment of the Divine Will, the single end of the diffusion of the knowledge of the Gospel over the whole earth.[41] The providence of God, Samuel Wilberforce, Archdeacon of Surrey, informed the Newfoundland School Society in 1842, had planned colonies in order that, together with the temporal advantages that might accrue to the mother country, God's Word might be spread throughout 'the lengthening chain of [Britain's] vast colonial occupation'. There were, however, two kinds of colonisation. The first was one in which countries drove out the natives and seized their inheritance (and here he cited the example of the extermination of the Newfoundland Indians), in which case, though the colonisers might be Christians, they were no better than 'murderers and robbers'. In Christian colonisation, however, it was incumbent upon the colonist, as the justification for conquest, to impart to the colonised peoples not only a knowledge of God but also education in the arts and sciences.[42] Similar sentiments had been voiced at the inaugural meeting of the Society twenty years earlier, when speakers had stressed the importance of Newfoundland's trade to the prosperity of Britain and the urgent need to counter the 'moral degradation' of the people of the island by the provision of education and the spread of vital Christianity.[43] The Bishop of Sierra Leone, The Bishop of Meath and the Revd Hugh Stowell of Manchester, in Anniversary Sermons before the Society in the mid-1850s, elaborated on the theme of the contrast between the commerce, wealth and enterprise of the Empire — granted by 'God in his gracious providence' to 'Protestant Evangelical England' — and the spiritual destitution of the colonists.[44]

If, to the modern mind, the concept of providence smacks of self-justification, a convenient device by which supporters of missions could ignore, or retrospectively accept, the harshness and rapacity of imperial conquest, it also gave to its adherents a self-confidence which sustained, against all difficulties and opposition, even the humblest missionary or teacher in the field. Armed with a conviction that they were part of a larger design, they felt they had the spiritual resources to combat not only the heathen, but also an enemy they came to recognise as even more formidable — Rome.

Though the civilising of colonial peoples remained the main objective of Protestant missionaries, much of their effort in the mid-nineteenth century went into opposing what they took to be the encroachment of the Roman Catholic Church on Britain's colonial preserves. In 1840 the *Colonial Magazine* had urged Protestants to unite to enforce the formation of an established church — including Dissenters — in each of the colonies; the alternative, it warned, would be the triumph of 'the Romanist Church', and the 'irremediable destruction' of the Protestant realm.[45] Alarm at 'Popery in the Colonies' was fed by the anti-Catholic phobia which engulfed Protestantism in the years following the Catholic Emancipation

Act of 1829, which granted access to 'offices, franchises and civil rights' to Roman Catholics in Britain and her colonies;[46] grants towards the salaries of colonial Catholic bishops, highlighted by the Protestant press,[47] increased Protestant fears. In both Britain and Newfoundland, the 'No Popery' crusade involved little less than the defence of the British Empire.

The crusade was prosecuted particularly fiercely in Newfoundland, where half the population consisted of Irish Catholics led by a militant bishop, Michael Antony Fleming, friend and follower of Daniel O'Connell. The Tory–Protestant élite, backed by all the Protestant churches and organisations, waged a furious campaign against the legislative activities of the Catholic radical–liberals in the Legislative Assembly (founded in 1832 under the newly-granted Representative Government), against the alleged attempts of Irish Catholic 'mobs' to intimidate electors at by-elections, and above all against Catholic support for the non-denominational schools for the poor established under the Education Act of 1836, and patterned on the Irish system inaugurated five years earlier.[48] The *Record*, organ of militant English Evangelicalism, interpreted these events as part of a world-wide design to foment rebellion in the British colonies,[49] and the London *Standard*, reflecting the Protestant investment in both missionary work and commerce, was aghast at the possibility of 'refugee Ribbonmen' converting Newfoundland into 'a buccaneering station for the ruin of our American trade'.[50]

Warning that 'Nowhere is Popery more active than in Newfoundland', the Revd Henry Melvill urged the Society, in his Anniversary Sermon of 1838, to oppose the Catholic-supported non-denominational system of education. Neither the Society, its supporters nor Bishop Spencer needed much encouragement; they took part in a campaign to force the Authorised Version of the Bible as a reading book into schools attended by both Catholic and Protestant children and in which religious instruction was given out of school hours. Under the slogan 'No Bible — No Schools', Protestant school board members resigned, Protestant parents were ordered to keep their children at home and the Society helped to set up independent Protestant schools.[51] In this fashion guerrilla war was waged, on and off, for seven years, much to the detriment of the education of innocent children. Ultimately the Protestant forces were successful; Newfoundland's new constitution of 1842, establishing an Amalgamated Assembly, narrowing the franchise and limiting the legislative role of Catholics, was in large part due to the effect of the 'No Popery' crusade on the British government's perception of the situation in Newfoundland. The Education Act of the following year, passed on Protestant initiative, divided the education grant between Protestants and Catholics,[52] thus inaugurating a denominational system of education which, with some additions and modifications, remains in Newfoundland to this day. Successes in this campaign, the Society had claimed, were due to 'the combined exertion of some influential persons, most of the clergy, some of the Wesleyan missionaries and the entire body of your teachers', and in 1845 the Revd Hugh Stowell of Manchester, in an Annual Sermon, congratulated the Society on keeping Antichrist at bay and preventing 'Romanism' from spreading across the whole of the island.[53]

This accolade, though something of an exaggeration — the Wesleyan Methodists, growing in strength and with numerous missionaries and schools, had been pursuing similar policies[54] — was significant of the position of power and influence which the Society had reached by the mid-1840s. It had profited from the relative weakness of the Church of England, which was without a diocese until 1839, and the Evangelical sympathies of Aubrey Spencer, the first bishop, also contributed to an advance which had been given an impetus by the material support of the British government. Moreover, the Society had taken advantage of the disruption of the public educational system by sectarian strife in the late 1830s to forge ahead with the opening of its own schools. By 1840 the number of schools established by the Society had reached fifty-two (though not all were in operation at any one time), and five years later the number of children under instruction totalled 3,907, nearly twice the figure of 1830.[55] As early as 1836 the Society claimed to have opened forty-three day schools, mainly in the more thickly-populated east coast areas; the total number who had received or were receiving instruction was 16,500 children and adults.[56] Thus, in a population of 75,000,[57] no less than twenty-two per cent had been or were being educated by the Society in the first dozen years of its existence.

The year 1844, however, marked the beginning of a change in the Society's fortunes. Spencer left Newfoundland for the warmer climate of Jamaica and was replaced by Edward Feild, described by a recent biographer as 'a convinced High Churchman of the tough, rigid and unbending type' who 'set out to build a strong, independent and decidedly Anglo-Catholic church.'[58] Though opposed to the pan-Protestantism and anti-Catholicism of Spencer and the Society, Feild initially gave the latter (as the only nominally Anglican school organisation) critical support, became its Vice-President and to some extent influenced its policies.[59] In 1846, at the instigation of both home and colonial bishops, the Society broadened its base and became the Church of England Society for Educating the Poor of Newfoundland and the Colonies.[60] Under modified regulations, the bishop of each diocese was given direct contol over the teachers and schools.[61] This may have satisfied Feild, but it infuriated the *Record*, which alleged the Society was becoming overly influenced by Puseyism, and dismayed the English subscribers, a strong body organised in over sixty local Associations and Auxiliaries.[62] Faced with the resignation of Feild and declining financial support in Britain, the Society had little choice but to re-adopt, in 1849, its original constitution.[63] In 1851 it reasserted its evangelical principles by amalgamating with the Colonial Church Society, another evangelical missionary organisation. As the Colonial Church and School Society[64] it was involved in a number of clashes with Feild on doctrinal and organisational issues,[65] and there is no doubt that from mid-century onwards the Society entered a period of decline. The number of its schools decreased,[66] and it began to concentrate more on raising the level of its pedagogical work — opening an infant and a model school[67] — than on proselytisation. After the death of Feild in 1876, the Society drew closer to the Church of England.[68]

In its heyday, however, the zeal and devotion of the Society's teachers had given it a distinctive place in Newfoundland education. Their efforts had contributed to a rise in the literacy rate from thirty-five to fifty-seven per cent between the years 1836 and 1857,[69] and had also led to a modest measure of social mobility — there were reports of former pupils of the Society's schools becoming teachers, taking up apprenticeships to trades or clerical work and filling 'positions of trust' in St John's. A taste for reading had developed in some outports.[70] But was the unremitting drill in the schools, the provision of libraries, the braving of snow, ice, storms and bogs to give fireside Bible readings,[71] directed solely to educational advance? Ford K. Brown has maintained that Evangelicals believed that activities of this kind did nothing for the 'best interests' of the people; such acts were done 'by the way' and the true object was to gain access to their homes and hearts, the better to make them disposed to receive religious counsel and instruction.[72]

Little in the work of the Society in Newfoundland contradicts this assessment. Bishop Spencer devoted a sermon to elaborating the means by which access to children's hearts might be obtained. Not only were the normal monitorial methods of 'scholastic dispositions, enforced obedience, the mere mechanical operation of learning' to be employed, but feelings of awe, if not of outright fear, should be invoked in the pupil in order that the lessons of Scripture 'may recur to him in some acceptable season with all their awful and all their saving force'.[73] These methods of religious instruction were inspired by the Evangelicals' characterisation of children as corrupt and evil creatures. The Revd Henry Melvill, in a sermon of 1838, echoing the words of the Revd Cooper uttered twelve years earlier,[74] declared that there was corruption at the very core of human nature, 'Away with all the dream and delusion of the innocence of childhood,' he cried, 'there are the seeds of every kind of evil in the smiling little one......'[75]

This typical Evangelical attitude led to the evaluation of disobedience, pride, lying and profanity not as childish misbehaviour to be overcome by kindness and firmness, but as examples of an inherent tendency to sinfulness, to be eradicated by the most extreme methods of spiritual terror. The shy and simple children of Newfoundland fishermen were early made familiar with these methods. Teachers wrote to the Society in England giving harrowing examples of repentance induced in pupils by fear of divine punishment. One teacher reassured his charges that although lying was not now punished with instant death as in the case of Ananias and Sapphira, yet the day was approaching when every liar would be sentenced to everlasting woe. Two scholars who had committed childish misdemeanours took this to heart, and recalling the line in the hymn, 'every liar must have his portion in the lake that burns with brimstone and fire', resolved henceforward to memorise the fifth chapter of Acts to keep themselves on the path of truth. Conversely, children were taught to regard death as a welcome event, to be looked forward to 'happily' or 'with pleasure'.[76]

The spiritual offensive against the realities of children's lives (and deaths) in the Newfoundland fishery was expressive of the fundamental Evangelical tendency to transform social and economic reality into moral terms. Education became less a means of generating economic achievement, even in the limited sense of the benefit accruing from the creation of literate planters and a few commercial clerks, or a means of enriching the intellect of children whose lives were bounded by the seasonal work in the fishery, than making young people 'wise unto salvation'. The social conditions which gave rise to childish misbehaviour, truancy and illness, or the economic exploitation by merchants which forced their parents into starvation, were dissolved into the universal and unavoidable moral predicament of man from which only spiritual grace could bring deliverance.

The assumption of the Society's teachers that they had the right to propagate their doctrines in another country was complementary to their moral position. Having satisfied itself that the people of the colonies were, by and large, spiritually destitute,[77] the Society felt it a duty to 'transplant England's laws, England's language, England's children, England's Church from the mother country, and give them room and opportunity to develop abroad'.[78] Attitudes such as those have led modern historians to view the missionary movement as an expression of cultural imperialism,[79] and the attempt of the Society's teachers to impose the values and attitudes of their homeland upon the social and secular culture of the Newfoundland fishery can hardly be seen in any other light. The teachers arrived on the island intent upon giving Newfoundlanders 'a participation in all the religious and intellectual privileges of this pre-eminently happy land, emphatically *their* Mother Country'.[80] This standpoint took little account of the customs and outlook engendered by the exigencies of small fishing communities. Work was seasonal, involving hecty activity in the summer months, when the men (assisted by young boys) fished incessantly and the woman cleaned, cured and dried the fish, followed by retirement to the woods in winter when fuel was cut and boats and fishing gear prepared for the following spring.

The values endangered by this existence were those of co-operation, in house building, in fishing, and at times of natural calamity, rather than those the teachers took for granted — competition, the division of labour, year-round regularity and the fixed working week characteristic of industrial life. to the fisherman, Sunday labour conformed to the ecconomic necessity of working seven days a week to catch and prepare the fish in season. To the Evangelical it constituted an infraction of God's law. 'Spoke to them on the sin they were committing and distributed many tracts', reported a teacher who observed people busily at work on a Sunday spreading fish, caulking boats and working in their gardens.[81] To the children, monitorial instruction, the system *par exellence* of industrial capatalism, must have seemed alien to the rhythm of their lives. Monitorial schooling demaded regular attendance, uniformity of behaviour and graded progression from one task to another, practices which conflicted with those of social environment regulated by the seasons and the availability of fish.

It is difficult to compile a balance sheet of the Society's progress. Though many Newfoundlanders were indifferent or hostile to the society's teaching, and though teachers' reports would suggest that drinking, dancing and card-playing remained the staple recreations of fishing communities, teachers from places as far apart as Hermitage Bay, Greenspond and Harbour Buffet could report dramatic decreases in Sabbath-breaking, profanity, disobedience and more worldly sins.[82] Ultimately, of course, the fisherman became reconciled to the six-day week and the majority of childeren to regular schooling. In the second half of the nineteenth century, despite the decline in the number of the Society's schools, the impulses towards imperial patriotism and religious observance which the Society had fostered came to fruition. Newfoundland's loyalty to the Empire was publicly validated in 1987 by no less a figure than

Rudyard Kipling,[83] and underlined by Premier William Whiteway, who declared that 'when England may be in difficulties, Newfoundland will not be backward in shedding its blood for her'.[84] Beckles Willson, a visiting Canadian author, found Newfoundland to be 'wonderously religious' and St John's 'the most religious town on earth',[85] and the Census of 1901 revealed the existence of 529 churches, one to every 410 of the population.[86] Although the Newfoundland School Society must be seen as only one component of the forces which engendered these developments, their existence was testimony to the part played by the Society in the island's social and religious life.

Notes

1 The Society's operations in Newfoundland ended in 1923.
2 Revd J. D. Mullins, *Our Beginnings: Being a Short Sketch of the History of the Colonial and Continental Church Society*, London, n.d., but 1823, p. 4; Canon G. H. Bolt, *The Codner Centenary*, St. John's, 1923, p. 1.
3 Monthly extracts from the Correspondence of the British and Foreign Bible Society, No. 52, 30 November 1821; report entitled *Society for Educating the Poor of Newfoundland*, London, n.d., but 1823, p. 13.
4 St John Chadwick, *Newfoundland: Island into Province*, Cambridge, 1967, pp. 8, 10.
5 J. J. Mannion (ed.), *The Peopling of Newfoundland*, St John's, 1977, *passim*.
6 Provincial Archives of Newfoundland and Labrador, GN2/2/A, Governor Pickmore to Lord Dalhousie, 13 November 1817; Proclamation of Governor Hamilton, 19 July 1819; PP 1817 VI, Report from the Select Committee on Newfoundland Trade, pp. 10, 11, 40; CO194/60, B. Lester to T. Goulburn, 15 March 1817, encl. Memorial from Merchants of Poole; Parl. Deb. XXXVI, 17 June 1817, 1294; CO194/65, Hamilton to Bathurst, 25 February 1822; Hamilton to Forbes, 4 May 1822; A Report of Certain Proceedings of the Inhabitants of the Town of St John's, in the Island of Newfoundland, St John's, 1821.
7 CO195/17, Bathurst to Hamilton, 14 March 1821; CO194/65, Hamilton to Bathurst, 25 February 1822.
8 *Society for Educating the Poor of Newfoundland*, p. 34.
9 D. M. Young, *The Colonial Office in the Early Nineteenth Century*, London, 1961, pp. 18, 58; P. Knaplund, *James Stephen and the British Colonial System 1813–1847*, Madison, 1953, pp. 14–18.
10 CO194/66, Codner to Wilmot Horton, 17 July 1823.
11 CO194/68, Memorial 'To the Right Honourable Earl Bathurst ...' (n.d.); CO195/17, Horton to Hamilton, 30 June 1824; CO43/64, Horton to Codner, 30 June 1864.
12 CO194/67, Hamilton to Horton, 5 July 1824; *Society for Educating the Poor of Newfoundland*, pp. 3–4; Methodist Missionary Society, Minutes of Missions Committee, 24 June 1823 (hereafter MMS).
13 A. H. McLintock, *The Establishment of Constitutional Government in Newfoundland 1783–1832*, London, 1941, pp. 158–61.
14 *Society for Educating the Poor of Newfoundland*, p. 12, 16–17; *The First Annual Report of the Committee of the Society for Educating the Poor of Newfoundland*, London, 1824, p. 13; *Christian Observer*, August 1823, p. 521.

Appendix
Newfoundland School Society: Schools and Scholars, 1830–1920*

Year	No. of day schools	No. of children under instruction	No. of Sunday schools	No. of children under instruction	No. of Adult schools	No. under instruction	Notes
1830	28	1,513	18	932	10	344	*Returns from 5 schools
1835	39	1,764	32	1,826	16	118*	
1840	52	3,234					
1845	44	3,907					
1850	34	2,552					
1855	29	3,000*					*Estimated
1860	28	2,500*	16				*Estimated
1865	19						
1870	20	2,324					
1875	20	2,543					
1880	20	2,287					
1885	17	1,874*					*Figures for 1885–6
1890	20	1,981					
1895	18	1,787*	16	1,451*			*Figures for 1894
1900	25	2,136*					*including 3 schools in Labrador
1905	22	1,880	20	1,964			
1910	19	1,337	17	1,165			
1915	18	1,242	16	959			
1920	14*		7*				*Figures for 1919

Source: Annual Reports, 1830–1920.

15 J. D. Rogers, *A Historical Geography of the British Colonies Vol. V — Part IV: Newfoundland*, Oxford, 1911, p. 206.

16 *Proceedings of the Society for Educating the Poor of Newfoundland*, 1824–25, London 1825, pp. 63–5 (hereafter SEPN); CO194/68, Codner to Horton, 22 May and 15 June 1824.

17 *Mercantile Journal*, St John's, 19 January 1826; *Proceedings SEPN*, 1825–26, p. 36.

18 *Proceedings SEPN*, 1824–25, p. 70; 1828–29, p. 39; *Proceedings of the Newfoundland and British North America Society for Educating the Poor*, 1829–30, London, 1830, p. 47 (hereafter NBNASEP); *Weekly Journal*, St John's, 29 October 1828.

19 *Mercantile Journal*, 16 September 1824.

20 *Society for Educating the Poor of Newfoundland*, p. 5.

21 *Proceedings SEPN*, 1827–28, Sermon of the Revd R. W. Sibthorp, p. 26.

22 *Proceedings NBNASEP*, 1842–43, p. 15; 1843–44, p. 16; *Proceedings of the Church of England School Society for Newfoundland and the Colonies, 1847–48*, London, 1848, p. 9 (hereafter CESSNC).

23 *Society for the Propagation of the Gospel*, C/CAN/NFL 4, W. Bullock to the Society, 8 July 1824; G. Coster to the Society, 9 November 1826 (hereafter SPG).

24 *Proceedings SEPN*, 1824–25, p. 56.

25 *Proceedings SEPN*, 1828–29, p. 25.

26 *Proceedings SEPN*, 1827–28, pp. 30–1.

27 *Record*, 3 May 1838.

28 *Proceedings SEPN*, 1825–26, p. 44; *Proceedings NBNASEP*, 1832–33, p. 7; 1833–34, p. 4; 1834–35, p. 8; 1837–38, pp. 2–3; *Proceedings CESSNC*, 1846–47, p. 23; 1847–48, p. 23.

29 F. K. Brown, *Fathers of the Victorians*, Cambridge, 1961, pp. 189–93.

30 *Proceedings NBNASEP*, 1830–1, p. 12.

31 *Proceedings NBNASEP*, 1836–37, p. 4.

32 Cf. MMS, Corres.N.AM. 3/30, S. Codner to J. Butterworth, 16 February 1822, encl. prospectus entitled 'Schools in Newfoundland, n.d., but 1822, signed by 120 individuals and merchant houses; CO 194/68, Memorial 'To the Right Honourable Earl Bathurst...' n.d., c. February 1824, signed by 125 Devon worthies with connection to the Newfoundland trade.

33 J. Bateman, *Life of the Right Rev. Daniel Wilson, D.D.*, London, 2 vols, 1860, I, pp. 269–71; *Proceedings NBNASEP*, 1830–31, p. 35; 1831–32, p. 10.

34 *Proceedings NBNASEP*, 1834–35, p. 4; 1835–36, p. 8; 1836–37, p. 3; 1837–38, pp. 6–7; 1839–40, p. 5; 1843–44, p. 24.

35 SPG C/CAN/NFL 4, A. Spencer to M. Campbell, 30 December 1840; A. Spencer to M. Campbell, 26 April 1841; *Proceedings NBNASEP*, 1842–43, pp. 9–10.

36 *Proceedings NBNASEP*, 1838–39, p. 11.

37 PP 1812–13 X, C. Grant, 'Observations on the State of Society Among the Asiatic Subjects of Great Britain', 1797, pp. 111–12.

38 Parl. Deb., N.S. XIX, 2 May 1828, 315.

39 'Extent and importance of the British colonies', *Colonial Magazine*, Vol. VI, No. 23, 1841, p. 258.

40 'England's Destiny — Colonisation', *Colonial Magazine*, Vol. VII, No. 26, 1842.

41 B. Stanley, 'Commerce and Christianity: providence theory, the missionary movement, and the imperialism of free trade, 1842–1860', *Historical Journal*, Vol. 26, No. 1, 1983, pp. 71–94.

42 *Proceedings NBNASEP*, 1841–42.

43 *Society for Educating the Poor of Newfoundland, passim.*

44 *Annual Report of the Colonial Church and School Society*, 1853–54; 1854–55; 1855–56 (hereafter CCSS).

45 'State of religion in the British colonies', *Colonial Magazine*, Vol. I, no. 2, 1840, pp. 241–2.

46 R. A. Billington, *The Protestant Crusade 1800–1860*, New York, 1938; E. R. Norman, *Anti-Catholicism in Victorian England*, London, 1958, pp. 13–21; G.F.A. Best, 'Popular Protestantism in Victorian Britain', in E.R. Robson (Ed.), *Ideas and Institutions of Victorian Britain*, London, 1967, pp. 115–42.

47 *Record*, 19 September 1839; 'Popery in the colonies', *Protestant Magazine*, Vol. I, March 1839, pp. 33–37; 'Colonial bishoprics', *Protestant Magazine*, Vol. III, June 1841, pp. 172–4.

48 Cf. Phillip McCann, 'The origins of denominational education in Newfoundland: 'No Popery' and the Education Acts, 1836–1843', in Phillip McCann, *Studies in the History of Education in Newfoundland, 1800–1855*, forthcoming.

49 *Record*, 20 September 1838. Cf. also *The Times*, 1 January 1841.

50 Standard, 24 September 1938. Cf. also 'Popery in Newfoundland', *Protestant Magazine*, Vol. III, February 1841, pp. 47–49.

51 *Proceedings NBNASEP*, 1837–38, pp. 10–11; McCann, 'Origins of denominational education', *loc. cit.*

52 VI Vic. cap 6, An Act for the Encouragement of Education in this Colony.

53 *Proceedings NBNASEP*, 1837–38, p. 12; 1844–45, p. 10.

54 Cf. McCann, 'Origins of denominational education', *loc. cit.*

55 Cf. Appendix.

56 *Proceedings NBNASEP*, 1836–37, p. 36.

57 Mannion, *Peopling of Newfoundland*, p. 13.

58 F. Jones, 'The church in nineteenth-century Newfoundland', *Bulletin of Canadian Studies*, Vol. V, No. 1 April 1981, p. 31. For Feild's life and activities, cf. F. Jones, 'Bishop Feild, a study in politics and religion in nineteenth-century Newfoundland', unpublished Ph. D. thesis, University of Cambridge, 1971.

59 *Record*, 29 April 1844; Jones, Feild, p. 140.

60 *Record*, 19 April 1847; 14 June 1849.

61 Leaflet entitled 'Statement Respecting the Extension of the Operations of the Newfoundland and British North American School Society to All Colonies of Great Britain', 30 July 1846.

62 *Record*, 19, 26 and 30 November, 7 December 1846; 19 April 1847.

63 *Record*, 29 April 1847; 14 June 1849; *Christian Remembrancer*, Vol. 2, 1850, pp. 499–500, Feild to the Society (1848).

64 Guildhall Library, Ms. 15674, Colonial Church and School Society. General Committee Minute Book 1850–55, Minutes of Special General Meeting, 27 December 1850. The amalgamation took place on 1 January of the following year.

65 Jones, Feild, pp. 137–9, 145ff, 217.

66 Cf. Appendix.

67 *Annual Report CCSS*, 1854–55, p. 59; 1855–56, p. 68.

68 *Annual Report, Colonial and Continental Church Society*, 1879, p. 82.

69 D. G. Alexander, 'Literacy and economic development in nineteenth-century Newfoundland', in E. W. Sager, L. R. Fischer, and S. O. Pierson, *Atlantic Canada and Confederation*, Toronto, 1983, pp. 122–3.

70 *Proceedings NBNASEP*, 1836–37, pp. 7–8; 1837–38, p. 5; 1838–39, p. 6, p. 14; 1840–41, p. 5; 1844–45, p. 16.

71 *Proceedings NBNASEP*, 1833–34, p. 3; 1834–35, p. 10; 1836–37, p. 8; 1843–44, p. 13; *Annual Report, CCSS*, 1851, pp. 31–2, p. 37.

72 Brown, *Fathers of the Victorians*, p. 231.
73 *Proceedings NBNASEP*, 1845–46, p. 13.
74 *Proceedings SEPN*, 1825–26, p. 20.
75 H. Melvill, *Religious Education; A Sermon*, London, 1838, pp. 10–11.
76 *Proceedings SEPN*, 1825–26, pp. 45–6, p. 53; 1827–28, pp. 45–6; *Proceedings NBNASEP*, 1825–26, p. 5; 1832–33, p. 10.
77 Cf. e.g., *Proceedings CESSNC*, 1846–7, Sermon of the Revd J. Harding, pp. 6–8.
78 *Record*, 2 January 1851, Speech of the Revd T. Nolan at the Annual Meeting of the Society.
79 Cf. K. E. Knorr, *British Colonial Theories 1570–1750*, Toronto, 1944, p. 388.
80 *Proceedings SEPN*, 1825–26, p. 65.
81 *Proceedings NBNASEP*, 1832–33, p. 3.
82 *Proceedings NBNASEP*, 1845–46, p. 18; *Proceedings CESSNC*, 1846–47, p. 30; 1848–49, p. 6, pp. 10–13, p. 16. p. 21; 1849–50, p. 6, p. 16.
83 R. Kipling to G. F. Bearn (n.d.) in the preface to B. Willson, *The Tenth Island*, London, 1897, pp. vi-viii.
84 W. Whiteway, in the foreword to Willson, *Tenth Island*, pp. xi-xiii.
85 Willson, *Tenth Island*, p. 42.
86 Census of Newfoundland and Labrador, 1901, Table 1, St John's, 1903, pp. vi, xxiv.

CHAPTER SIX

Imperialism, patriotism and Kiwi primary schooling between the wars

R. Openshaw

The years after World War One witnessed an upsurge of patriotism in New Zealand which had considerable impact on both primary and secondary schools. It was the primary schools, however, by virtue of the compulsory attendance requirements, which were regarded as the nurseries of future citizens. In addition, primary-school patriotism constitutes a unique historical problem. Although it represented to a degree a continuation of pre-1914 concepts, it also differed markedly in intensity and in impact from the earlier period. There is a need to consider the immediate causes which brought about this situation. This having been accomplished, the evidence utilised must be critically reassessed in an attempt to understand the underlying function of the New Zealand education system. The first part of this chapter, therefore, is both descriptive and explanatory, while the second part is more purely analytical.

The zenith of patriotic zeal

The renewed interest in history and civics teaching, the provision made for elaborate commemorative school assemblies on days of imperial or national significance, and the officially-sanctioned Navy League activities in schools all constitute evidence of an ongoing primary school patriotism after 1918. An even more significant aspect of post-war school patriotism was the growing emphasis on loyalty, enforced through legislation. In particular the introduction of compulsory flag-saluting and loyalty oaths for teachers provide strong indications of a new belligerency.

One reason for the grim new mood was New Zealand's bitter war experience. Proportionately speaking, few countries shouldered as intensive a war burden.[1] From 1916 there were constant exhortations to set aside political and class differences in the interests of unity. Instruction in the primary school reflected the new tone: during 1916, issues of the *School Journal* began to stress the need for sacrifice over the earlier notion of simply being 'right'. Bluntness in informing children about total war became common. 'Every little task performed at home' was now claimed to be vital to the imperial war effort.[2] Expressions of mass loyalty and individual conformity were increasingly regarded as true patriotism. In 1917, following a recommendation of the National Efficiency Board, many schools introduced weekly flag-saluting ceremonies on the assumption that children would thus be encouraged to regard themselves as an integral part of wartime society.[3]

After World War One this mood remained. Many schools continued to hold regular flag-saluting ceremonies, though they were not compelled to do so. The war became the inspiration for an increased emphasis on patriotic instruction. A number of school committees supported the construction of war memorials in school grounds, aided by a government subsidy. An ongoing determination to teach children about the war was aptly illustrated by the phenomenal success of the multi-volume *Children's Story of the War*, which received the backing of the Education Department and the education boards.[4] W. F. Massey, the Prime Minister, was adamant that the new history syllabus should make adequate provision for the inculcation of patriotism, 'especially through the study of great men from whom the race had sprung'. He wanted specific reference made to the heroes of the Great War, including Haig, Foch and Beatty.[5] The 1919 syllabus went some distance towards this and although the history and civics section was in many respects similar to the earlier revised syllabus of 1913, it differed in giving more emphasis to the personal, military, political and racial qualities which were believed to have contributed to British victory.[6] These concepts were reinforced through patriotic observances and ceremonies which fused war commemoration with wider patriotic and imperial sentiment. Anzac Day became the dominion's major national day and, in addition to taking part in school services, deputations from schools attended dawn parades in the main centres. Empire Day was another occasion for the display of patriotism in the schools. Special models were distributed to school pupils and in 1921 the Chief Inspector of Primary Schools, T. B. Strong, utilised the *Education Gazette* to give teachers details of an elaborate Empire Day ceremony which was to include singing, readings, choral speaking and flag-saluting.[7]

In addition to increasing the prestige of school patriotism, the war had another, more sinister impact. The last years of the conflict saw a growing intolerance. Germans living in New Zealand were singled out as potential traitors. As early as 1915, the Alien Enemy Teacher's Act forbade the employment of any teacher who was not a British citizen, who had at any time been a citizen of an enemy state.[8] Collective anger was also directed at any teacher who, through careless word or deed, appeared to have abused the trust of society. A few months before the armistice, A. W. Mayo, a mathematics teacher at Seddon Memorial Technical College, was dismissed by the Auckland Education Board for allegedly making statements critical of the allies. Only in September 1920, when it was discovered that the principal witness against him had a criminal record, was Mayo given an opportunity to seek re-employment as a teacher, though he was not reinstated to his old position.[9]

Teachers who had been military defaulters during World War One were regarded with both hostility and fear lest they passed on their sentiments to children.[10] Education authorities had long memories. One unfortunate teacher, imprisoned as a military defaulter until 1918, was unable to gain employment with any education board until 1932, despite possessing a favourable teaching report prior to his arrest.[11]

The war thus had two main effects on school patriotism; firstly, it stimulated an increased awareness of the school's role in sustaining national and imperial unity, and secondly, it predisposed society to regard outward expressions of loyalty and conformity as being truly patriotic. Both were of ongoing significance, yet it was the presence of other, equally important factors which were to reshape primary-school patriotism in the post-war period.

One of these factors was the continuation of strategic insecurity in New Zealand. After 1918, strategic insecurity stemmed from two major causes; fear of Asian aggression, and anxiety concerning the level of British naval commitment in the Pacific. Each of these served to strengthen the role of school patriotism. The *School Journal* during the early post-war years made frequent reference to the special relationship between the dominions and Britain. In part, this reflected the New Zealand Government's own position. Even as Massey was reiterating his country's support for closer imperial defence ties at the 1921 Imperial Conference, the Minister of Education, C. J. Parr, was preparing a special article for the *School Journal* illustrating how Britain, Australia and New Zealand were bound by 'a common language, common ideals and an Anglo-Saxon love of the sea'.[12] A *School Journal* article in May 1923 outlined the obligations of dominion status. Freedom, it was alleged, carried a burden of responsibility. In return for protection, New Zealand had a dual obligation; to supply food to a hungry Britain, and to provide a new home for the surplus British population.[13] Another *School Journal* article referred to the potential threat posed by China and Japan. The answer was to be found in attracting more British migrants as a bulwark against a land-starved Asia.[14]

Victory in 1918 had not brought security. There was increasing concern at the rapid growth of United States and Japanese naval strength in the Pacific.[15] Although the Imperial Government stressed its determination to maintain the Royal Navy at a strength at least equal to that of any other single power, in reality this meant the official abandonment of the two-power standard. Massey returned to New Zealand fron the 1921 Imperial Conference fearful that Britain was about to sacrifice its slim margin of naval superiority at the twin altars of international understanding and financial economy. Something of his anxiety crept into an article he wrote for the *School Journal* which argued that it was imperative that Britain possess the largest fleet in the world.[16]

Given the degree of New Zealand interest in naval affairs, it was hardly surprising that the Navy League was officially encouraged to assume a leading role in promoting an awareness of naval problems as an integral part of school patriotism. During the early 1920s the Navy League took advantage of frequent visits by Royal Navy vessels, planning visits to schools by ship's officers and organising conducted tours of vessels for school children. The Navy League's effort in the schools was facilitated by the goodwill of education boards and school committees.[17] In 1919 co-operation with these bodies had enabled the Navy League to enrol some 10,000 school children as honorary members, and the organisation's lecturers were frequent speakers at school patriotic ceremonies, such as Anzac Day and Empire Day.[18] By contrast, the League of Nations Union during this period found it considerably more difficult to convince educational authorities that it had a worthwhile message for primary-school children. For many, perhaps most, New Zealanders during the early post-war years, universal human brotherhood seemed a remote even dangerous concept, when compared with the tangible bulwark of the Royal Navy.

While continuation of wartime modes of thought, along with the heightened sense of insecurity in New Zealand, were important for the development of school patriotism, one further factor played a significant part in producing the changes which occurred during the early post-war period. Fear of militant socialism was strong in early post-war New Zealand. Stories of world-wide Bolshevik activities were treated as major news items by the press, even though they were often ill-founded rumours.[19] The effect was to encourage speculation about Bolshevism at home. The enigmatic New Zealand Welfare League warned workers against heeding the arguments of 'heady socialist advocates'.[20] Some economists gloomily predicted the consequences of organised Labour's apparently '"... idealistic and revolutionary" stance'.[21] Equally passionate denunciations of socialism came from the pulpit, typified by the Rev C. H. Grant-Lowen's warning to an Auckland Anzac Day gathering that there was a 'great deal of disloyalty in our midst'.[22] Deteriorating industrial relations during the early post-war years served to confirm the worst fears. The Government, not unmindful of electorate feeling, was determined to act strongly. By the end of 1920, comprehensive legislation had been introduced, expressly designed to counter militant socialist influence. The new bill brought together many of the old wartime regulations dealing with the distribution of subversive literature, the efficient operation of wharves and the suppression of subversive strikes, only now the enemy was not Prussian militarism, but militant socialism. While most of the bill's clauses met with Labour opposition, the most controversial clause was that dealing with subversive literature: 'No person shall print, publish, sell, distribute, have in his possession for sale or distribution, or bring or cause to be brought or sent into New Zealand, any document which incites, encourages, advises or expresses any seditious intention.'[23]

The following year saw a rising number of convictions under the subversive literature clause of the new legislation. Thorough press coverage of each individual case was often freely mixed with accounts of left-wing violence overseas, and did much to encourage the pessimistic view that the dominion itself was grappling with a well-organised group of subversives, determined to bring the country to its knees.[24] Typical was the reaction of R. H. A. Potter, Chairman of the Mount Eden School Committee, Auckland. Potter, incensed by a paper's account of a May Day parade in the Sydney Domain at which a Union Jack was burned, complained: 'never has the devil's propaganda been so strong, so shrewd, so involved with anarchy and revolution as at present'.[25] This was a spectre which loomed ever larger for educationists. Indeed, the possibility that socialist subversion might make considerable inroads amongst politically unsophisticated youths had not been lost on teachers. Delegates at the New Zealand Educational Institute's first post-war conference in February 1919 were told that 'every child should be supplied with the mental and moral equipment that would enable him to meet the influences that would be brought to bear on him from without'.[26] A remit calling for the school-leaving age to be raised to sixteen was supported by delegates on the grounds that too many pupils left school lacking even an elementary knowledge of the industrialised world, and 'thus more easily fell prey to the arguments of agitators whose fallacies they were unable to detect, and in a few years they were members of that class which was a source of unrest to the community'.[27] The first issue of National Education suggested that education could make a valuable contribution towards discouraging the state of mind which saw 'Red Labour' on one side and 'Big Money' on the other, and instead encouraged the view that society was based on 'unity and co-operation'.[28] Over the next few years, school inspectors enthusiastically pressed for more classroom recognition of the value of history and civics in creating more responsible citizens, better able to resist the blandishments of extremists. The Canterbury inspectors, for instance, deplored what they considered to be an excessive reliance on text-book civics, and went on to stress: 'It is very necessary that the feet of our pupils should be guided to the openings of the road to good citizenship, as strong and insidious forces are at work in certain quarters which may lead sooner or later to the disruption of society and of the general happiness of our people.'[29] Some politicians, however, remained unconvinced that education alone would be sufficient to ensure loyalty. Parr was particularly alarmed at the activities of the Socialist Sunday Schools; small, privately-run, weekend schools which offered a broadly socialist curriculum as a counterweight to what its proponents saw as the dangerous dose of imperialism and militarism administered by the state schools.[30] Although the Socialist Sunday Schools attracted comparatively few pupils, and were more inclined to stress human brotherhood than bloody revolution, Parr regarded them as a blatant challenge. In May 1921, he retaliated by instituting regulations making weekly flag-saluting compulsory in all New Zealand schools. In justification, he argued that if children were to be taught effectively, 'disruptive influences in the community had to be countered, especially the Socialist Sunday Schools, where ideas were inculcated which treated with contempt national feeling and tended strongly towards revolutionary socialism'.[31]

These regulations marked a watershed in the teaching of patriotism because they encapsulated the view that instruction alone was insufficient to ensure loyalty. Their introduction also indicated a willingness to resort to coercion in order to safeguard the school's role in political socialisation, and this in itself underlined a shift from a defensive strategy to one which was primarily offensive. Only a small spark was now needed to initiate still more drastic measures.

On 19 June 1921, Hedwig Weitzel, a university graduate and a student at the Wellington Teachers' College was arrested for distributing subversive literature. The publication concerned was *The Communist*, a pamphlet of Australian origin which advocated revolution and the creation of a Marxist state. In court the police alleged that Weitzel 'knew quite well all the risks she was taking in dabbling in a matter of this kind'. In addition, she had frequently been observed in the company of 'well-known communists'. Such evidence made the verdict a formality. Weitzel was fined £10, and her studentship was terminated.[32]

While this constituted the end of Weitzel's teaching career, her case was not easily forgotten. A number of features distinguished the Weitzel case from similar offences;[33] Weitzel's German ancestry aroused waretime animosities,[34] and, worse, her position as student-teacher underlined for many New Zealanders the urgency of ensuring that all teachers were loyal, for, as Parr himself was to put it some weeks later, 'if you are going to have disloyal teachers, you are going to have disloyal children'.[35] The implications of the Weitzel case were ominous, but the whole incident was further inflamed when the constable in attendance at the hearing claimed that seventeen female students from the Wellington Training College had been present in court and had contributed money to Weitzel's fine. This

E

brought the whole, hitherto latent question of socialist influences at both the training college and Victoria University College into prominence.[36] Parr pressed immediately for full inquiries into the activities of both institutions.[37]

The Wellington Training College inquiry was completed in early September, but uncovered no tangible evidence that students had contributed to Weitzel's fine, or had sympathy for her political views. Still more embarrassing from the Minister's point of view, one of the Committee members, the Chairman of the Wellington Education Board, D. Forsyth, strongly criticised what he regarded as the unnecessary circulation through the press of ... 'mischievous rumours before the slightest investigations'.[39]

By this stage, however, it was too late for cautionary statements. Parr's suspicions remained stronger than ever, and with Massey back from the Imperial Conference, the Government was ready to deal with the disloyalty issue once and for all. On 13 October, with public interest in the Weitzel case still high, Parr informed the House of his intention to make loyalty oaths for all teachers a prerequisite for employment in the schools. Ten days later, the promised clause was incorporated in a new Education Amendment bill:

> On and after the first day of April, nineteen hundred and twenty two, no person shall be employed or shall continue to be employed or shall act as a teacher, in any public school, secondary school, technical school, Native school, or primary school unless, in the case of a British subject, he has since the passing of this Act made and subscribed the Oath of Allegiance, and, in any case, he has since the passing of this Act made and subscribed in the prescribed form an oath that he will not, directly or indirectly, use words or be concerned in any act which would be disloyal to His Majesty if such words were spoken or written or such Act was committed, by a subject of His Majesty.[39]

Parr justified loyalty oaths on the grounds that there was creeping into the teaching service, 'a spirit of Bolshevism that needs to be suppressed'.[40] Labour members, supported by a number of Liberals, attacked the clause bitterly, with Fraser accusing the Minister of leading a 'heresy hunt' against the entire teaching service because of the Weitzel case.[41] Despite fierce opposition and the last-minute defection of two Government members, however, the bill, with its controversial clause, became law.[42]

Reinterpreting school patriotism

Thus far, we know 'what happened', and some of the immediate causes.

The question now becomes, 'Is this enough?' When I first examined school patriotism, I attributed its post-war growth solely to several more or less equal causes; the desire to see youth commemorate the war, the projection of wartime hysteria well into the following decade, the continuing naval rivalry between the Great Powers which necessitated a public sympathetic to future naval requirements, and the fear of militant socialist subversion.[43] In a society where overt school patriotism was now rare, it was all too easy to dismiss school patriotism as a fascinating but irrelevant specialist study. By 1980, however, anti-union and anti-socialist sentiment was rising and the Business and Economic Education Committee (BEEC), set up by the combined New Zealand Chambers of Commerce, had promoted a new series of economic studies booklets for secondary schools on the grounds that 'For too long the business community has allowed its foes to report it, its critics to judge it, and its enemies to define it.'[44] Educational rhetoric was sounding rather familiar. I began to reorder the causes of school patriotism during the 1920s and to assign a key role to the fear of socialism. Now I stressed the role of the press in creating an atmosphere of fear and loathing towards militant socialism, the willingness of the government to utilise the Bolshevik bogeyman as a political weapon and the signal impact of the Weitzel case as a catalyst in provoking further legislation on school patriotism.[45]

Even then it seemed simply common-sense to back these assumptions with Murray's claim that, as in the United States over a broadly similar period, '... harassed by the rantings and ravings of a small group of business and employers' organisations and assaulted daily by the scare propaganda of the patriotic societies, and the general press, the national mind ultimately succumbed to hysteria'.[46] In any case, sociologists of the structural-functionalist school, such as N. J. Smelser, appeared to have demonstrated conclusively that, in terms of collective behaviour theory, school patriotism could be best seen as a value-orientated movement, '... a collective attempt to restore, protect, modify or create values (love of country, loyalty, obedience) in the name of a generalised belief' (that New Zealand was filled with Bolshevik agitators against whom youth had no skills of counteraction).[47]

Today, such explanations seem inadequate. This is not to deny that, like their British and American counterparts, many New Zealanders firmly believed that '... a tidal wave of revolution seemed to be curling westward'. The difficulty with this as a complete explanation, however, is that we learnt very little about the work that the education system in general or school patriotism in particular was intended to perform during this period; almost nothing about the nature of education with its hierarchical relationships between decision-makers, bureaucrats, teachers and pupils, and even less regarding the interaction of school patriotism with those whom it was supposed to shape. In Williams' words: 'The pattern of meanings and values through which people conduct their whole lives can be seen ... as autonomous, and as evolving within its own terms, but it is quite unreal, ultimately to separate this pattern from precise political and economic system, which can extend its influence into the most unexpected regions of feeling and behaviour.'[49]

Armed thus with new charts, and in collaboration with a sociologist colleague, I began to reinterpret the available evidence. The cruder economic realities of early post-World-War-One New Zealand were not difficult to uncover. Parr, Massey, the various education boards, even the New Zealand Educational Institute now became so much less the frightened, misguided patriots; so much more the cynical manipulators of class-consciousness through a school system designed to keep workers in their place. With the impending reintroduction of flag-honouring regulations (1984), we felt able to assert that 'During periods of economic recession, schools become major vehicles for the indoctrination of sets of patriotic ideologies, which promote the value of unity and loyalty in order to draw attention away from existing economic and social division'.[50] Prolonged economic recession during the twenties aggravated social and political divisions. Real wages in 1919 had fallen to their lowest since the turn of the century.[51] Massey, quite apart from being a British Israelite, obsessed with crackpot theories about the imminent decline of British greatness due to moral laxity, also epitomised the worldly code of the New Zealand primary producer in his assertion that 'the employer cannot be prosperous without the loyal cooperation of the worker, and the ... worker be prosperous without the cooperation of the employer'.[52] The first post-war annual Institute conference and *National Education* reflected political concern about youth susceptibility. This ideology of organicist harmony was reflected in the 1919 history syllabus revision, which gave explicit directions to teachers on how a lesson on colonial expansion, for instance, could be utilised as a basis for further instruction on the causes of British greatness: her strength, unity and harmony. Likewise, flag-saluting and numerous school assemblies for Empire Day, Trafalgar Day and Anzac Day were excellent examples of what Hobsbawm termed invented tradition, 'with its ritual, its evocative symbolism and almost feudal notion of duties and obligations'.[53] It seemed common-sense (once again) to postulate that in an increasingly grim post-war world, faced with a rising New Zealand proletarian consciousness, conservative politicians and conservative educationalists became disciples of the new patriotism, with its heady doses of uncritical emotionalism. In this they were joined by more than a few liberals, who felt more comfortable defending the established order, especially since much of the patriotic rhetoric borrowed heavily from the new child psychology, then gaining ground. T. B. Strong, Chief Inspector of Primary Schools, for example, in the process of justifying flag-saluting to teachers, stressed the plasticity of the child's mind, and the high development of the capacity for self-sacrifice in the young.[54] Further evidence of the official respectability of patriotic ideology stemmed from its intellectual links with the intelligence-testing movement. Researchers such as Thorndike, Goddard and Terman on occasion utilised similar phrases concerning the malleability of children, the importance of harmony in society and the necessity for social hierachy.[55]

The above analysis provides a more rigorous conceptualisation of school patriotism. It acknowledges that patriotism can no longer be dismissed as unfinished business. It permits a dialogue, of sorts, between the historian, the past and the present. Notwithstanding these advantages, however, the analysis contains serious flaws. A major shortcoming is that it does not fit subsequent events. If, for instance, 'there is a close relationship between the ideology of patriotism and economic recession',[56] then logically school patriotism should have reached a new peak in 1929–35 with the Great Depression. Yet exactly the opposite occurred. Patriotism and its entire role in the school were increasingly bitterly debated.[57] Many educationalists advocated internationalist teaching and became more critical of school patriotism. It is instructive to trace attitudinal changes through the *New Zealand School Journal*. In March 1919, a *School Journal* article on the Versailles Conference laid heavy emphasis on the justice of the allied cause and the corresponding 'wickedness' of Germany.[58] Over the following five years numerous patriotic articles appeared in the *School Journal* which explored the underlying reasons for British superiority in empire-building and the greatness of the British race, whilst others praised the exploits of New Zealand soldiers. By the end of the decade, however, anti-war sentiment was more noticeable and during the early 1930s pacifism was a strong feature. Now the real patriot was '... he/Who knows no boundary, race or creed/Whose nation is humility/Whose dearest flag is brotherhood'.[59] By contrast, the real enemies of mankind were '... not aggressive foreign powers but ignorance, prejudice and disease'.[60]

The development of internationalism as a reaction to earlier patriotic zeal in the primary schools militates against the wholesale acceptance of economic determinants. In addition, the utilisation of rather more sophisticated Neo-Marxist analyses would appear to offer more fruitful lines of enquiry. Central here is the concept of hegemony as defined by

Gramsci and refined by subsequent Neo-Marxist scholars. Viewed historically, hegemony is a process. It is, therefore, dynamic and has been constantly defined, created and modified. Connell has attempted to illustrate the hegemonic process at work in an Australian context.[61] In New Zealand less work is available, but specific studies within the Neo-Marxist tradition are of value in applying theory to particular historical problems. Hill, for instance, examining film censorship, demonstrates the role of public opinion in changing concepts of censorship, whilst also pointing out that the decisions of the censors have continued to reflect the interests of the ruling class.[62]

Applying Hill's conclusions to school patriotism during the 1920s, we can identify fairly readily the growth of a crisis in public opinion. This is particularly evident as school syllabus and curriculum changes were superseded by coercion, in the form of regulations, legislation, trials and public enquiries. Even the more conservative provincial newspapers such as the *Waikato Times* and the *Manawatu Daily Times*, which had exhibited concern over the activities of socialist booksellers and the revelations made during the Weitzel case, displayed unease over the imposition of loyalty oaths for teachers and were hostile to further controls on them.[63] Likewise, political opinion was changing and, by 1927, even conservative MPs were sufficiently critical to block a proposed Education Amendment Bill which would have given boards the right to fine teachers 'up to 10 pounds for various unspecified minor offences'.[64]

While coercive measures against teachers met increasing public resistance, public concern over youth, in itself a strong feature of school patriotism, appears to have gradually subsided after 1930. Butchers's comment about the '... deplorable moral laxity of the present generation', which attracted parliamentary criticism at the time, represented the swansong of this concern which, at its height in the 1920s, reached considerable proportions.[65] The part concern over youth morality played in sustaining the momentum of school patriotism during the early 1920s can best be illuminated through the utilisation of Cohen's theory of moral panic. Of particular relevance here is the concept of the boundary crisis. According to Cohen, the boundary crisis is characterised by the dominant class attempting to establish more clearly moral boundaries during a period of moral and social uncertainty.[66] Accordingly, the patriotic over-reaction of politicians and educational administrators in the early 1920s can be typified as reactions in terms of '... positions, status, interests, ideologies and values', rather than as undifferentiated acts of collective fear.[67] Obviously, there are difficulties. From an evidential perspective we need to know more about New Zealand youth during the 1920s, the various influences upon it and the reactions to the youth problem as it was perceived by society. Furthermore, the utilisation of critical social theory to explain patriotic zeal must allow that not every education board member, Reform Party politician or magistrate acted like a component in an ideological blueprint. Forsyth, the previously-cited Chairman of the Wellington Board was a case in point. Forsyth was a member of Massey's own Conservative Reform Party, yet he not only resisted 'jingoist' sentiment, but stood up to the redoubtable R. A. Wright, a senior Reform Party spokesman and a future Minister of Education, in the course of defending the rights of teachers accused of disloyalty.[68] Similar comments can be made of several Conservative administrators, not to mention many Liberals.

Despite these qualifications, the 'notion of moral panic' is a useful one, permitting questions to be asked about the nature of the educational decision-making process, and its interplay with 'public pressure'. To some extent, it also focuses on the changing ideology of the decision-makers. It seems evident that the change of heart among the majority of educational decision-makers concerning school patriotism from the end of the twenties had complex, underlying causes. Further utilisation of critical theory may provide crucial insights into social processes. Gouldner, in another context, has described the rise of the British new 'middle class of intellectuals and technocrats, along with that class's distinctive ideology'.[69] In New Zealand, Mueli, utilising the work of the American, C. Wright-Mills, has examined the rise of the new middle class over the 1896–1926 period. He concludes that 'Social pressures of modern urban existence required that schools produce well adjusted and socially aware young citizens, as well as useful and reliable employees'.[70] Despite a superficial liberalism, educational progressivism endorsed these values. It is possible to trace the rise of liberal progressivist influence within the New Zealand education system, from relative obscurity in the early 1920s to respectability, and then, after World War Two, to orthodoxy.[71] In 1952, F. C. Lopdell, looking back on a long career, justifiably claimed that '... in the twenties ... education began to set itself the wider objective of developing the whole person for life in a democracy ...'[72]

The careers of both Lopdell himself and F. L. Combs illustrate this process.[73] The inter-war period witnessed an upsurge in domestic progressivist writing.[74] Progressives were reaching positions of responsibility in the New Zealand education system during the 1930s and frequently they disliked school patriotism, with its overt indoctrination through the history syllabus and its blatant coercion of teachers and pupils. For them, social studies was to offer a much more acceptable and more effective vehicle for proselytisation.[75] To use Gouldner's terminology, senior teacher and curriculum designers were, as members of the new middle class, busily engaged in producing their own culture of critical discourse. This evolved set of values, scientific, organicist and internationalist in rhetoric, displaced the coercive structure of school patriotism. It is precisely these values that are reflected so clearly in the *School Journal* during the 1929–34 period. Likewise, it was the adoption of these values that lay behind the anti-war activism of the Institute over the same period. It seems apparent that the decline of school patriotism was also hastened by the movement of the new middle class into the administrative and bureaucratic infrastructure of education. The support of this infrastructure was vital to school patriotism.

A recent example provides an apt illustration. In 1984, the Minister of Education, M. Wellington, was unable to gain significant support from teachers or from the educational bureaucracy for flag-honouring regulations, despite having the backing of caucus. That educational circles commonly regarded flag-honouring as unnecessary and even as irrational, 'may well have foredoomed the measure even without the change of government'.[76] As far as the inter-war educational infrastructure is concerned, a clear illustration of the respective outcomes of 'control-maintenance' and 'control-loss' for school patriotism is provided by two incidents, thirteen years apart. Each involved the Navy League, an organisation which often enjoyed liberal terms of entry into schools for the purpose of fostering naval awareness.

In October 1921, the Navy League was refused entry to three city schools controlled by the Auckland City Schools' Committee on the grounds that the League encouraged '... the fostering of the military spirit' among children. This was the first time in which an educational body had publicly refused the League and almost immediately the Committee faced formidable pressure. Other school committees were quick to acknowledge their own support for Navy League activity. An editorial in the *New Zealand Herald* attacked the committee's decision. The Auckland Education Board expressed its concern, as did the Department. Following the receipt of a letter from Massey, the isolated committee capitulated. The educational infrastructure had rallied behind the Navy League and dissent was crushed.[77]

In May 1934, however, with school patriotism under attack in the wider community, these roles were reversed. The League was made acutely aware that times had changed. Under the Navy League's auspices, Rear Admiral Burges Watson, Commander of the New Zealand Division, Royal Navy, had warned pupils of several Wellington schools about the impending Japanese threat. Now though, there was no friendly infrastructure. Instead there were protests concerning the Admiral's remarks from various educational bodies. In the House, the Navy League had to endure criticism from the Labour Opposition, while the government remained pointedly silent on the issue.[78]

All this is not to say that social control in schools had ceased or even that patriotism itself did not remain an integral part of the education system. Rather, they assumed different forms and an important indication of this process lies elsewhere in the school curriculum. While school patriotism and its history vehicle were unable to accommodate themselves to decisive changes in society and education, moral instruction displayed an evolutionary continuity. In 1919, the moral instruction syllabus (senior division) contained references to behaviour in public places, 'obedience, order (the value of system, punctuality and promptness)', 'moral courage (including the "heroism" of common life) and industry' ('the dignity of honest labour, especially manual labour').[79] The 1929 syllabus softened these strictures by subordinating them under general headings and concepts. 'Improvements in social welfare (English and Norman serfs, labourers in the Middle Ages, the Industrial Revolution, childworkers in modern times, how the worker is safeguarded today)'. In addition, there were topics such as the 'History of Useful Inventions', 'the Growth of the British Constitution' and 'Citizenship (elections, churches, rights of citizens, elementary ideas regarding free trade and protection)'.[80] By contrast, the 1929 history prescription attempted, unconvincingly, to juxtapose both 'old' patriotism and 'new' internationalism.[81]

Unbeset by such philosophical problems, moral instruction was well on the way to becoming part of post-war social studies, with its quasi-scientific platitudes of co-operation, social justice and social concern. Where I wrote optimistically in 1980 that 'the second post-war world would be shaped around an altogether different ideal', I would now add in 1988 the somewhat more pessimistic proviso that this ideal corresponds rather well with the cultural process described by Willis, which is aimed at producing '... a less skilled work force, open to greater systemisation and higher working pace, coupled with a degree of flexibility to allow interchange between increasingly standardised processes'.[82] While there are obvious discrepancies between official syllabus prescriptions and what actually occurred in the classroom, it is equally clear that the intervening years have made cynics of us all.

Notes

1 Casualties were fearful. During the abortive Somme offensive in late 1916, for instance, New Zealand troops suffered nearly 7000 casualties in just twenty-three days of

fighting. By 1918, over forty-three per cent of New Zealand men of military age had enlisted, and nearly half of these served overseas.

2 See, for instance, 'The Earl of Meath, an Empire Day message', *SJ* 11(3), June 1917, p. 154. For further details on patriotism and *School Journals*, see E. P. Malone, 'The New Zealand Journal and the imperial ideology', *New Zealand Journal of History*, 7, April 1973, pp. 12–27.

3 *SJ* 11(3), August 1917, p. 226.

4 See especially A. H. Reed to J. N. O. Caughley, Director of Education, 8 June 1922, Personal Files of A. H. Reed, Dunedin.

5 *New Zealand Parliamentary Debates*, 183, 1918, pp. 186–7 (hereinafter cited as *NZPD*).

6 Education Department, *Regulations for the Organisation, Examination and Inspection of Public Schools and the Syllabus of Instruction*, Wellington, 1919, p. 82.

7 T. B. Strong, 'The inculcation of patriotism', *Education Gazette*, 1 November 1921, pp.2–4 and Saluting the flag, *Education Gazette*, 1 December 1922, pp. 138–40.

8 Alien Enemy Teachers Act, 1915, Geo. V., *New Zealand Status*, p. 361. The Act's most notable victim was Professor von Zeditz, who was removed from this position at Victoria College. For further accounts of individual victimisation, see L. H. Barber, 'The Twenties: New Zealand's xenophobic years', *New Zealand Law Journal*, No. 4, 2 March 1976, pp. 95–6.

9 Minutes of the Auckland Education Board, XX, 7 September, 5 October and 19 October 1920.

10 Note, for instance, the case of R. O. Page, cited in W. J. Gardner, E. T. Beardsley and T. E. Carter, *A History of the University of Canterbury, 1873–1971*, Christchurch, 1973, p. 213.

11 This teacher's experience was recalled by C. W. Boswell, the Labour Member for Bay of Islands as late as 1941, *NZPD*, 260, 1941, p. 61.

12 C. J. Parr, 'The British Empire', *SJ*, 15(2) June 1921, p. 18.

13 'The value of empire', *SJ*, 17(2), May 1923, pp. 54–7. Although no author was cited the tone and placement of the article suggests that the author was, again, Parr.

14 'The British Empire Exhibition', *SJ*, 17(3), May 1923, p. 116.

15 See S. Roskill, *Naval Policy Between the Wars*, London, 1968, I, p. 283.

16 W. F. Massey, 'The Imperial Conference', *SJ*, 13(3), February 1922, p. 17.

17 With one notable exception, provided by the Auckland City Schools' Committee, in October 1921. See below.

18 See R. Openshaw, 'Patriotism and the New Zealand primary school: the decisive years of the twenties', Ph.D. dissertation, University of Waikato, 1978, pp. 75-80.

19 See, for instance, *The Waikato Times*, 4–8 March 1919 inclusive, which carried reports of Bolshevik armies, a million strong, preparing to march into Eastern Europe, of Bolshevik activity in China, Western Europe and Britain, of Spartacist leaflets being handed out to New Zealand soldiers with the occupation forces in Germany.

20 *New Zealand Herald*, 19 January 1921.

21 Professor B. C. Murphy of the Economics Department at University College thus warned the Wellington Accounts Students' Society in April 1921, basing his conclusions on the rising incidence of industrial unrest in the dominion. *New Zealand Herald*, 9 April 1921.

22 *New Zealand Herald*, 9 April 1921.

23 War Regulations Continuance Act, 1920, 11, Geo. V., *New Zealand Statutes*, Clause 2, p. 58.

24 See, for instance, the *New Zealand Herald*, March–May 1921, *passim*.

25 *New Zealand Herald*, 9 May 1921.
26 *National Education*, Wellington, 1919, p. 2.
27 *Ibid*. p. 3.
28 *Ibid*. p. 21.
29 *AJHR*, 1920, E-2, Appendix B, p. xvi.
30 By May 1921 there were three Socialist Sunday Schools in operation; one in Christchurch, one in Palmerston North and one in Auckland.
31 *New Zealand Herald*, 27 May 1921.
32 *New Zealand*, 20 August 1921.
33 The trivial nature of the fine by comparison with others collected for a similar offence suggests that, judged purely as a disseminator of subversive literature, Weitzel was a comparatively small catch.
34 When the case was discussed in the House, Parr countered Labour objections to Weitzel's dismissal by demanding to know where Weitzel's father had been during the German War. *NZPD*, 191, 1921, p. 970.
35 *Ibid*.
36 Parr had become particularly suspicious of the Victoria University College Debating Society, which he felt to be left-wing in its sympathies. See especially J. C. Beaglehole, *Victoria University College*, Wellington, 1949, pp. 182–99.
37 He had, of course, a statutory right to demand an inquiry into the Wellington Training College and his public criticism of the University College and its alleged links with militant Socialism obliged that institution to conduct its own inquiry.
38 *New Zealand Herald*, 10 September 1921.
39 Education Amendment Act 1921–22, 12 Geo. V., *New Zealand Statutes*, Clause 2, pp. 263–4.
40 *NZPD*, 191, 1921, p. 948.
41 *Ibid*. p. 953.
42 The final division was thirty-eight votes to twenty-seven. The dissenting votes included ten Liberal and two Reform votes. For a more complete analysis of voting patterns, see R. Openshaw, 'Patriotism and the New Zealand primary school: the decisive years of the twenties', pp. 153–4.
43 See R. Openshaw, 'The highest expression of devotion: New Zealand primary schools and patriotic zeal during the early 1920s', *History of Education*, Vol. 19, No. 4, 1980 pp. 333-4.
44 New Zealand Chambers of Commerce, *Economic Education Programme — How it Works*, foldover pamphlet, Wellington, *c*. 1978.
45 See R. Openshaw, '"A spirit of Bolshevism": the Weitzel case of 1921 and its impact on the New Zealand educational system', *Political Science*, Vol. 33, No. 2, December 1981, p. 127–39.
46 R. K. Murray, *Red Scare. A Study in National Hysteria*, New York, McGraw Hill, 1964, Preface, pp. ix-xii.
47 N. J. Smelser, *Theory of Collective Behaviour,* London, Routledge and Kegan Paul, 1962, p. 313.
48 D. Mitchell, *1919: Red Mirage*, London, Jonathan Cape, 1970.
49 R. Williams, *The Long Revolution*, London, Chatto and Windus, 1961, pp. 119–20. See also, M. W. Apple, *Ideology and Curriculum*, London, Routledge and Kegan Paul, 1979, pp. 27–8.
50 L. Gordon and R. Openshaw, 'The social significance of flag-raising in schools', *Delta*, 3–4 July, p. 55.
51 See L. Richardson, 'Parties and political change', in W. H. Oliver (ed.), *The Oxford History of New Zealand*, Wellington, Oxford University Press, 1981, p. 213.

52 *NZPD*, 184, 1919, p. 87.
53 E.Hobsbawn and T. Ranger (eds), *The Invention of Tradition*, Past and Present publications, Cambridge University Press, 1983, p. 1.
54 T. B. Strong, 'The inculcation of patriotism', *Education Gazette*, 1 November 1921, p. 3.
55 D. McKenzie, 'Little and lightly. The New Zealand Department of Education and Mental Testing, 1920–1930'. A paper presented to the NZARE Conference, Dunedin, 1984.
56 Gordon and Openshaw, p. 61.
57 R. Openshaw, 'New Zealand state primary schools and the growth of internationalism and anti-war feeling, 1929–1934', *ANZHES Journal*, Vol. 19, No. 1, Autumn, 1980, pp. 1–14.
58 'The Armistice and the peace conference', *New Zealand School Journal*, 13, Part Two, March 1919, p. 6.
59 F. C. Knowles, 'The New Patriot', *School Journal 23*, Part Two, June 1929, p. 295.
60 P. Myers, 'The League of Nations', *School Journal 24*, Part Three, August 1930, p. 295.
61 R. W. Connell, *Ruling Class, Ruling Culture: Studies of Collective Power and Hegemony in Australian Life*, Cambridge, Cambridge University Press, 1977, p. 206.
62 A. N. Hill, 'In the public good. Film censorship, the state and hegemony', M.A. dissertation, Massey University, 1983, pp. 66–7.
63 See, for instance, *Waikato Times*, 1 November 1921, Editorial.
64 *NZPD*, Vol. 216, 1927, pp. 395–6.
65 A. G. Butchers, *The Education System*, Auckland, National Printing Company, 1932, p. 99.
66 S. Cohen, *Folk Devils and Moral Panics. The Creation of the Mods and Rockers*, Oxford, Martin Robertson, 1980.
67 *Ibid*. p. 191.
68 See *Waikato Times*, 1 November 1921, and *New Zealand Herald*, 15 December 1921.
69 A. Gouldner, *The Future of Intellectuals and the Rise of the New Class*, London, Macmillan, 1979, pp. 28–30.
70 P. M. Mueli, 'Occupational change and bourgeoisie proliferation: a study of new middle class expansion in New Zealand 1896–1926', M.A. dissertation, Victoria University, 1977, p. 149.
71 A process paralleled in the United Kingdom. See R. J. W. Selleck, *English Primary Education and the Progressives, 1914–1939*, London, Routledge and Kegan Paul, 1972.
72 *AJHR*, 1952, e-2, pp. 1–2.
73 G. W. Parkyn, *Sight of that Immortal Sea. The Combs-Lopdell Memorial Address*, Wellington, NZCER, 1964.
74 See, for instance, H. McClune and G. H. Lord, *Democracy in the Classroom*, Auckland, Whitcombe and Tombs, 1919; C. A. Batt, *Hands the Child*, Wellington, 1927, and N. M. Bell, *Education of Freedom*, Greymouth, 1921.
75 The decline of history is considered in H. J. A. Diorio, 'The decline of history as a tool of moral training', *c*. 1984. University of Otago.
76 Gouldner, p. 51.
77 *New Zealand Herald*, 11, 14 and 22 October 1921.
78 *Evening Post*, 4, 16 and 21 May 1934.
79 Senior Division, Moral Instruction, in *Regulations for the Organisation, Examination and Inspection of Public Schools and the Syllabus of Instruction*, Wellington, Government Printers, 1919.

80 History (Introduction), Standard VI (Form II), in *Syllabus of Instruction for Public Schools, 1929*, Wellington, Government Printers, 1930.

81 History (Appendix), *Syllabus of Instruction, 1929*.

82 P. E. Willis, *Learning to Labour. How Working class Kids get Working Class Jobs*, London, Saxon House, 1978, p. 180. The oath or affirmation of loyalty must still be taken by intending New Zealand teachers. The flag-honouring regulations (1941), which, likewise, itself replaced the older regulations on flag-saluting have never been withdrawn.

CHAPTER SEVEN

Socialisation, imperialism and war: ideology and ethnicity in Australian corporate schools

Geoffrey Sherington and Mark Connellan

As with the other white dominions of the British Empire, the Australian colonies had, by the late nineteenth century, developed institutions and cultural forms that had their origins in the British Isles. Until the early twentieth century, the majority of the adult population were born overseas and much of their early socialisation had taken place in a specific British environment and context. Ethnic loyalty intersected with the emerging class structure in the colonies. Many sons and daughters of the professional and commercial classes were brought up in Protestant communities with attachment to English and sometimes Scottish ways of their forefathers. Others were suspicious of interests that seemed to be merely serving the ruling class in England; a feeling that was most marked amongst the one-third of the population whose ethnic origins lay in Catholic Ireland.

These issues of attachment and commitment were most clearly seen in formalised education. During the early nineteenth century the state had provided aid for the schools of the various religious denominations. In the late nineteenth century, such aid was withdrawn. The various Protestant sects united on the ethic of common British Christianity to support state-run elementary schools whose curriculum would emphasise a loyalty to the spreading British Empire and race. The major Protestant denominations were now to concentrate on creating secondary schools inspired by the examples of English public-school reform. In contrast, the Catholic community remained outside the late nineteenth-century educational settlement. The Catholic hierarchy set out to establish a school system which would be dependent on religious teaching orders, many of whom would arrive from overseas. The values of the Catholic schools often reflected a deliberate attachment to an Irish past and distrust of English imperialism. But within the Catholic secondary schools there remained also tensions of the specific origins of the various religious teaching orders and the need for social acceptance with others of similar social class in the Protestant communities.[1]

Within this colonial context, the following study of two individual schools illuminates the effect of Imperialism in various forms upon the socialisation of the potential male leaders of society. Both schools were founded in late nineteenth-century Sydney, the oldest of the colonial capitals. By the early twentieth century, each was recognised as forming part of an elite group of schools whose social interaction had been primarily focused on the organisation of sporting competitions. One was a Church of England foundation whose commitment to specific English institutions, ideologies and practices was quite clear from the beginning. The other was a Catholic foundation in which social and educational influences acted more subtly. In the end Imperial commitment through war would test both in different ways but with similar outcomes.

Sydney Church of England Grammar School was established as a late nineteenth-century antipodean public school under the influence of the English reforms of the mid-century. Its founder was Alfred Barry, Bishop of Sydney and Primate of Australia, 1884-9. Son of the architect of the Houses of Parliament, Barry himself had been educated at King's College, London and Trinity College, Cambridge. After his ordination he had become Vice-Principal of Trinity College, Glenalmond, the seminary of the Scottish Episcopal Church.[2] In 1854, at the age of twenty-eight, he became headmaster of Leeds Grammar. Barry transformed the school, moving it from its old site in the centre of Leeds to the expanding middle-class suburbs.[3] When he left to become Principal of the newly-founded Cheltenham College in 1862, Leeds Grammar was on the verge of achieving public-school status. Only at Cheltenham for six years, Barry showed equal commitment to this new proprietary foundation as he had to the old endowed Leeds Grammar. He started a system of boarding houses, created prefects, improved its academic standing, formed a cadet corps and opened a gymnasium and racquet courts.[4] He deserves recognition as one of those post-Arnold English school headmasters who did so much to create the machinery, if not the ideology, of reform.

Barry was not merely an architect of English public-school traditions. He was also a proselytiser for the Imperial English Church. Associated with the Broad Church Movement, he recognised the need for Anglicans to come to terms with the modern world. For Barry, education was the means whereby the Church could understand modernism. He had a particular faith in institutions, and specifically English institutions such as the public schools, to provide the unity between the individual and the commonality of family, nation, race and mankind. In his Hulsean lectures at Cambridge, delivered after his return from Australia, Barry reviewed the *Ecclesiastical Expansion of England in the Growth of the Anglican Communion,* writing of the Empire as being all part of a united family. The white colonies were growing up, seeking not to become independent, but rather to be recognised as full members of the family. He looked forward to the growth of the 'many new Englands with which we have fairly girdled the world'.[5]

In Sydney, as other Englishmen did elsewhere, Barry provided the inspiration. An earlier English episcopalian, William Broughton, had founded The King's School, just outside Sydney. The school had generally languished. Barry reconstituted the council of that school and, as new headmaster, brought out the Rev Arthur St John Gray, an old boy of

Clifton College and graduate of Magdalen College, Oxford. Gray introduced reforms based on his own experience at Clifton, initiating a school magazine and office-holders and building a chapel.[6] Barry also took advantage of the new relations between the Church and State which now pertained in New South Wales. The State itself had acquired a number of former church-school sites. From the compensation paid for one of these, Barry was able to persuade the local Anglican community, through a series of complicated and astute financial moves, to devote much of the funds arising to establishing another major boys' school in Sydney. It was to be a school founded on English public-school ideals. As Barry told his audience at the opening of the school in May 1889:

> He thought that they ought, as far as possible, to make this a school which should have the impress of the old public school system of England. He knew, of course, that the English Public School system was not without its imperfections, but it was notwithstanding an English system, which thoroughly suited the English character, and which educated Englishmen for that which would be during their lifetime their doctrine and manner of life in this free country . The system of education which they intended to adopt here was one which would develop a lad's character and draw out all his faculties, and above all, the great old schools insisted on one grand feature which had often astonished the great teachers of the Continent, and this was the free use of the religious power and influence.[7]

Barry did not stay to see the new institution prosper. He returned to England a week after the formal foundation. Another Englishman would develop the school in its first decade. If Barry was a representative of the mid-nineteenth-century English public school reforming clerics, then Ernest Iliff Robson, the first headmaster, was the product of much of the reform itself. Son of a Sunderland shipbuilder, Robson had attended Repton, in the wake of the reforms which the legendary Dr Stuart Pears had instituted in his twenty-year reign from the mid-1850s. Robson's headmaster was Henry Robert Huckin who built on the reforms of Pears by introducing a modern side, encouraging science and also 'practical subjects' through a laboratory and carpenter's shop. Robson was also caught up in the new athleticism. His experience of organised games at Repton was reinforced in the residential college life of Cambridge where he became a prominent oarsman.[8]

The imperialism of Robson was both direct and diffuse. As a young Englishman in the colonies, he often simply transferred his own experiences into the new environment. He designed a crest for the new school even before it was opened, outlining it in blue and white, the colours of his old college, Christ's, Cambridge. The school song bore the title 'Vitai lampada tradunt', the Lucretian motto which had been popular in his days at Cambridge and which was later to be immortalised through the imagery of Henry Newbolt. The last verse of Robson's composition reminded his boys of the wider world of which their school was a part:

> Here's to the Queen, may she long live to reign
> O'er this land where old England is youthful again,
> O'er an Empire as wide as the world-circling main,
>   Tradit, lampada vitai.

The school song had been composed as a celebration of the school's first victory in a regatta. Much of its imagery mirrored Newbolt's later appeal, but without its sensitivity.

> Here's to the fellow who never says die,
> Though his oar may be sprung or his bowling awry,
> Five lengths to make up, or four goals to our try,
>   Tradit, lampada vitai.[9]

The ideology of athleticism was well-entrenched in the school magazine, *The Torch Bearer,* which Robson had established within two years of the school's foundation. It's first editorial, written by an assistant master, McCulloch Hughes, a former exhibitioner at Oriel College, Oxford, emphasised the need for the boys to create 'sound traditions' and 'unwritten laws in school life' founded on the true principles of 'the triple cord of love' which embraced the 'tie of school work', 'the tie of school games' and the 'moral standard or "tone" that springs up and flourishes in every school worthy of the name'.[10] Machinery reinforced ideology. A prefect system was soon established with a special ceremony requiring a special oath of office; a General Sports Committee composed of both masters and boys awarded 'colours' for sporting prowess.

Yet the new school could not simply be an English institution in the antipodes. In the first place, it was initially a small, primarily day-boy school, located on the slowly expanding north shore of Sydney Harbour. It was the hope of Robson that it could become 'the Clifton of Australia', but this was not easily achieved.[11] He found that Australian youth were often too seduced by a healthy outdoor climate to respond to his moral ideals; rather than showing initiative they tended towards laziness, he suggested in an article written in 1895.[12] Moreover, the social structure was different from England. The boys at the school were generally the sons of professionals and businessmen who expected some results for the schooling for which they were paying. Even athleticism was transformed in the colonial environment. Playing the game for its own sake soon faded. As a new and small college, the school required recognition and success. It was to be a founding member of the Athletic Association of Great Public Schools (AAGPS) in New South Wales, a body which would become the regulator of sporting competitions and, indirectly, the arbiter of the social status of a school.[13] There were also specific meritocratic and conservative expectations amongst the social clientele. Earlier colonial headmasters had found that they had to adapt the curriculum to Australian circumstances by introducing modern languages and commercial subjects. In the difficult climate of the 1890s, in the wake of an economic depression in the colony, Robson had to abandon curricula reforms such as the integrated physics and carpentry programme which he had known at Repton. In the end, poor results at the university examinations would lead to dissatisfaction within the school and ultimately to Robson's resignation as headmaster.[14]

A more coherent imperial ideology arrived in the school in the early twentieth century. The second headmaster was C. H. Hodges, previously assistant master at Rugby in the 1880s and then, for a decade, head of Townsville Grammar in North Queensland. Hodges had served under Jex-Blake at Rugby; he was one of the Rugby 'colonisers' sent throughout the Empire in the late nineteenth century.[15] By marriage he was related to the Hawtrey family which had produced the former provost and headmaster of Eton. Poor health had brought him to the Australian colonies, but his imperial connections remained strong; so did his commitment to much of the ideology that the school had previously espoused. The 'instinct' of sport had helped to create the British Empire he claimed at his first speech day in 1901: 'Opportunities for the practice of those virtues which stamp the real man — courage, vigour, chivalry, straightforwardness — are found perhaps more frequently in the playing field than upon the school benches.'[16]

Under Hodges, and his successor, English-born W. A. Purves, who had worked under the former at Townsville Grammar and regarded him as mentor, the school would retain a particular orientation to the ways of the late nineteenth-century English public school. In common with other headmasters of similar schools in Sydney, both resisted the efforts of the State to modernise the curricula and introduce state-controlled examinations. The classics still remained the focus of education for those who wished to aspire to become gentlemen. Some of the staff also resisted the corruption of earlier English ideals. The sporting competitions in which the school was now actively engaged had become excessive, suggested J. Lee Pulling, son of the former master of Corpus Christi, Cambridge.

Team games 'have done much to make the kind of Briton with whom we are proud to be fellow countrymen', but the demands for premierships were 'too exacting and too constant'.[17]

Already socialisation was assuming new forms of imperial commitment which were related to the specific circumstances of the new Australian Federation in the early twentieth century. The celebration of an Australian-British nation within the empire became more prominent. During 1899-1900 a number of old boys of the new school had fought in South Africa. In 1901 the school council supported the proposal of the Old Boys' Union that there should be erected a library in memory of those who had fought and the three who had been killed. Four years later the school recognised the 'Empire Day' instituted on the occasion of the birthday of Queen Victoria. The headmaster appealed to the boys to show even greater love for their school, so 'learning what the patriotic spirit really meant, hereafter extend towards our country, and that Motherland from which we were sprung, the same spirit of devotion'. This first occasion ended, as it would in succeeding years, with a master leading the school in 'Rule Britannia'.[18]

Militarism became the test of both imperial and new national loyalty. The school council had discussed the formation of a cadet corps in the 1890s but had taken no action. The circumstances of the new century brought a new urgency. Defence became a prominent concern of the new Australian Federal Government. The Japanese defeat of the Russian fleet at Port Arthur in 1905 reinforced Australian fears of the threat from the Asian North. In 1908 the school formed a cadet company as part of a battalion of Great Public Schools in the Sydney area. A Sergeant-Major Cooke Russell, former member of the Scots Guards who had served with Kitchener in Egypt and in the Boer War and who had been in charge of cadets in Queensland, became the prime instructor. The initial enrolment in the corps was half the school numbers.[19]

Participation in the cadets provided the training for the big event of 1914. At the outbreak of hostilities, an old boy of the school was the first Australian officer killed; a medical doctor, he had been fatally wounded when he gave up his red cross brassard to another soldier carrying wounded during the invasion of the German island of New Britain. His example was held up to the school as one to emulate. As the Archbishop of Sydney said at the 1914 speech day: 'There was the intellectual attainment, the athletic ability and bodily strength and behind all that which gave to each their value — character.'[20]

About one half of the boys who had been at the school in the decade before the war would join up and one-sixth would be killed. There was hardly a questioning of the need for this commitment to the defence of the empire. It was the war which united much of the ideology and purpose of the school founded over a quarter of a century earlier. The hope of Barry that the school would reflect a religious life had not been fully achieved until the foundation of a chapel had been laid in May 1914. The chapel, opened in 1915, soon became lined with war memorial windows. At each service the chaplain would read out the list of fallen. In the memory of a boy at the time: 'Years after I could give the list almost completely. It made a lasting impression on my memory of the great number of the school's best boys who had laid down their life for their country and their school.'[21] Military service had become Christian sacrifice.

In England the war brought a revulsion against both organised games and militarism. Perhaps too many young officers had carried forward lessons learnt on the playing field on to the fields of Flanders. At Sydney Church of England Grammar School, the war not only strengthened a commitment to games-playing, but left a legacy and tradition. It was a legacy that was now more Australian than English in orientation. Many had sometimes drawn parallels between war and games but it was significant that when Sir William Cullen, the Lieutenant-Governor of New South Wales and himself Australian-born, spoke to the school in 1917, he would use a specific ethnic reference — 'Sport had been left out in the genius of Germany but how magnificently the Australian boys had played up to it.'[22] The old boys of the school would have agreed too. In the post-war years the war memorial to the fallen would not be a library as in 1901 but large playing fields.

Sydney Church of England Grammar School was quite clear of its origins upon its foundation in 1889. In contrast, the Sydney Catholic Marist School, St Joseph's College, Hunters Hill, had a number of competing influences. Denied resources from the State following the educational settlements and legislation in late nineteenth-century Australia, the colonial Catholic hierarchy had come to depend on overseas religious orders to establish secondary schools as the basis for creating a Catholic social élite. At St Joseph's, the French director, Brother Emilian, and his superior, Brother Ludovic, had, from the outset, determined that their school would be French Catholic in orientation with the necessary insularity from colonial society and its pernicious influence that they believed to be of fundamental importance. The geographical locale of the college was to act as a safeguard; it was situated on the opposite side of the harbour to the city of Sydney, accessible only by ferry, and with the nearest settlement inhabited by predominately French emigrants.

The dominance of the French-Marist educational system in the early years at St Joseph's relied heavily on the availability of French Brothers to staff the College. Out of an initial staff of eight Brothers, five were French, two were Australian and one was Irish.[23] The College was to be run according to the methods prescribed in the canon of Marist pedagogics, the 'Guide d'Ecole'.[24] Most of the French Bothers in Australia had first-hand experience of this system and its successful missionary application in the French colonies of the Pacific.[25] They undoubtedly erred in believing that similar results could be obtained in Australia without altering their approach. From the outset, and throughout the 1880s and 1890s, the French Brothers and their pedagogy were the subject of unfavourable comparisons with the English public-school system. These critical evaluations of practices at St Joseph's emanated primarily from the Irish and Australian Brothers, often with the support of the boys, and reflected their dissatisfaction with Brother Emilian and his intransigent attitude towards reforms.

Friction over the question of organised games was a feature of the first fifteen years at St Joseph's. Other areas of conflict existed between the French Brothers and their Irish and Australian colleagues, but sport proved to be the area in which the battle-lines were most clearly drawn. Initially it would seem that the French Brothers' opposition to sport stemmed from a sincere effort to establish the Order's educational priorities in a foreign land. The later arguments over sport at St. Joseph's provided a marked contrast to this sincerity, with both French and Irish-Australian factions resorting to acrimonious and petty debate in support of their respective beliefs. A central figure in this controversy was the Irishman, Brother Basil. He was the patron of the St Joseph's Rugby and Cricket Clubs from their earliest inception and also served as sub-director under Brother Emilian. In 1887, after several clashes with Brother Emilian, he referred to his sub-directorship as a 'farce'.[26] Brother Basil welcomed the enthusiasm for games amongst the boys and, in 1890, supported their petition to Brother Emilian, requesting a Wednesday half-holiday so that fixtures could be organised against outside teams.[27] The request was refused, ostensibly because it would interfere with St. Joseph's timetable of five full days schooling as well as a half-day on Saturdays. Brother Emilian clearly had little regard for the resentment that his decision would lead to. He may not have been aware of the experience of the Vincentian Order at St Stanislaus in Bathurst in Central New South Wales, who had precipitated a local crisis owing to fears that they were 'against football'.[28] More importantly, he did not seem to comprehend the effect that prohibiting inter-school sport could have on the status of St Joseph's College. As was seen in the case of Sydney Church of England Grammar School, the late nineteenth century in Sydney was a period when a school's sporting facilities and its fixture lists were held to be as important as examination results in determining its reputation.

The rivalry over sport at St Joseph's seldom found its way into the official documentation of the college. The college magazine occasionally refers to unsuitable playing-fields and the inability to travel outside the college as impediments limiting contact with other schools and teams. Apart from these tentative complaints, the magazine, from its inception in 1888, contained numerous elaborate rhetorical justifications, similar to those associated with the English public-school cult of athleticism, in support of the physical, moral and character-building efficacy of games. The St Joseph's cricket report of 1891 reflected the extent to which the English public-school attitudes to sport had been so readily assimilated by the boys: 'Apart from the physical strength which it develops, cricket is quite an educative power. To play it thoroughly a boy must be patient, self-denying, brave and obedient;...It is therefore not surprising that such an amusement meets with the Brothers' highest approval and warmest encouragements.'[29]

This form of rhetoric had little effect on the French Brothers and their attitudes. As late as 1895, after some years of games between St Joseph's and other élite schools, the French Superior of the Marist Order in Australia, Brother Felix, wrote to his superiors in France to complain about sport: 'I have decided...to take a firm stand against the excessive tendency to sports, which is the greatest plague of our colonies.'[30] By the end of his period as Superior, in 1896, Brother Felix still maintained that the major evils confronting young boys were, 'the world, sports, flesh and the devil.'[31]

Much of the content in the early editions of the magazine seems curiously at odds with the official line at St Joseph's. The editors seemed determined to present the college as an antipodean version of the English public school, and to claim the élite status attributed to such institutions. At first this was achieved by a defensive mixture of self-congratulation allied with the anti-secular rhetoric of the Catholic hierarchy. The first issue of the magazine, reflecting on the seven years that the college had been in existence, concluded that the year 1885 '... was a singularly eventful one in the annals of the College, both for its successes at the public examinations and victories gained in the cricket field.'[32]

The Catholic primate in Sydney, Cardinal Moran, presiding over the 1887 Speech Day, backed this sort of rhetoric with his own firmly-held views: 'Such results should prove to the public that St Joseph's College, without receiving a penny of aid from the State, was able to hold its own against all the schools endowed and otherwise of the whole colony.'[33]

[141]

Within the next few years the tone of the magazine portrayed the growing confidence of the college through its association with other élite schools. Older institutions, such as the Methodist Newington College, which had long followed the English public-school example, were presented as kindred institutions rather than sectarian rivals. The St Joseph's' cricket correspondent of 1889 could barely disguise the self-congratulatory feeling within the college that was occasioned by the successful organisaton of a match against Newington:'As an educational institution, Newington has been very prominent for a great many years past. More than once have its boys distinguished themselves in the cricket field. A sort of rival claim for supremacy has for some time existed ...'.[34]

Clearly the magazine had become a valuable ideological instrument, useful for forging the bonds of association with other élite schools, while at the same time reminding the public at large that St Joseph's should enjoy the same élite status accorded to those schools.

It was not only adulation of games, however, that appeared in the St Joseph's College magazines of the late-nineteenth century. There was also a strong current of anti-British opinion over the Irish question. In 1889, John Dillon 'the great campaigner'[35] visited St Joseph's and was assured by a College spokesman: 'During the past few years we have followed, with intense and painful anxiety, the fierce but unequal battle that you and your Colleagues have been waging there [Ireland].'[36]

A donation of £40 was presented to Dillon by the students of St Joseph's College, as a contribution to the 'Irish fund'.[37] The existence of anti-British sentiment at St Joseph's also inspired the editors of the 1889 magazine to publish an essay on 'Imperial Federation' by a St Joseph's student, William Donnelly.[38] Donnelly argued that Australia should be guided by the Irish experience in its future dealings with England:

It was not until England forced her to federate and be governed by a Parliament at Westminster that Ireland's troubles really began ... they are persistently outvoted by the Conservative Party, in their pompous stupidity and dense ignorance of everything pertaining to a just settlement of the great Irish question. Australia would gain nothing and would only be a loser by having any closer connections with England ...[39]

Overall, St Joseph's stood alone amongst the élite Catholic schools in openly criticising the British for their actions in Ireland. The degree of anglo-conformity at the Jesuit St Ignatius College, the other élite Catholic institution in Sydney at this time, precluded such an open expression of 'Irishness'. A report on the reception accorded to a similar Irish delegation at St Ignatius' contains no overt pledges of financial and political support, although its author takes pains to assert that 'the rounds of applause that greeted mention of Home Rule were sincere and enthusiastic.'[40]

Resistance to British imperialism in Ireland, however, did not lead to any diminution of the desire to emulate the more publicised features of the English public-school model. Both boys and the sympathetic Brothers tended to disassociate such political considerations from the educational model that they so admired.

The emergence of an Irish-Australian character at the college, initially as a challenge to the ascendency of French values, provided significant support for the belief that conditions at St Joseph's must be the equal of those existing in any other élite school in the colony. The departure of Brother Emilian in 1890 and the installation of St Joseph's first Australian director, Brother Stanislaus, seemed likely to provide an ideal environment in which this syncretic mixture of Irish-Australian values and English public-school practices could flourish. In fact, his directorship was marred from the outset by claims of anti-French bias and calls for his resignation. The two French Brothers who most resented the appointment of Brother Stanislaus as director, Brothers Theobald and Vales, also launched an attack on the school magazine. They wrote to the Brother Superior in France, criticising the magazine for the financial loss it had incurred, its lack of acknowledgement for their help in producing it, and its over-emphasis on sport.[41] The dispute over the magazine was essentially a symptom of the rivalry between the French and Irish-Australian factions at the college. The magazine was a prime target for the French Brothers' grievances because it strengthened the bonds between the Irish and Australian Brothers and the boys, while further alienating the French Brothers, who showed little understanding or sympathy for the college life that it portrayed.

In 1892 the French Superior placed a ban on the St Joseph's College magazine that was to last until 1897. Deprived of their formal means of disseminating propaganda, the boys nonetheless continued to agitate for adequate playing facilities and increased sporting opportunities. Brother Stanislaus, his effectiveness as a director severely compromised by the collapse of the primary and business sectors of the economy, supported his dwindling number of students in their sporting endeavours. In 1892 Brother Stanislaus was able to negotiate the purchase of sixteen acres of ground, in close proximity to the college and suitable for playing-fields, for the sum of £3,000.[42] During his directorship the St Joseph's cricket teams travelled to other schools for fixtures, despite the fact that the French Brothers attempted officially to censure this activity.

The gradual erosion of French influence at St Joseph's was undoubtedly hastened by St Joseph's becoming a member, along with Sydney Church of England Grammar and St Ignatius, of the Athletic Association of the Great Public Schools.[43] As elsewhere, such membership confirmed the acceptance of athleticism as part of the educational orthodoxy at these schools and, at the same time, provided a distinction between member schools and all other schools in the colony. Inter-school sport was, from the outset, the major agent of conformity amongst Australian schools. The setting up of AAGPS provided a forum for the interchange of sporting and pedagogic ideas and practices, to some extent mirroring the work of the Headmasters' Conference which had been initiated by Thring in 1869. By the time of the first Headmasters' Conference of Australia in 1931, the AAGPS of New South Wales and the Associated Public Schools of Victoria had been the arbiters of public school conformity for some forty years.

St Joseph's membership of the AAGPS met with a predictable measure of French opposition within the college and Marist hierarchy. The vestiges of French influence were instrumental in keeping St Joseph's out of the early AAGPS activities. Having experienced one year of fielding a College cricket XI in 1893, the French Brothers protested about the necessity for such teams to leave the college grounds. In 1894 no teams were entered, following a ruling by the French Superior of the Marist Order. This ruling allowed games to proceed only under the following guidelines: that they were only to be played in the college grounds; that such play would be 'moderate'; that opponents would only be respectable young men, and that no results should be published.[44]

These edicts, issued in March 1894, were totally impractical if the college wished to be actively involved in the AAGPS. The moral provisions could be subjectively adhered to but the inability to leave the college grounds made involvement impossible. The last point, given the enthusiasm of the press for such sporting contests, was also impossible to enforce. Brother Basil, returning to St Joseph's in 1895 to take over the directorship from the beleaguered Brother Stanislaus, sought and gained permission for a one-year trial period of games involvement. A rugby XV from St Joseph's entered the 1895 AAGPS competition, a well-publicised competiton with home and away matches, thus patently ignoring the conditions that the French Superior had placed on their entry.

With the original French influence at St Joseph's totally dissipated, and little prospect of more French Brothers being sent to the college, Brother Basil and his successors substantially altered the temporal and financial priorities of the college. For the first time since St Joseph's foundation, the college authorities began openly to emulate antipodean copies of the

English public school. Much of this process was involved in the acquisition of what Thring called the 'machinery' of the public school. St Joseph's already possessed its own fine buildings, playing fields, school colours and religious life. In 1897 the college magazine returned fron exile to lend the ideological support to the innovations being introduced at the college. An Old Boys Union was established in 1898, initially as a sporting institution, but later providing financial support to the college, establishing a network of patronage, and playing an active role in defining the direction of college policy. Apart from supporting the re-entry of the St Joseph's cricket XI into the AAGPS competition in 1901, the Old Boys were instrumental in introducing the costly and élitist sport of rowing to the college in 1906. With the introduction of rowing, St Joseph's could at last claim to be a fully active member of the AAGPS. In 1908 the college adopted its own badge which included the motto 'In meliora contende', or 'Strive after better things', a singularly appropriate motto to exemplify the struggles of the preceding period.

Freed from the insularity that characterised the 'French' period at St Joseph's, the attitudes and perceptions of the Brothers and boys were significantly broadened through contact with the masters and boys of other GPS schools. Brother Clement, the St Joseph's director from 1902–9, sought to attract lay masters to the college who would support the growing 'esprit de corps' and sense of college tradition amongst the boys. One such master, the ex-England rugby forward B. I. Swannell, elevated St Joseph's to a pre-eminent position in the AAGPS by coaching the college rugby XV to three successive premierships between 1905 and 1907. Masters such as Swannell, a Boer War veteran who later died at Gallipoli, left a lasting impression on the boys at St Joseph's: 'Swannell was such a strong straight character that he made a distinct impression upon all those he met; he was blunt and open in the expression of his opinions, ... [one] could not help admiring the man's courage and sincerity ...'.[45] Through the work of men such as Swannell, St Joseph's College and its pupils began to internalise, rather than merely to imitate, the values and practices of the English public school.

From 1910 onwards, militarism superseded athleticism as the dominant rationale for the inculcation of imperial values at St Joseph's. St Joseph's College ex-students were first involved in the defence of the Empire during the Boer War. Opinions throughout the college on this involvement were sometimes critically anti-British. Bernard J. Grogan, an old boy, wrote a scathing anti-Boer-War statement for the college magazine in 1899, supporting Australian federation as a means of avoiding such imperial conflicts.[46] The English, according to Grogan, needed to learn 'how to settle international differences without the arbitrament of the sword'.[47] There were many at St Joseph's who actively disagreed with Grogan's pronouncements on the war in South Africa. The 1900 magazine proudly acknowledged the enlistment of a popular old boy 'Barney' Barnes, who served in Kitchener's Light Horse throughout the Boer War.[48] In the following year an heroic obituary appeared in the college magazine for one Daniel Hogan, killed in action in South Africa.[49] St Joseph's College with its own dead to be inscribed on yet to be erected honour boards, shed its initial ambivalence towards supporting Britain in its imperial wars. Gradually the rhetoric of military preparedness at St Joseph's began to display a level of intensity that foreshadowed the unprecedented severity of the upcoming conflict.

As in the other GPS schools, the St Joseph's Brothers applauded the government decision to introduce compulsory cadet service.[50] The result was a fairly unprecedented amount of rifle and drill work, with the juniors practising for three hours per week and the seniors for half a day each week.[51] The inauguration of the cadet movement, and the additional half-hour drill administered by Brother Bernard before breakfast, were seen as part of the 'duty and nobility of patriotism.'[52] In assessing the military preparedness of the boys at St Joseph's, the editor of the 1912 annual remarked quite prophetically: 'In this, Our Country's hour of apprehension, our Alma Mater stands shoulder to shoulder with the great secondary schools in an effort to turn out a hardy body of young men, robust and hardy in physique, strong in character, with minds disciplined by the finest studies ...'[53]

As the approach of the war became more imminent, the athlete began to merge with the soldier in the minds of college ideologies. The sporting report in the 1913 *Cerise and Blue,* the old boys' magazine, contained an article by a writer calling himself 'Warrior', putting forward the highly agnostic view that:

> ... the determined and high-motivated athlete is always morally safe, even though he be indifferent as regards religion; he must be careful to avoid excesses of all kinds ... he must live ascetically ... When the day of reckoning comes [he] will be much more capable of undertaking a long forced march in war time than the old woman in the semblance of a young man who never takes any exercise.[54]

When the hostilities erupted in 1914, St Joseph's boys were not faced with any dilemma regarding their involvement in the war. Membership of the AAGPS ensured the comformity of patriotic response that led to the enlistment of 401 St Joseph's boys; fifty were killed and 110 wounded.[55] As far as the élite Catholic schools were concerned, the Great War offered an unparalleled opportunity to consolidate their acceptance among the great secondary schools. Despite a previously aggressive stance on issues such as Home Rule and Federation, the boys, old boys, Brothers and Masters of St Joseph's displayed a whole hearted support for the war effort. Amidst anti-British feeling within the Irish community following the events in Dublin in 1916, St Joseph's preferred to stand amongst the other AAGPS schools in asserting their new found Australian conservatism and its concomitant of imperial loyalty.[56]

The most readily identifiable characteristic of the growth of élite secondary schooling in Australia during the mid-to-late-nineteenth century, was undoubtedly the widespread diffusion of ideals and practices commonly associated with the English public schools. An earlier commentator, C. E. W. Bean, has suggested that 'the more one studies them, the more one is impressed by the fact that the main institutions and principles of these schools in Australia ... stem directly from the reform of Dr Arnold at Rugby'.[57] Recent historians of the English public schools have taken issue with the 'Arnoldian' tradition and its use as an essentially reductivist explanation for a variety of innovations and practices that had emerged by the late nineteenth century. The major positive contribution of this debate has been the realisation that the impact of diffusion can most accurately be assessed by looking at individual schools and the variations that may arise due to prevailing conditions or existing and sometimes conflicting ideologies.[58]

From the two case studies presented above, it is quite clear that the situation was often complex. Both ideals and practices may have had their origin overseas but the adaptation was set within a local colonial context. Even the prominent ideology of athleticism would be transformed into a different ethic based on competition and the need for social recognition. It was the interaction on the games field that helped to build a relationship between the schools which had dissimilar origins and loyalties. By the early twentieth century, although the forms of an antipodean public school were well in place at both of the schools, commitments were beginning to alter. Boys socialised in ways and habits drawn from overseas were to go to fight a war beyond Australian shores; they would return not as pale imitations of Englishmen, Irishmen or even Frenchmen but as Australian Britons.

Notes

1 A history of the Australian corporate schools influenced by English ideals is C. E. W. Bean, *Here, My Son*, Sydney, 1950. Son of Edwin Bean, old boy of Clifton who became a headmaster in Australia and later in England, C. E. W. Bean, also a Clifton old boy, was later author of the multi—volumed history of the Australians' effort in the imperial conflict of 1914–18.

2 See E. H. P., 'Barry, Alfred' in Sir Sidney Lee (ed.), *Dictionary of National Biography, Second Supplement*, 1, 1901–11, London, 1912, pp. 103–4, and K. J. Cable 'Barry, Alfred' in N. B. Nairn, G. R. Serle and R. W. Ward (eds.), *Australian Dictionary of Biography*, 3 ,Melbourne, 1969, pp. 105–7.

3 A. C. Price, *A History of the Leeds Grammar School*, Leeds, 1919, pp. 193–217.

4 M. C. Morgan, *Cheltenham College*, Cheltenham, 1968, pp. 42–53.

5 Alfred Barry, 'The loyalty of the colonies', *The Nineteenth Century*, November 1890, p. 811.

6 S. M. Johnstone, *A History of the King's School*, Sydney, 1932, pp. 202–11.

7 *Sydney Morning Herald*, 6 May 1889.

8 See *Repton School Register 1557–1910*, Repton, 1916, p. 232 and *Biographical Register of Christ's College 1505–1905*, Cambridge, 1913, II, pp.672–3.

9 Reproduced in *The Torch Bearer* (hereafter T.B.), June 1891.

10 T.B., June 1891.

11 Sydney Church of England Grammar School, Council Minutes, 12 August 1891, and Ernest I. Robson Memorandum of 3 August 1891.

12 E. I. Robson, 'Education from the point of view of moral training', *The Australian Teacher*, September 1895, pp. 1–5.

13 Geoffrey Sherington, 'Athleticism in the Antipodes. The AAGPS of New South Wales', *History of Education Review* 12, 2, 1983, pp. 16–28.

14 Geoffrey Sherington, *Shore, A History of Sydney Church of England Grammar School*, Sydney, 1983, pp. 50–8.

15 *Rugby School Register*, III, reviewed and annotated by Rev A. T. Mitchell, Rugby, 1904, p.x and J. B. Hope Simpson, *Rugby Since Arnold,* London, 1967, pp. 101–13.

16 T. B., December 1901.

17 *The Australian Journal of Education*, 15 November 1909, pp. 12–13.

18 T. B., June 1905.

19 Sherington, *Shore*, pp. 79–81.

20 T. B., October 1914.

21 Memoirs of Athol D'Ombrain, T. B., May 1964.

22 T. B., October 1917.

23 Br M. Naughton, *A Century of Striving 1881–1981*, Hunters Hill, 1981, p. 30

24 *Ibid*. p. 56.

25 Br A. Doyle, *The Story of the Marist Brothers in Australia 1874–1974*, Sydney, 1974.

26 Naughton, *A Century of Striving*, p. 70.

27 *Ibid*. p. 96.

28 Bean, *Here My Son*, p. 71.

29 *SJC Annual*, 1891, p. 36.

30 Naughton, *A Century of Striving*, p. 97.

31 *Ibid*.

32 *SJC Annual*, 1888, p. 10.

33 *Ibid*. p. 37.

34 *SJC Annual*, 1889, p. 72.

35 *SJC Annual*, 1889, p. 28.
36 *Ibid*. pp. 28–9.
37 *Ibid*. p. 29.
38 *Ibid*. p. 37.
39 *Ibid*. pp. 38–9.
40 *St. Ignatius College Riverview Jubilee Book 1880–1930*, Sydney, 1930 (hereafter called *SIC Jubilee*), p. 175.
41 Naughtin, *A Century of Striving*, p. 85.
42 *Ibid*. p. 89.
43 See Sherington, 'Athleticism in the Antipodes', p. 16.
44 Naughtin, *A Century of Striving*, p. 97.
45 *SJC Annual*, June 1915, p. 24.
46 *SJC Annual*, 1899, p. 25.
47 *Ibid*. p. 25.
48 *SJC Annual*, 1900, p. 68.
49 *SJC Annual*, 1901, p. 66.
50 C. E. W. Bean, *Here My Son*, p. 178.
51 Naughtin, *A Century of Striving*, p. 141.
52 *SJC Annual*, 1911, p. 5.
53 *SJC Annual*, 1912, p. 6.
54 *Cerise and Blue*, 1913, p. 41.
55 Naughtin, *A Century of Striving*, p. 160.
56 For the general response of the Irish in Australia during the war, see Alan Gilbert, 'The conscription referenda 1916–17. The impact of the Irish crisis', *Historical Studies*, 14, 53, 1969.
57 Bean, *Here My Son*, p. 3. See also C. Turney, The advent and adaptation of the Arnold public school tradition in New South Wales', *Australian Journal of Education*, 10, 2, 1966 and 11, 1, 1967.
58 J. A. Mangan, *Athleticism in the Victorian and Edwardian Public School*, Cambridge, 1981. See also J. R. de S. Honey, *Tom Brown's Universe*, London, 1977.

CHAPTER EIGHT

Race, gender and imperialism: a century of black girls' education in South Africa

Deborah Gaitskell

Introduction

It is striking how relatively absent women are from John MacKenzie's recent discussion of popular imperialism, that late nineteenth-century cluster of 'monarchism, militarism and Social Darwinism' infusing and propagated by every organ of British life. The relative dearth of research on women and empire partly reflects, of course, what masculine activities war and conquest have been, but it is still surprising that, after pointing to female emigration schemes, he has only two other — admirable — pieces of work to refer to: Brian Harrison's on the imperial enthusiasm of the Girls' Friendly Society and Anna Davin's portrayal of the concern for a healthy race of imperial sons which informed much schooling for motherhood and social projects for women at the turn of the century.[1]

British socio-educational research, however, has been underlining how for both boys and girls very gender-specific emphases have been stressed in education, with some relevance for empire. Male public school 'athleticism' aimed to foster 'manliness' of character, embracing 'antithetical values — success, aggression and ruthlessness, yet victory within the rules, courtesy in triumph, compassion for the defeated'. As athleticism fused in the late Victorian period with imperial Darwinism, it prepared boys for military and administrative service to empire.[2] By contrast, girls' education of the same period was still, after a generation of pioneering expansion, a preparation for 'women's mission' — femininity and domesticity.[3] While the empire wanted boys to be manly, girls must be womanly. This applied no less to the British colonies in South Africa, hence Natal Prime Minister Sir John Robinson exhorted schools in 1895 to turn out 'the good old-fashioned, true English type of woman who had made England what it was.'[4]

A further important twist operated in the case of African girls in South Africa. Unlike the situation in much of the rest of Africa, female pupils often outnumbered male in time, especially in the pre-teenage years; but while gender assumptions that a woman's place is in the home applied to them too, race and class discrimination meant that they were frequently propelled into domestic service in white settler homes. Indeed, within the wider restrictions of a colonial economy, Western and African stereotypes of women's role combined to limit many educated girls either to paid employment as maids, primary school teachers and, in this century, nurses, or to unpaid labour as housewives and mothers within marriage.

Within this volume's broad focus on imperialism, this chapter explores three questions: the ideology of the educators; the experiences of girl pupils; and official attitudes and assumptions. First of all, to what extent did

[151]

the women sent out from Britain to teach and convert African girls see themselves as part of an imperial as much as a missionary movement? How much of a contrast emerges with American and continental European missionaries, or were shared assumptions about racial, technical and religious superiority more important than different national loyalties? Secondly, how much was loyalty to the British empire and familiarity with all things British a prominent part of African girls' education? Finally, imperial social engineers from Sir George Grey to Lord Milner attempted to shape African education in ways that, for women, led to a stress on 'industrial education' of a domestic sort: sewing, laundry work, cookery. In a racially stratified colonial society, which South Africa had already become by the time Britain assumed control during the Napoleonic Wars, these skills were seen not simply as enabling black girls to become good Christian wives but also as rendering them useful potential employees in white settler homes. Missionaries varied in their commitment to such training, and the debate around African girls' education should help throw light on the role of gender-differentiated schooling in extending and maintaining imperial control.

Two main periods will be looked at in the century of mission-controlled African education prior to the assumption of total government direction under the Afrikaner Nationalists' Bantu Education Act of 1953. The first, the hey-day of imperial certainty and influence, lasted broadly until the end of the First World War, by which time the devoted imperialists among the small African educated élite had lost their first love. The second, the remaining three decades under mission leadership from the 1920s, saw diminished African loyalty to the empire, despite the persistence of royal ceremonial in black schools and teacher-led youth movements.

This exploratory piece will draw its major examples from two of the country's four provinces, the Cape and the Transvaal. The shift in dominance and importance between them in a sense encapsulates the declining resonance of imperial ideology, for its most ardent supporters among Africans had always been the Cape-educated aspirant petty bourgeoisie, many from the Mfengu people who had, as rootless underdogs in Xhosa society, responded most positively to the triple package of Christianity, commerce and civilisation. The overwhelming dominance of Cape education in 1920, at the end of the first period, is striking. A third of the African population lived in the Cape at that time, but it had some sixty per cent of the schools, teachers and pupils, plus three-quarters of the funding. Transvaal education was worst off — one-sixth of pupils and teachers nationally in an area with nearly a third of the total African population. Natal lagged behind slightly less badly, while the Orange Free

State fared well proportionately: it had just under ten per cent of the African population and between 7.5 and ten per cent of schools, teachers and enrolment. By 1953, with the Free State's position remarkably unchanged — still about one-tenth of total numbers on all counts — Natal had caught up almost entirely, representing one-fifth both of the population and educational provision. Cape enrolment had nearly trebled, but its overall share of pupils and funds was almost halved. Meanwhile, Transvaal pupil numbers had increased some tenfold and its share of expenditure had trebled. Tremendous educational expansion in the 1930s and 1940s, in the Transvaal particularly, had therefore begun to challenge Cape dominance: a quarter of all African schools were to be found in the northern province and a third of the pupils, while the Cape figures were forty-three and forty-six per cent respectively.[5]

From imperial domination to African disillusion (1850-1920)

The imperialism of mission educators

For progressive educational researchers in South Africa today, there is little doubt that African Christian schooling was part of a process of conquest and dispossession. 'The colonised peoples of Southern Africa', writes Kallaway, 'were not simply conquered in a military sense; did not lose only their political independence; were not simply divorced from an independent economic base; were not just drawn into new systems of social and economic life as urban dwellers or wage labour ... colonisation ... also entailed cultural and ideological transformation, in which the schools were major agents.'[6]

Yet one can accumulate evidence of the contrary convictions of the nineteenth-century mission pioneers of the beneficent connection between mission and empire. John Philip, generally seen by white settlers as, if anything, too biased in favour of the indigenous population, was already articulating this view in the 1820s: 'While our missionaries, beyond the borders of the Colony of the Cape of Good Hope, are everywhere scattering the seeds of civilisation, social order and happiness,' he wrote, 'they are, by the most unexceptionable means, extending British interest, British influence, and the British empire.'[7] The *Christian Express*, the journal of the outstanding Scottish mission settlement at Lovedale in the eastern Cape, was even more chauvinistic in the 1880s. While confirming the imperial citizenship of the African population in, for example, an article on 'Her Majesty's Subjects: Black and White', it also voiced its conviction of the 'undoubted superiority' of the British who, as a race, had not only had what Africans had not, 'the priceless possession of Christianity and civilisation', but had also been 'wonderful colonizers', dealing with subjugated races with a degree of 'mildness, compassion and pity' lacking in the Iberian powers, for instance.[8]

Both consciously and by personal example, as is well known, missionaries frequently recreated, with their converts, patterns of community life from the imperial heartland. As the early Lovedale settlement imitated the missionaries 'in their building, gardening, dress and manners', for instance, the missionary Thomson reported in 1827 that 'If you except the black faces, a stranger would almost think he had dropped into a little Scotch village.'[9] Government particularly encouraged them to foster plough agriculture, industrial habits, the wearing of clothes and use of money in order that, as Sir George Grey (Cape Governor, 1854–61) put it, Africans might become part of colonial society with a common faith and common interests, 'useful servants, consumers of our goods, contributors to our revenue'.[10] The colonial state then came to expect accountability from its aided mission schools on such goals, even though very varied responses resulted. The Natal Inspector of Native Education (appointed in 1885), for example, detailed 'the means taken to encourage conformity with European habits', which ranged 'from such profound measures as "constant reflection upon the infallible truth that Europe, though one of the smallest of the four quarters of the globe, is the greatest in spiritual, scientific, and military power" (St John's School, Ladysmith) to such matter-of-fact methods as "a daily bath and a weekly washing of clothes", (Adams' Training College, Amanzimoti)'.[11]

Despite Grey's references to a common society, it was clear by the 1890s that Cape government thinking was anti-assimilationist. An 1892 education commission report pointed to the debate on 'the real aims of an education intended for an intellectually inferior and socially distinct race such as the South African Aborigenes'.[12] Indeed, Hunt Davis points to a crucial change in the late Victorian age as mission (and general European) convictions of racial superiority ousted the belief in cultural and religious superiority. Thus instead of wanting to 'civilise' Africans by contact with superior Christian culture, missionaries began to see it as more important to 'improve' Africans, make them 'useful' because they could never, on account of race, become 'equal'.[13]

The important religious and educational contribution of missionaries outside the British imperial network — the Swiss Protestants among the Tsonga of the Northern Transvaal, German Lutherans in the Transvaal and Scandinavian Lutherans in Natal and Zululand, the American Board Congregationalists in Natal and later Johannesburg — meant that while Western superiority might be and frequently was stressed, there was no specific patriotic brief held for *Britain*, its monarchy and empire in such areas. Curiously, though, the prestige of English literature might still be upheld — so Sol Plaatje, who translated some of Shakespeare's plays into Tswana, was apparently first introduced to the Bard by his German missionary teacher at Pniel, Elizabeth Westphal.[14] But while members of the Wesleyan Methodist settlements at Driefontein and Edendale in Natal fought on the British side in the Anglo-Zulu war and some even against the Bambatha rebels in 1906, this was noticeably *not* true of American Board converts on either occasion. Indeed, the Governor of Natal in 1906 said suspiciously that the American pastors 'could not be expected to advocate the principle of honouring the king as much as that of fearing God'.[15]

All this notwithstanding, Natal evidence suggests that local conditions determined missionary methods despite denominational differences. Etherington claims that the American missionaries, like the frustrated and formerly anti-imperialist Norwegian and Hermannsburg societies, all became imperialists by the late nineteenth century in the sense of supporting the extension of British rule, because they hoped it would overcome African opposition to their message.[16]

Surprisingly little overt discussion of imperialism emerges from the late nineteenth-century reports of female missionary associations of either the Free Church of Scotland (which worked at Lovedale) or the Anglican United Society for the Propagation of the Gospel (SPG), although assumptions of cultural and class superiority are more numerous. Jane Waterston's letters — she founded the Girls' School at Lovedale in 1868 — testify to her enthusiastic interest in the career of General Gordon and her passionate support of Milner's imperial ideal in South Africa, but by that high point of strident imperialism she had been gone from Lovedale over a decade. The male secretary of the Free Church's Ladies' Society wrote unusually reflectively to one of their women missionaries in Natal in the 1890s about the ever 'larger and heavier' burden of empire; and of Rhodes and his ilk, he feared 'there is too good ground for the allegation that they have simply one object in view — namely, gold, and that to gain it they are very unscrupulous ... This imperialism, which has become so popular, seems just to mean grabbing as much of the world's surface as possible.'[17]

The female monarch could be an important touchstone for British women mobilising others to support female education abroad. Sometimes, inclusive imperial citizenship was emphasised, as when a penny booklet of the 1880s referred to the pitiable condition of 'millions of heathen women in our own Queen's dominions ... Those women of India are our fellow-subjects. Two hundred and fifty of them pass into eternity every hour.'[18] The most sustained paeon of praise for Victoria came, not surprisingly, in her diamond jubilee year: 'the most wonderful year in the history of the great British Empire', said the SPG. It attributed the growth of the Women's Missionary Association to the example of the Queen who, 'by uniting true womanliness with a high sense of duty, religious, political, and social, has enabled women to attain a position, undreamt of before her reign.'[19]

How the African elite viewed imperialism

Much innovative recent South African historical research has documented the growth of a prosperous, largely Christian, African peasantry responsive to market opportunities in the Cape and Natal, working towards full inclusion in colonial society and, with the urban growth sparked off by the gold and diamond discoveries of the 1860s and 1880s, building up aspirant petty bourgeois communities in Kimberley and, later, Johannesburg.[20] This African intelligentsia was, as Shula Marks has pointed out, 'both the most ardent believers in the new colonial order and its most vociferous critics',[21] although in fact much of the criticism became overt only from the 1920s.

It is important to emphasise gender difference in the African relationship with imperialism. The educative, 'civilising' and Christianising effect of the missionary's own home was a widespread article of faith for Victorian evangelisers. Especially in the rural Cape (by contrast with increasingly tightly segregated urban twentieth-century South Africa), a small group of black women learned their Christianity and then lived or studied in Britain through being attached to mission households. Lovedale's first African ordinand illustrates this: Mpambani Mzimba's mother had come under Christian influence and learned to read and write while in domestic service in Somerset East; after marriage, she converted her husband and shared her literacy. Their son's bride, Martha Kwatsha, and her bridesmaid, Tause Soga, were among the first girls educated at the Girls' School at Lovedale and both went with the missionary Mrs Thomson to Glasgow in 1874-76 to complete their education.[22] Two other Lovedale graduates went to Scotland for extended periods with the principal's wife, Mrs Stewart: Sana Mzimba, as nurse to the growing family (1872–75), and Letty Ncheni from 1876–79, after she had already been in service with the Stewarts from 1868–73, simultaneously attending evening classes at the Institution. Such girls went on to marry male members of the new élite.[23] But personal contact with the imperial heartland came in very different ways for the young men. For the young women, the setting and purpose of their long journey was basically domestic, underlining yet again that women's sphere was that of the home and home training was most desirable.

For African men, although some like Tiyo Soga went in order to study, trips to England could be much more explicitly political. A vital series of — ultimately fruitless — journeys were undertaken in the early twentieth century to try to get the imperial government to intervene on behalf of Africans in South Africa. These trips were predicated partly on the fact that *male* Africans in the Cape who fulfilled certain property, income and educational qualifications had a right until 1936 to vote alongside whites for the same Cape members of parliament. Such men could be seen as having more of a 'claim' on the imperial power than did their wives and daughters, although the whole family was caught up to some extent in their aspirations to a common citizenship with white settlers.

Sol Plaatje's biographer has described very sympathetically the small, mission-educated African community in Kimberley in the 1890s, admiring both the Cape franchise and equality before the law, and earnestly improving their command of English. Their optimistic vision of a society in which merit and hard work, not race, would determine Africans' place was frequently expressed in symbolic terms, 'above all through expression of loyalty to the figure of Queen Victoria; her name, and the image of the great white queen, were inextricably associated with notions of justice, progress, and opportunities for education and advancement'.[24] Particularly in a context of represssive local colonial interests, imperial control was believed to be an essential protection for non-racialism.[25]

Another ANC notable, the Revd John Dube of Natal, had already seized on an alternative — and, for many, vital — model for African 'belonging' and aspiration: the black American. Educated at American Board schools in Natal, Dube accompanied a missionary back to the USA in 1887, worked his way through Oberlin College and later raised funds in America for his Zulu industrial school, Ohlange, opened in 1901 and following the example of Booker T. Washington's Tuskegee in Alabama.[26]

Among the Africans who also took advantage of the religious and educational networks of the black South were two outstanding women, a generation apart and reflecting in their different involvements much about the pre- and post-1920 contrast around which this chapter is structured. Charlotte Maxeke went from Cape schools to graduate from Wilberforce University, Ohio, round the turn of the century under the auspices of the African Methodist Episcopal Church, for whom she then did pioneering educational work back in South Africa. Active in a female adjunct of the ANC, the Bantu Women's League from 1918, she participated in inter-racial joint councils and conferences in the 1920s, speaking from her experience as an urban social worker. Sibusisiwe Violet Makanya from Natal, by contrast, went to the USA in the late 1920s under the aegis of the educationalist Loram and the Phelps-Stokes Fund, returning to do more rural community upliftment work, focusing on women in order to build up African home life. American female social activism and contact with white American missionaries in South Africa remained important to both women and others like them, providing strong alternative ties and models to those of the British imperial network.

But for the ordinary female pupils of Scottish and Anglican mission schools in the Cape and Natal, schooling at the turn of the century had a very 'English' flavour. Take the senior boys' and girls' curriculum at Lovedale, for example. For English it included Gray's *Odes and Elegies* and Goldsmith's *Vicar of Wakefield,* while History comprised Green's *Short History of the English People* and Smith's *Greece.* Others were reading Scott's *Ivanhoe, Julius Caesar* and *Tom Brown's Schooldays* in English and Meiklejohn's *British Empire* in Geography.[27]

Some signs of female absorption of the message of imperial loyalty are worth highlighting briefly. The symbolic power of Queen Victoria was reaching even isolated rural areas. Thus Maria, wife of a Natal catechist in the 1880s, prayed for 'the great Inkosikase [female chief] of us all, who takes care of us — bless her greatly, O Lord'.[28] Britain's wars evoked sacrificial giving and compassion from African schoolgirls. At St Matthew's, Keiskamahoek, during the Boer War, for example, many gave up sugar for Lent to send the proceeds to wounded soldiers, or knitted and sewed for Belgian refugees 'eagerly' during the First World War.[29]

Domesticity or domestic service for girls?

In the two historical chapters of her outstanding study of domestic service in contemporary South Africa, Jacklyn Cock argues for a connection between black female employment and education patterns in the Eastern Cape up to 1880. She documents the very early entry of African women into the colonial labour market and their growing domination of domestic service. Because she is able to chronicle the founding of several missionary training institutions in that same region which taught domestic skills — cooking, sewing, laundry work — to girls in industrial departments like those at Lovedale, Blythswood, Healdtown and St Matthew's, and couple this with examples of missionary eagerness to place African pupils as servants, she concludes that mission education for girls was 'vocational, domestic and subservient', suited 'to Africans, to women and to subordinate classes'.[30]

The relevance of this to imperialism concerns the role which mission educators saw African women playing in settler society. Cock underplays the extent to which missionaries were aiming at a transformation of African domestic life in order that the Gospel might take root in expanding Christian villages of square cottages (round African huts, Jane Waterston declared, 'utterly' prevented 'the growth of refinement without which you can never have an educated woman').[31] Missionaries did not just see African girls as potentially useful to white settlers, servants of imperial conquerors. The two aims — creating Christian wives and training domestic servants — were frequently held together, or seen as mutually compatible (a girl might earn some money in service and then marry), or seen as applicable to intellectually different levels of ability: the brightest girls were wanted for more advanced academic schooling to train them as teachers and equip them to marry teachers and preachers from the male élite.

The early Christian concern with homemaking merits some illustration. As regards Lovedale, the original aim of the Free Church Ladies' Society was certainly to find a 'highly qualified Christian lady' to train the most promising girls from the elementary station schools: 'Some of these will in due time become the best teachers of their countrywomen; and others will do service of perhaps equal importance when they come to be settled in homes of their own as educated wives and mothers.'[32] Domestic service was not even mentioned. Jane Waterston, as first Head there, repeatedly emphasised that *homes* were what were needed, and hence she set much store by creating a 'home character' for the school that she might turn out not schoolgirls, but women able to make homes because they had understood and seen what a home was. Her correspondence fascinatingly confirms her personal concern to encourage Christian marriages characterised by a new companionship and partnership. To retain the confidence of their most gifted young male converts by recognising their manhood, she helped pair off her star pupils with them and followed the fluctuating fortunes of these relationships with close interest.[33] She was frank about not wanting a totally vocational schooling for the brightest girls: the 'Work Department' established in 1871 'to meet the demand for servants and thoroughly taught workers among the native girls', was not what she would encourage a 'clever, capable scholar' to enter.[34] But she did expect the housework of the girls' school to be done by the girls themselves as far as possible — an educative experience.

A common early missionary ideal was the establishment of a boarding school in order to separate the children from what were seen as corrupting or distracting home and community influences. Yet such a school, especially in the case of girls, was often called a 'home', because it was very much a rival *domestic* establishment, giving intimate daily contact with alternative 'maternal' figures and Western cultural norms. Home life (rather than, say, team games) was character-forming for girls.[35] So, for instance, by 1878, Anglican women missionaries established St Margaret's Home for Native Girls in Pietermaritzburg, with the familiar two-pronged aim: 'receiving a certain number of young native girls into the house to be trained up either for useful servants or wives for native Christians'. A decade on, this had split into two, with younger girls receiving at St Margaret's a Christian education plus industrial training for marriage, while a companion home, St Agnes's, provided a hostel 'sheltering' some twenty domestic servants (by 1893) who also received some domestic instruction.[36]

The Anglicans of this era seem to have been more servant-minded than Scottish or Methodist missionaries, perhaps because of their social background. As Miss Lucas of the Industrial School at St Matthew's wrote at the beginning of the 1880s, having taught girls between six and twenty years of age there for four years:

On the whole I find these girls amiable, obedient, intelligent, and quick to learn, for after some months' training the most ignorant, taken from the wild heathen state, soon fall into the cleanly habits and daily routine of industry followed by the regular inmates of the Mission, such as washing and ironing, baking, household work, sewing, &c., &c. Some of the girls turn out really excellent laundresses, and a few of those who attend to my rooms are quite equal to many English ladies' maids, so thoroughly clean and neat — mending, and even making my underlinen, and keeping everything in the greatest order. They also make good parlour-maids, Mrs Taberer having them in her house as such when occasion requires. It is our object to render them good, useful servants, and therefore we insist upon work of every description being done, from hoeing in the mealie fields to attending upon me personally.[37]

Despite the fascination and importance of this material on acquiring domestic skills in the 1880s, there is a danger of applying it ahistorically. In a sense, as far as women were concerned, this was a time of pioneer instruction in Christian homemaking which subsequent indigenous cultural transmission made less centrally a female mission task. And as regards the mission production of servants for settlers, explicit courses in domestic skills, when looked at over a century-long perspective, had a miniscule impact. It would be wrong to overstate the utility to imperial settlement and rule of black female education. Indeed, at a formal level, it is easy to discount female industrial training before 1953 as making any significant contribution to African women's employment patterns. First of all the actual numbers involved are so small. By the 1950s they still did not exceed a couple of thousand *in toto*: 2,239 African boys and girls were receiving vocational training in 1955 out of the over one million pupils then at school. In 1914, 606 boys and 394 girls attended the Cape's industrial departments and schools; for the country as a whole in 1936, the figures were only 543 male and 621 female students. By 1946, the total had not quite doubled to 2,105, of whom 542 in the Cape and 213 in Natal were female, the other two provinces providing no gender breakdown.[38]

Africans attending mission boarding institutions were always a minority within the Christian minority. The vast majority of African scholars attended much more rudimentary, often one-teacher, day schools, clustering largely in the first three or four years of instruction. Although Victorian Christian aspirations as well as the emerging African converts' conceptions of the natural and proper roles for men and women must have shaped this elementary schooling, the actual sex-specific slant of the curriculum was minimal. The only subject taught to all girls exclusively was sewing. Needlework and the role of clothing in conversion and 'Christian civilisation' generally, constitute one of the great unresearched subjects of South African women's history! It was for sewing teachers that governments were ready, from the 1860s and 1870s, in line with current practice in Britain, to give (very small) grants. Sewing continued to be so central to primary school inspection and funding that into the 1920s in Transvaal schools, for example, white women missionaries might spend a considerable part of their time in its proper supervision.

Once sewing machines and commercial clothes retailing spread, sewing became less clearly domestic: it might lead to an independent dressmaking income rather than either domestic service or the care of a family home. More specific housewifery training was long confined to the upper school standards which the mass of pupils never reached. As the educationalist Loram, an enthusiast for industrial and adapted education, commented years ago, 'the number of pupils in Standards IV and higher is so small that less than 1 per cent of the pupils in Native schools are receiving anything like adequate industrial training'.[39] Even when, in the 1930s, domestic education in Standards V and VI was being extended to more and more mission schools,[40] as only 2.5 per cent of African pupils were in Standard VI in 1935, the extent was still very small.[41]

Secondly, what little evidence we have of the results of such training shows the perennial gap between educational aims and actual achievements. The marvellously rich record of 538 pupils who attended Lovedale Girls' School in the twenty years after its opening in 1868 shows that, by contrast with the industrial course, more girls took the academic course which was intended to lead, if not to intelligent and companionate Christian marriage and motherhood, then to teaching rather than domestic service. Figures from the 1890s highlight the alternatives to service even more (see table 1).

Table 1
Occupations of Lovedale Girls' School pupils

	1886	1896
Teachers	158	269
Domestic servants	53	84
Married (excluding teachers)	79	232
At home or keeping house	71	165
At school elsewhere and miscellaneous	9	19

Source: R. Hunt Davis, 'Nineteenth-century African education', p. 107.

Cock finds (as do I), eighty-five rather than fifty-three who had some experience of service by 1887.[42] But these bald statistics fail to draw out far more significant aspects of these unique personal records. If we distinguish between the fate of those in the academic 'classes' and those in the Industrial Department (started in 1871), it emerges that more girls went into service from the supposedly purely scholarly education than from the vocational training: fifty-three of the eighty-five pupils who worked as servants for any period after leaving Lovedale were girls who had only attended the 'classes'. Rather than confirm Cock's reasoning about the overriding slant of girls' education, this underlines the narrow occupational options open to black women in the British settler heartland of a colonial economy. From the records we see that 159 girls spent some time in the Industrial Department, several of them after anything from six months to four years in the classes: twenty-two were still there. Only some forty-five of the 137 who had left the Institution had actually completed the intended three-year indenture period, and only one-fifth of that small group had been in service, five out of those nine at Lovedale. In fact, full industrial training seems to have ensured *more* responsible, 'élite' status — two-thirds, thirty out of the forty-five who had done the full course, were or had been teaching. Of course, in some — perhaps most — cases, they were employed as the statutory sewing mistress, but this still needs to be distinguished from working as a maid in a white home. When one goes on to discover that less than a quarter of Industrial Department trainees had actually been in service, the shortcomings of such education as a means of supplying settler household labour needs are confirmed.[43]

It is also vital to appreciate that many a biography will combine short periods of at least two of the four 'occupations': service, teaching, time at home, and marriage. Simple tabulation fails to capture this variety and mobility. But domestic service seemed to be a short-term occupation for such girls, if indeed it featured at all. Lovedale transformed the course in 1922, raising the educational qualifications and increasingly framing the course 'to fit girls to make comfortable homes' which meant learning to make use of slender resources instead of learning skills more appropriate to a more prosperous settler setting.[44]

The other vignette showing the mixed fate of industrial training comes from the post-Boer War Transvaal. The Anglican St Agnes's School in Johannesburg started off as an Industrial School where, again, African girls would board and serve three-year indentures as apprentices, afterwards being placed in domestic service. This was meant to tie in with Milner's imperial reconstruction plans for the Transvaal: trained black women would replace the African males who had hitherto, as so-called houseboys, performed household labour for whites and this would begin to free more male labour for the gold mines which faced a crisis of labour supply. Within a year or two of St Agnes's foundation in 1908–09, however, after a walk-out by mutinous older girls who thought they were being worked too hard doing laundry for white families, the ambiguous status of household training in the eyes of African adolescent girls and Christian families became clear. By 1913, a new headmistress was trying to stress the academic teaching more to attract the 'better-class' Africans who felt their wives could teach their daughters housework now, and a boarding school should offer different, more advanced schooling. By the early 1920s, St Agnes's pupils were making 'fitting wives for educated native men' rather than becoming servants, although others became nurses, teachers and even, in one case, a nun. By the 1930s, in response to the ever-rising levels of education and expectation among black middle-class Anglicans, St Agnes's provided boarding accommodation for girls studying alongside the boys of the prestigious St Peter's School, although its small industrial department still prepared a few for a domestic training certificate which could lead to a job as a servant. By then its pupils could also try for the Junior Certificate examination in domestic science.[45]

This section has demonstrated that, while a 'home atmosphere' and encouragement of Western domestic skills were particularly central to the first generation experience of African female education, this cannot be interpreted unambiguously as race and class differentiation of Africans to make them useful to white settlers. Following Victorian domestic norms and possessing at least basic education were also a desirable part of being a Christian matron from the prosperous African peasantry or aspirant petty bougeoisie who demonstrated such loyalty to monarchy and empire. Increasing efforts were put into training African girls to teach these skills to others, a point further explored in the next section.

Imperialism muted and marginalised (1920–53)

Developments in African girls' education

Although only a series of pointers rather than exhaustive analysis can be offered here, this section seeks to emphasise that Cock's characterisation of black girls' education as 'vocational, domestic and subservient' is decreasingly true to the twentieth-century reality. The 'higher' education of girls by the inter-war period contributed to a growing feminisation of especially primary school teaching, the implications of which still need working out in historical research and educational analysis in South Africa. Certainly, as regards imperialism, it seems likely it played a part in the decreasing resonance of imperial ideology, as Cape African male voters, it was argued above, rather than their spouses, had the greatest stake in imperial political and legal assumptions. Yet, as the Cape still trained nearly two-thirds of all women student teachers in 1935, most female trainees continued to be exposed to the empire loyalty of the by then somewhat attenuated 'Cape liberal tradition'. But the growing political, social and economic exclusion of Africans from a common society by whites in these decades, and the sharply diminished power and will of the British government to intervene were even more important curbs on imperial feeling than were female schoolteachers. Likewise, a growing separatist African nationalism, urban radicalism and embryonic socialism superseded imperial ties.

By 1935, female enrolment figures for Standard VI in African schools in the Cape and Natal well outnumbered the boys, at 2,664 and 820 to 1,766 and 561 respectively (whereas Transvaal boys were slightly in the majority at 1,038 to 937),[46] suggesting girls' education was not just catching up but in some respects overtaking boys'. Standard VI pupils represented the 'finished' product and survivors of the African primary school system; a pass in that year was the minimum requirement for teacher training colleges and increasingly for nursing. Cape domination was still striking: not only were over half of all Standard VI pupils at Cape schools,[47] but the Cape was also training some sixty-four per cent of all African women student teachers in 1935.[48] By a decade later, this had altered markedly, with the Cape only responsible for some forty-five per cent of female student teachers (but, by contrast downwards, twenty-five per cent of males in training), as table 2 shows. It also shows that nearly three-fifths of those in training were girls.

Initially, things were different: at St Matthew's Training School, male students well outnumbered female, by ninety-nine to fifty-five in 1918, for example. But in 1932 the position was reversed for the first time and, because 'experience taught from year to year' that women tended to make

Table 2
African teacher training, 1946

Province	Training schools	Students		
		Male	Female	Total
Cape	14	545	1,345	2,190
Natal	5	388	438	826
Transvaal	9	756	610	1,366
OFS	4	520	326	846
	32	2,209	3,019	5,218

Source: P. A. W. Cook, 'Non-European education' in Hellmann, Handbook, p. 376.

better teachers than men for children in lower primary classes, men were then encouraged to follow the primary higher course; from 1945, the lower teacher's course there was restricted to women.[49] A numerical breakdown for the three dominant Eastern Cape mission institutions at the time of government handover illustrates gender educational developments at a local level. It is noteworthy that at Healdtown twice as many girls as boys, at St Matthew's three times as many, were in teacher training (table 3).

Table 3
Enrolment at three key Cape institutions, 1955*

	Healdtown		Lovedale		St Matthew's	
	Boys	Girls	Boys	Girls	Boys	Girls
Training school	101	219	99	114	61	182
High school	226	205	182	112	84	54
Practising school	252	240	233	262	157	247

Note: *Figures for St Matthew's, 1949.
Sources: L. A. Hewson, 'Healdtown: a study of a Methodist experiment in African education', Ph.D. thesis, Rhodes University, 1959, p. 297a; R. H. W. Shepherd, Lovedale, 1824–1955, p. 144, St. Matthew's College Reports, 1949.

Imperialism in inter-war African education: some examples

Having established the growing importance of female students at prominent institutions, the relevance to girls of selected episodes of 'empire loyalty' in those schools can now be accepted. For by the 1930s and 1940s, the impact of the British monarchy on the trio of long-established Eastern Cape schools on which this chapter has particularly focused was largely restricted to rare and special ceremonial celebrations. These events were clearly very meaningful for the expatriate principals; a more refracted message must inevitably have been received by pupils. Two such highlights were the Coronation in 1937 and the Royal Visit of 1947.

The St Matthew's Warden recorded the full timetable of Coronation Day in his (semi-official) journal. The previous evening, a staff service was held, following a form of prayer and dedication commended for general use by the Archbishops of Canterbury and York. May 12 1937 was a holiday and College uniform was worn. The day began with a college service of Holy Communion at 7 a.m. At 10.30 a.m. all the pupils assembled for a flagstaff ceremony. After singing *Nkosi Sikelel'i Afrika* ('God Bless Africa', now the ANC anthem), the breaking of the Union Jack was followed by a hymn and prayers, then all joined in affirming 'God Save the King'. Refreshments for the schoolchildren were then provided at the Flag while staff and representative students planted eighty commemorative pine trees at the Sports Field, before receiving tea and buns respectively. Celebrations continued, after a special meat dinner, with dormitory and table matches, a Servants' Feast, and Evensong at 6 p.m. as usual. The whole College listened to the Empire Radio Programme at 8 p.m. that night, although the planned bonfire and sing-song were postponed because of rain. But such isolated moments of patriotic solidarity could not shield St Matthew's from serious disturbance, particularly in the Girls' Hostel. Through the early months of 1936, for instance, the Warden was attempting to cope with unhappy staff, complaining girls and suspected arson to a white staff member's room.[50]

Lovedale similarly had just been through a traumatic year when King George VI, Queen Elizabeth and the Princesses Elizabeth and Margaret toured South Africa. In 1944–45 some twenty student riots took place at mission institutions (including St Matthew's) in August 1946 some 150 men students at Lovedale rioted, breaking 600 panes of glass. The school was closed for two months, and half the convicted rioters were then debarred from returning.[51]

The royal family met a gathering of 5,000 Africans on the Lovedale sports field on 1 March 1947: staff and students of Lovedale, Healdtown and St Matthew's together with the nearby agricultural college, Fort Cox, and the University College of Fort Hare, plus several hundred pupils from day schools in the vicinity. It must indeed have been a stirring and historic occasion, one of the last symbolic flourishes of all that the old Cape liberal tradition meant, occurring in the midst of changes in the political outlook of educated Africans and only a year before the Afrikaner Nationalist victory, which was to lead to the severing in 1961 of links with the British Commonwealth as South Africa became a republic. Most fittingly, Professor D. D. T. Jabavu of Fort Hare, son of the distinguished editor of the formative generation of African Cape liberals, John Tengo Jabavu, had trained a massed choir from the five institutions and led them in three

African songs, including *Nkosi Sikilel'i*. The royal family then left the dais and moved among the various sections for nearly an hour in 'one of the most informal occasions of the whole tour'. Shepherd, the Principal of Lovedale, wrote enthusiastically that 'Nothing could have been more delightful. The Royal Family left an indelible impression of graciousness, dignity and unfeigned interest.' Noting the extensive press coverage, he proudly recorded how Queen Elizabeth II later recalled this occasion to him at Balmoral Castle.[52] The St Matthew's Warden too described the event as a 'great occasion' which would 'long remain an outstanding memory in the minds of all who were privileged to share in it', commenting that the students deserved 'special congratulation for their fine bearing and their exemplary behaviour'.[53]

For the heads of these institutions, the British connection still had great resonance and they needed to acquit themselves worthily in the royal presence. The same applied to Africans of Jabavu's vintage and background. His energetic and meticulous preparation for this occasion would have helped impress on a much younger generation of black schoolchildren the elevated importance of the royal visitors.

Yet albeit in a more muted and perhaps contested way, identification with British values had continued to characterise these three Cape schools in the inter-war years. In Healdtown's Sunday morning parade of the 1930s, for instance, African nationalism, imperial patriotism and Christian zeal were suitably fused: the school band would march to fetch the girls from their hostel, then all would muster in the large square made by the impressive school buildings, for The King, *Nkosi Sikilel'i*, and a prayer. Obviously, such occasions were intended to build up pride in the school and general *esprit de corps*, even more than loyalty to the British monarch, but links with Britain were also maintained through continued staff recruitment from there and the provision of well-built flats for visitors from all over the Commonwealth.[54] At Lovedale too, the English ethos prevailed in the self-imposed rule of the students that English would be the language of the playground, while the superb library provided, in addition to every English-language South African newspaper, the airmail London *Times*, the *Illustrated London News*, *The Tatler* and *Punch*.[55] The St Matthew's Warden of 1923–34 consciously developed the house and prefect system, sports competitions (for girls too) and school reunions on an English public school model.[56]

Despite some valuable recent personal accounts of African women's lives, virtually no black women's autobiographies of any historical depth or detail exist. Ellen Kuzwayo's *Call Me Woman* provides a fascinating exception. What she recalls of her education at mission schools in the 1920s and 1930s is enlightening: the highlights of her early schooling were 'action songs and physical exercises which I was good at and loved'. She went to Methodist schools in the Free State, a Catholic college at Marianhill in Natal and the Americans' Adams College, and then on to Lovedale in the Cape, a very varied and perhaps unusually peripatetic training. But despite the variety of denominations and national origins of those in overall charge of these schools, she expresses a standard liberal pro-British and anti-Afrikaner stance. Also, while deploring the segregated education and its belittling of African custom, she asserts loyally that the churches 'have been a vehicle for progress, growth and development for all black women educated before the mid-1950s'. Her positive verdict is endorsed by the career path she followed, which was all that mission educators could have wanted: she became a teacher, trained as a social worker and gave long service to the Young Women's Christian Association among African girls, remaining a prominent Anglican. Yet it is worth underlining too that her role models were no longer mainly imported British teachers and missionary wives, as was the case with the girls around Jane Waterston and Mrs Stewart, to a large extent. The outstanding teachers whom Ellen Kuzwayo remembers at each institution were black, a number of them female; student girl friends were also an important inspiration to greater educational endeavour, an important reminder that the ethos of inter-war African education in the big institutions was increasingly being shaped by black staff, as had long been the case in the small, purely African-taught primary schools scattered through the countryside and attached to dispersed urban congregations.[57] To a greater degree than in the late nineteenth century, Christianity and African identity outstripped imperialism and Britishness as dominant values in the socialisation and education of African schoolgirls, a point underlined in a brief consideration of the impact of an African adaptation of Girl Guides.

The Girl Wayfarers' Association

The Girl Guide movement started in South Africa only a year after its 1909 British launch and spread rapidly once the Governor-General's wife, Lady Buxton, agreed during the First World War to become President, with her daughter as Organising Commissioner.[58] But this was among white girls — the inclusion of African girls was discussed, but shelved in 1925 on the grounds that it was premature. Instead, a mission-dominated, school-linked African version of Guides developed, the Girl Wayfarers' Association, which maintained its separate existence in the Transvaal on into the 1970s, although its branches in the other provinces were absorbed into the Guide movement from 1936. Its importance in the socialisation of

African schoolgirls and the training of their teachers in extra-curricular leadership was considerable, although in line with other developments of the inter-war period, the value of this movement to the empire was indirect and implicit, rather than as explicitly conceived as Baden-Powell's sister's first — apparently none too successful — efforts at British recruitment through a patriotic charter, *How Girls can help Build up the Empire*.[59]

Christian youth movements were a far more significant part of learning outside school life for both female pupils and teachers than for their male counterparts. In 1937 in the Transvaal, for example, sixty-three per cent of African women teachers in goverment-aided schools helped with youth movements.[60] Wayfaring had some 30,000 members throughout southern Africa by 1935, double the number of its male equivalent, the Pathfinders.[61]

Women missionaries hoped Wayfaring would 'help in the adjustment to civilised conditions of these girls, and be for their spiritual, moral and physical well-being'; it 'would teach the right use of leisure, give wholesome discipline through teamwork and games, and inculcate loyalty to authority and the idea of sisterhood for service'.[62]

The GWA's aims, as set out in its 1926 handbook, stress deference, usefulness and domesticity, within the rubric of making African girls 'better Christians', rather than the 'good citizenship' stressed by Guiding. Wayfaring's Christian foundation and leadership was a disinguishing mark.[63] 'Upward' was its motto, encouraging aspirations of self-improvement, but the 'really smart' GWA uniform and the enjoyable games and songs learnt had the deepest impact.[64]

At the start, some objected in the African press at the 'mock militarism' and public parading of girls; Wayfarer leaders insisted they too believed 'ardently ... that the place of Native womenfolk is in the home'.[65] Nevertheless, girls took part in regular big rallies which, with bands playing and flags and banners flying, inspired the Christian youth movements and held up imperial notables who came to inspect them, for particular respect. In 1932 it was the Chief Scout, and on another occasion the Governor General, Lord Clarendon.[66]

After the rest of the movement joined the Guides, where imperial as opposed to Christian loyalty would have been more central, the 'adapted' version in the Transvaal continued to boom, claiming over 22,000 members in 1939 and 500 officers, whereas for the whole Union there were only 5,460 Wayfarer Guides and 3,907 Sunbeam Brownies that year.[67] Yet both movements, while offering much that was positive and enriching for black girls, simultaneously shored up settler security by inculcating the many African schoolteacher leaders of Wayfarers with unquestioning values of loyalty to authority and co-operation with white Christians.

Conclusion

This chapter has tried to show how the concept of imperialism lost some of its resonance for Africans in South Africa, in large part because of the political dominance of the white settler population. But the idea of equal access through education and Christianity to imperial citizenship rights was very influential, reaffirmed at sporadic ceremonial intervals in the schools and climaxing in the enthusiastic expression of loyalty to the monarch in 1947. For girls, predictably, their domestic role was never far from the mind of educators and Christian socialisers. But a range of destinies for African schoolgirls were in mind at various times: domestic servant, peasant wife and mother, teacher, nurse, literate though racially inferior worker, as racial attitudes entwined with gender expectations to determine the place of black girls in colonial, imperial and then dominion-status South Africa.

Notes

I gratefully acknowledge grants towards my research from the Institute for Advanced Studies in the Humanities, Edinburgh University, and from the British Academy.

1 J. M. MacKenzie, *Propaganda and Empire: The Manipulation of British Public Opinion 1880–1960*, Manchester, 1984, p. 7; Brian Harrison, 'For Church, Queen and Family: the Girls' Friendly Society, 1874–1920', *Past and Present*, 61, 1973, pp. 107-38 and Anna Davin, 'Imperialism and Motherhood', *History Workshop*, 5, 1978, pp. 9–65.

2 J. A. Mangan, *Athleticism in the Victorian and Edwardian Public School: The Emergence and Consolidation of an Educational Ideology*, Cambridge, 1981, pp. 135–6.

3 D. Gorham, *The Victorian Girl and the Feminine deal*, London, 1982, p. 109.

4 Quoted in P. Randall, *Little England on the Veld: The English Private School System in South Africa*, Johannesburg, 1982, p. 82.

5 See tables in R. Hunt Davis, 'The administration and financing of African education in South Africa 1910–1953' in P. Kallaway (ed.), *Apartheid and Education: The Education of Black South Africans*, Johannesburg, 1984, pp. 136–7

6 P. Kallaway, 'An introduction to the study of education for blacks in South Africa' in Kallaway (ed.), *Apartheid and Education*, pp. 8–9.

7 J. Philip, *Researches in South Africa*, London, 1828, 1, pp. ix–x, quoted in L. Bean and E. van Heyningen (eds.), *The Letters of Jane Elizabth Waterston 1866–1905*, Cape Town, 1983, p. 7.

8 R. H. W. Shepherd, *Lovedale, South Africa: The Story of a Century, 1841–1941*, Lovedale, 1940, p. 302.

9 *Ibid.* p. 67.

10 Quoted in P. Christie, *The Right to Learn: The Struggle for Education in South Africa*, Johannesburg, 1985, p. 37.

11 Quoted in C. T. Loram, *The Education of the South African Native*, London, 1917, p. 58.

12 Quoted in B. Rose and R. Tunmer (eds.), *Documents in South African Education*, Johannesburg, 1975, p. 216.

13 R. Hunt Davis, 'Nineteenth-century African education in the Cape Colony: a historical analysis', unpublished Ph.D. thesis, University of Wisconsin, 1969, pp. 172–4.

14 B. Willan, *Sol Plaatje: A Biography,* Johannesburg, 1984, p. 21.

15 S. Marks, *The Ambiguities of Dependence in South Africa: Class, Nationalism and the State in the Twentieth-Century Natal*, Johannesburg, 1986, p. 59.

16 N. Etherington, *Preachers, Peasants and Politics in South East Africa 1835–1880*, London, 1978, pp. 28–9.

17 National Library of Scotland, MS 8011, W. Stevenson to Miss Lorimer, 9 March 1894 and 27 March 1896.

18 *Woman's Work in India and Africa. In connection with the Free Church of Scotland*, pam., Paisley, 1882, pp. 3 and 27.

19 Archives of the United Society for the Propagation of the Gospel in Foreign Parts (herafter USPG), Women's Missionary Association of the SPG (hereafter WMA), *Annual Report 1897*, p. 9. Many would dispute the Queen's contribution to women's advance!

20 Marks, *The Ambiguities of Dependence*, p. 47.

21 *Ibid*. p. 13.

22 S. Brock, 'James Stewart and Lovedale,' unpublished Ph.D. thesis, University of Edinburgh, 1974–5, pp. 345–6.

23 Bean and van Heyningen (eds.), *The Letters of Jane Elizabeth Waterston*, pp. 26 and 31.

24 Willan, *Plaatje*, p. 34.

25 B. Willan, 'An African in Kimberley: Sol T. Plaatje, 1894–1898' in S. Marks and R. Rathbone (eds.), *Industrialisation and Social Change in South Afrca: African Class Formation, Culture and Consciousness, 1870–1930*, Harlow, 1982, pp. 241–2.

26 Marks, *The Ambiguities of Dependence*, pp. 43–4 and 69.

27 Cory Library for Historical Research, Rhodes University, Grahamstown (hereafter Cory), MS 16 292, *Roll of Classes Lovedale Institution Second Session 1893*, pp. 2–3, 14 and *passim*; *Ibid. First Session 1896*, p. 3; *1905*, p. 5; *1909*, pp. 5–6.

28 Free Church of Scotland Women's Work pamphlets, 19, *Zulu Homes by Mrs Dalzell of the Gordon Mission*, Paisley, 1886, p. 25.

29 USPG, WMA, *Annual Report 1900*, p. 39; SPG, *Annual Report 1914*, p. 110.

30 J. Cock, *Maids & Madams: A Study in the Politics of Exploitation*, Johannesburg, 1980, Ch. 6 and p. 305.

31 *Christian Express*, August 1883, p. 121, quoted in Shepherd, *Lovedale, South Africa*, p. 436.

32 Free Church of Scotland, *Report on Foreign Missions*,VI, 1864, pp. 8–9.

33 Bean and van Heyningen (eds.), *The Letters of Jane Elizabeth Waterston*, pp. 14–15, 25–7, 37, 114, 120 and 125.

34 *Ibid*. pp. 124 and 119.

35 USPG, Ladies Association for the Promotion of Female Education among the Heathen in connexion with the Missions of the Society for the Propagation of the Gospel, *Annual Report 1871*, p. 10.

36 *Ibid. Annual Report 1879*, p. 21; *Ibid. 1893*, p. 34; *Ibid. 1895*, p. 21.

37 USPG, *Grain of Mustard Seed*, June 1881, p. 13.

38 Figures from Loram, *The Education of the South African Native*, p. 151; P. A. W. Cook, 'Non-European education' in E. Hellmann (ed.), *Handbook on Race Relations in South Africa*, Cape Town, 1949, p. 353; Malherbe, *Education in South Africa, Vol. 2, 1923–1975*, Capetown 1977, p. 193–4.

39 Loram, *The Education of the South African Native*, p. 153.

40 A. H. Dodd, *Native Vocational Training*, Lovedale, 1939, p. 39, quoted Cock, *Maids & Madams*, p. 298.

41 P. A. W. Cook, *The Native Std. VI Pupil*, Pretoria, 1939, p. viii.

42 Cock, *Maids & Madams*, p. 300, and note the misprint of 838 instead of 538.

43 Calculations drawn from *Lovedale Past and Present: A Register of 2,000 Names*, Lovedale, 1887, pp. 397–534.

44 Shepherd, *Lovedale, South Africa*, pp. 475–6.

45 D. Gaitskell, 'Housewives, Maids or Mothers: some contradictions of domesticity for Christian Women in Johannesburg, 1903–39', *Journal of African History*, 24, 1983, pp. 244–5.

46 Cook, *Std. VI Pupil*, pp. ix and 1. He relates this to the predominance of rural schools in the Cape and Natal, in a situation in which boys' services are in greater demand than girls' in the country (particularly for herding), and to the supposed greater readiness of Nguni girls, as opposed to Sotho-Tswana females, to go to school and become teachers.

47 *Ibid.* pp. 1–2.

48 P.A.W. Cook, *The Native Student Teacher*, Pretoria, 1940, p. 65.

49 P. M. Fihla, 'The development of Bantu education at the St Matthew's Mission Station, Keiskama Hoek, 1853–1959. (an historical survey)', unpublished M. Ed. thesis, University of South Africa, 1962, p. 144.

50 Cory, MS 14 831, Warden's Journal, St Matthew's Mission, 12 May 1937 and 25 March – 16 May 1935 *passim*.

51 R. H. W. Shepherd, *Lovedale, South Africa, 1824–1955*, Lovedale, 1971, pp. 128–9.

52 *Ibid.* p. 140.

53 Cory, MS 14 838, *St Matthew's Occasional News*, No. 110, 7 March 1947.

54 Interview with Lionel Webster, 5 December 1985, Grahamstown, who was on the Healdtown staff 1937–40 and 1946–8.

55 Interview with Mrs Ruth White, 6 December 1985, Grahamstown, who was on the Lovedale staff 1938–78.

56 Fihla, Bantu Education, pp. 35–7 and 185.

57 E. Kuzwayo, *Call Me Woman*, London, 1985, pp. 78–9 and 251.

58 R. Kerr (comp.), *The Story of a Million Girls: Guiding and Girl Scouting around the World*, London, 1936, pp. 58–70; A Liddell, *The First Fifty Years*, London, 1960, pp. 17 and 24–7.

59 J. Springhall, *Youth, Empire and Society: British Youth Movements 1883–1940*, London, 1977, pp. 131–2.

60 P. A. W. Cook, *The Transvaal Native Teacher*, Pretoria, 1939, pp. 77–8. There were 2,082 government-paid teachers that year and he obtained a seventy-three per cent return on his questionnaire.

61 Witwatersrand University Library, Rheinallt Jones Collection (hereafter WUL, RJC), AD843, B25.1, 'Pathfinder movement', 'The Wayfarer Movement'.

62 International Missionary Council Papers, School of Oriental and African Studies, London (hereafter IMC), 1229, File, 'Wayfarers and Pathfinders', 'The Girl Wayfarers' Association in South Africa', n.d. For a much fuller account of the movement, see D. Gaitskell, 'Upward all and play the game: The Girl Wayfarers'

Association in the Transvaal, 1925–1975' in Kallaway (ed.), *Apartheid and Education*, pp. 243-55.

63 IMC, 1229, *Girl Wayfarers' Association. Handbook of Rules and Organisation. Revised November, 1926*, Lovedale, n.d.

64 J. B. Blacking, *Black Background: The Childhood of a South African Girl*, New York, 1964, pp. 101–7.

65 Letters in *Umteteli wa Bantu*, Johannesburg, from Archibald M'belle, 23 May 1925, 23 June 1928; from Iris Northam for Organising Secretary GWA, Cape Town, and Edith Jones, 6 and 20 June 1925.

66 Cory, *Transvaal Methodist*, November 1933, January and June 1934.

67 Girl Guide Association, *Directory of the British Isles, Overseas Dominions and Colonies, and Foreign Lands 1940, also report for 1939,* London, pp. 9–19; WUL, RJC, Mrs Jones to Secretary, Mining and Finance Corporation, 25 April 1939.

CHAPTER NINE

Public-school freemasonry in the empire: 'mafia of the mediocre'?

Paul J. Rich

An English lodge is still to be found on every continent, and most possess many. Of course, the spread of English, Irish and Scottish masonry was largely the result of British colonialism, and in particular the vast expansion of the British Empire in the nineteenth century. [K. W. Henderson, *Masonic World Guide*]

The contribution of public-school freemasonry to the British Empire has been largely unnoted.[1] A Shrewsbury housemaster told a departing prefect: 'I want your school to be a kind of minor religion with you, ranked by the side of patriotism. Make it a sort of bond, a freemasonry between you and all of those who have been here.'[2] Often, the freemasonry was not only an illusion to the bonds of old-boy fellowship, but actual membership in that secret society.[3] Whether first joining while at school or thereafter, the old boys who became masons gained access to a network that reinforced a collective identity and emphasised the difference between the 'initiated' and the 'uninitiated'.[4] Public-school fagging experience and the masonic initiation ordeals both derived their force from the gulf that they created between those who endured and those who did not, the creation of a 'tribal mystic peculiar to a caste in England which flourished from the eighteenth and reached its meridian in the second half of the nineteenth century'.[5]

The public-school lodges were part of the empire's power structure[6] and provided an introduction to arcane topics presumably useful in the darker corners of the colonies. Much has been said about the old-boy network, but nothing about the old-boy network when it combined with masonry.[7] When masonry combined with the public-school ethos to reinforce élitism, the result was particularly potent, compounding the mystique which was a necessity in the imperial administrator's portfolio of tricks.[8] In overseas possessions where public schools were established, so too were public-school masonic lodges.

The activities of a large secret association with its own legal system and insistence on privileged communications raises questions, especially since masonic authorities have advised members to obfuscate when queried about their masonic obligations.[9] The same penchant for discretion is characteristic of public schools. When Michael McCrum was appointed to Eton from the Tonbridge headmastership, *The Times Educational Supplement* carried a brief biography that concluded, 'Tonbridge has never been in the news, and you can't ask more of a headmaster than that.'[10]

Symbolism, ritual and secrecy were part of public-school life. Peter Earle wrote: '... few knew much about them. For public schools were secret places, isolated from the world and protected from that world by a code of secrecy and silence that was shared by masters and boys alike. No boy would tell his parents what really went on. If he had he probably would not have been believed.'[11] Through ritual, the public schools 'defined social position, emphasised the location of power, and moulded group behaviour'.[12] Ian Hansen discusses this moulding and myth-making, concluding: 'In any school, myth plays a crucial role in establishing and maintaining what is seen to be legitimate and in labelling certain beliefs as being unacceptable. Myths are employed to anchor the present in the past: myths have qualities that may reinforce the present solidarity and stability that the school is seen to have.'[13]

The myth-making was an important ingredient in maintaining British cultural hegemony throughout the empire, and so it is not surprising to find a connection between masonry, the public schools, and other *rites de passage* of imperialism. The masonic institution is compared with rebirth, as was joining the Indian Civil Service. Members of the I.C.S. were called 'the twice born'.[14] Initiation to the school as a small boy, progression through the ranks, elevation to the glories of a praepostor — all these degrees were marked by symbols and rituals.

Public-school life resounded in the rituals of empire. J. A. Mangan observes: '... what the public schoolboy did was to take his school world and its symbolic actions and trappings *with him* into the outside world'.[15] He relates how Old Uppinghamians in India incongruously attired themselves in 'Uppingham scarves, ties, cricket caps, and hat ribbons'.[16] The salutes, parades, decorations, and uniforms were instigated from the moment the British waded (or were carried) ashore. It would be a mistake to think that these symbols and rituals were based entirely on the house system and games. Behind the scenes, public-school freemasonry was a significant force.

Expansion of the British Empire and public schools in the nineteenth century coincided with growth in masonic activity, and with the 'poor man's masonry' of friendly societies such as the Odd Fellows, Shepherds, Druids, and Antediluvian Buffaloes: 'cermony and ritual were an essential part of the societies' life ... mostly in the imitation of freemasonry ... From an estimated 925,000 members in 1815 they grew to about four million in 1872 [compared with nearly 400,000 in the co-operative movement and 500,000 trade-unionists in the same year].'[17] The masonic historian, A. C. F. Jackson, emphasises that the nineteenth century was an era of ritualistic fraternalism:

'During the century the increase in masonry, both at home and abroad, was phenomenal. In 1844 there were 723 lodges under the United Grand Lodge of England with an annual intake of about 1,600 brethren. In 1885 the lodges totalled 1,936 of which 337 were in London, 1,066 in the Provinces and 527 overseas, and there were six military lodges with travelling warrants. The annual intake was about 10,000.[18] The public schools provided many of these new masonic brothers.[19]

The parallel growth of the public schools and masonry was partly because both drew from the emerging upper-middle classes who could afford school and lodge fees. In 1885 when the majority of the population earned less than 25s a week, the minimum masonic joining fee was five guineas.[20] Another reason was that passing through the complicated and archaic masonic initiation rites required a high level of education and self-confidence, which the public schools provided. Commenting on the close public-school connection, Jackson said: 'The product of the system was a young person, slightly intolerant but ambitious and capable. These were the breeding grounds of the masons of the late Victorian era.[21]

The public school initiated boys into a brotherhood and masonry initiated them into an even closer brotherhood. In Sir Shane Leslie's school novel, *The Oppidan*, A. C. Benson (who appeared disguised as the Eton housemaster, Mr Christopher) said about *The Eton Boating Song*: 'I do not say it is poetry, but it throws the Eton spirit into song, all her athletic grace and speed, social contempt, self-centred freemasonry.'[22] The similarity between school and the masonic bonds was duly noted in the Aldenham School magazine:

If you are an OA you may well be a member. If so, did you know that there is an OA lodge? ... We have a very small but very fraternal group who combine the value of Freemasonry with the common bond of OAs, which works out very well and much to our liking ... Now, to those of you who are still at the school, I'm afraid you will have to wait a wee bit but please remember that if your father is a mason (and I mean that in the nicest possible way) you are eligible, to join when you are eighteen ... It is not just a load of 'mumbo-jumbo' conducted behind closed doors with a lot of old men dressed up in funny outfits playing a game of secret agents; it could really be summed up as 'A Way of Life' ... I wonder if you really knew what life at the school was all about until you joined. You were lucky, and no doubt you are proud to be a member. I was lucky to join the OA Lodge in Freemasonry and I'm just as proud of that.[23]

Overseas lodges

Masonic imperialism followed on the heels of colonists and administrators, and overseas lodges were organised at an early date. St John's Lodge in

Boston was instituted at the 'Bunch of Grapes' Tavern on King Street (now State Street) in Boston in 1733, and still exists.[24] Calcutta's Star in the East Lodge No. 67 is of early-eighteenth-century origin[25] and Lodge of Perfect Unanimity No. 150 in Madras was established in 1786.[26] The United Grand Lodge of England and most other Grand Lodges number their subordinate lodges, and the number gives an idea of the founding date. There are 8,000 lodges in obedience to the Grand Lodge of England, so '150' identifies an old lodge. There were just over 300 English lodges by the end of the eighteenth century. No. 1000 was formed in 1864. No. 2000 was warranted in 1883 and No. 3000 in 1903. No. 4000 was chartered in 1919 and No. 5000 in 1926, and Lodge No. 6000 in 1944.[27]

Lodges were started in all parts of the empire amazingly soon after a rudimentary British presence had been achieved. Lagos Lodge No. 1171 of the English Grand Lodge was started in 1867, and Freetown Lodge of Good Intent No. 721 in 1820.[28] An English lodge was started in Guyana in 1813, although there were masonic lodges in the country during the eighteenth century.[29] Amity Lodge no. 309 was formed at Belize in 1763, Royal Victoria Lodge No. 443 at Nassau in the Bahamas in 1837, and Union Lodge No. 266 in Bermuda in 1761.[30] Sometimes, when a lodge was organised in England, the members took the lodge with them when they emigrated — freemasonry in South Australia started with the consecration of Lodge of Friendship No. 613 in London in 1834. After meeting in London a number of times, the lodge made its permanent home in Adelaide in 1838.[31] Occasionally, as the empire retreated, the lodge would be brought to Britain, e.g. Caledonian Lodge of Uganda No. 1389, which now meets in Edinburgh.[32]

This proliferation of lodges overseas was accompanied by the creation of lodges in England accommodating returned expatriates. London lodges with associations with India, Australia, Canada, and elsewhere in the empire, were made up both of those home temporarily and those back for good.[33] The Royal Colonial Institute had a lodge 'for the purpose of enhancing the ties of Empire and Craft and as an additional bond between the Resident and Non-Resident Fellows and Members'. Its first meeting was at Freemasons Hall in London in January 1912, 'when Lord Ampthill, the pro-grand master of English masonry, was the principal officiant. The first master of the lodge was the grand master, the Duke of Connaught, Governor-General of Canada and a former president of the institute'.[34] The institute's lodge, typical of the period for masonic organisations in the educational and learned bodies, flourished: 'The freemasons at the institute grew steadily in strength and the Royal Colonial Institute Lodge formed in 1912 was added to, until by 1924 there were a United Empire Lodge, a

Mark Lodge, a Royal Arch and Rose Croix Chapters.'[35]

Lodges in London were paired with sister lodges overseas so members in the colonies could enjoy a familiar setting when on leave — Lodge Zetland in the East No. 508 in Singapore for example, founded in 1845, was twinned with Zetland in London. Further examples of Lodges which provided a London 'home' for returned ex-patriates include Anglo-South American No. 3623, Anglo-Colonial No. 3175, Anglo-Overseas No. 4886, Bombay No. 3651, London West Africa No. 5485, Nile Valley No. 6306, and Overseas No. 4030.[36]

Hyam, whose figures are at variance with those of Jackson,[37] estimates that in 1862 there were 271 English masonic lodges overseas, in 1885 a total of 617, and 905 in 1914. Membership in 1909 included 50,000 Australians and 64,000 Canadians, and he adds: 'These figures considerably underestimate freemasonic activity because they do not include the Scottish and Irish lodges, each of which had several hundred branches overseas. During the period 1800 to 1914, 502 Scottish lodges were chartered in the empire, and 69 more outside it. By 1914 virtually half (48 per cent) of all Scottish lodges were overseas ...'.[38]

Advancement in masonry went with advancement in government office. Arguably, high masonic office went to those who were distinguished in civil life, but a reverse argument is that masonic associations inclined superiors to 'take a chance'. as a British Chief Constable remarked about promoting masonic officers 'And the more I know about you that causes me to be in sympathy to your cause — the school, the Rugby club, the golf club, Freemasonry or whatever it may be, the more I will be inclined to take a chance — life is about taking chances when you give appointments — on you, opposed to the man that I know nothing about'.[39] For brethren who were initiated in English lodges, the associations that continued over the years suggested a network that could be misused.

An item in The Old Melburnians, a newsletter of the old boys of Melbourne Grammar School which regularly carries masonic news, indicated the enduring significance of public-school masonry:

> Old Melburnians Lodge with its 90 members is just one cog in an organisation of 6 million members throughout the world with 70,000 in Victoria ... we offer our congratulations to the Right Worshipful Brother the Honourable Mr Justice Austin Asche Grand Master, who was installed as Grand Master of the United Grand Lodge of Victoria in March 1984. He is an Old Boy of the School (1934 to 1943) and a member of our Lodge.[40]

Not all old-boy masons would be in a school-affiliated lodge. They might join a lodge connected with their profession or with their London club or military unit. Dual membership was permitted so some affiliated with several lodges. Another issue of *The Old Melburnians* recorded an Old Melburnian joining the school lodge who had been a mason in another lodge for fifty-two years.[41]

Structure of public-school masonry

Stratification within the initiated circle is to be shown by the existence of *two* masonic lodges for the same school. Typically, one drew its membership from old boys and masters and met in a large city like London, with additional meetings at the school. This metropolitan old-boy lodge was eligible to join the Public School Lodges' Council, but not if a favourite groundskeeper or bursar was a member:

> ... the Sir Thomas White Lodge, No. 1820, associated with Merchant Taylors' School, was founded in 1879, eight years before the Old Westminsters' Lodge. However for some years the Lodge was apparently not considered eligible for membership of the Council, and it did not join until 1928. It has been and still is the practice to insist that to become members of the Council Lodges shall in practice unofficially restrict their membership to Old Boys of their School, and to masters and members of the governing body. The present writer had some correspondence on this point with the later Worshipful Brother J. R. Illingworth, Past Junior Grand Deacon, for many years the Secretary of the Sir Thomas White Lodge. He understood that at one time the Lodge admitted to membership some who while associated with the School, did not fall into one of these categories, and this precluded them from membership. This is no longer their practice.[42]

Another lodge would meet in a masonic temple near the school or on the school premises recruiting from an eclectic mixture of masters, old boys, 'lewises' (the masonic term for under-age masons who were allowed to join before the statutory age of twenty-one because of family masonic connections) and townspeople.[43] Instances of pairs of school lodges include Salopian Lodge of Charity No. 117 meeting in Shrewsbury, in contrast with Old Salopian No. 4790 meeting in London: St Wilfred No. 4453 in Oundle, in contrast with Old Oundelian No. 5682 in London; Taunton School No. 8215 in Taunton in contrast with Old Tauntonian No. 5785 in London, and Etonian Lodge of St John No. 209 in Windsor in contrast with Old Etonian No. 4500 in London. An Irish example would be Enniskillen No. 205 with associations with Portora Royal School in Northern Ireland and Old Portora No. 859 for old boys, meeting in Dublin.[44]

English lodges located at or near the school generally had lower numbers on the Grand Lodge roll than old boys' lodges in London, indicating that the first appearance of masonry was in a lodge serving the local school community with the old boys forming city 're-union' lodges later.[45] Schools governed by livery companies had further masonic connections because the companies had their own lodges.[46]

Public-school lodges were started wherever overseas public schools were founded. Old Georgian No. 5104 in Buenos Aires served the old boys of St George's College. Famous Australian schools like Hale, Scotch College, Guildford and many others had lodges.[47] A historian of Prince Alfred College in Adelaide recounted a pro-typical story of the founding of a public-school lodge:

> Towards the end of 1907 about thirty old boys who were members of the Order of Freemasons, after due deliberation, founded the Prince Alfred Collegians' Lodge. It was No. 51 on the roll of the Grand Lodge of South Australia, and was the first of the 'College' Lodges of this State. It was followed very quickly by a similar lodge formed by the old boys of St Peter's College ... The first new member to be elected and initiated into the rites of Freemasonry in the new Lodge was the veteran Headmaster, Mr Chapple.[48]

Public-school freemasonry supported a Public School Lodges Council.[49] Out of over 170 school lodges in England, only the leading schools belonged to the Council.[50] Many Council lodges used the old boys' designation in their name: Old Westminster No. 2233, Old Rugbeian Lodge No. 3551, Old Harrovian Lodge No. 4653, Old Alleynian Lodge (Dulwich College), Old Rossallian Lodge No. 5042.[51] Scottish school lodges affiliated with the separate Grand Lodge of Scotland: Edinburgh Academy Centenary No. 1327, The Watsonian No. 1375.[52] Other lodges joined old boys of several schools together in specialised masonic activities: The Public Schools Knight Templar Preceptory, The Eton and Harrow Lodge of Mark Master Masons, The Public Schools Council of Royal and Select Masters.[53]

Although school lodges were most frequently connected with Anglican foundations, and some denominations were hostile to masonry,[54] Methodist public schools like Taunton and The Leys had lodges. Strict Methodists were opposed to masonry and S. P. Record's list of founding members in his history of Taunton School indicates that the lodge chaplain, although an Old Tauntonian, was an Anglican canon.[55]

The Public Schools Lodge Council issued year-books separate from the general masonic ones and published the masonic histories of schools. Yearly it sponsored a masonic festival at one of the schools, a large-scale gathering of public-school masons from all over Britain and overseas.[56] Public-school lodges were notable for the prominence of their members, as the addresses at the festivals enjoyed mentioning with some smugness. The master of Old Alleynian Lodge remarked at a Dulwich festival:

> In every walk of life, in the Services, in the Church, in politics, in literature, in art and music, and, as especially appropriate when we consider to whom we owe our foundation, in the drama, Alleynians have been eminent and by their efforts and success have helped to secure for Dulwich its rightful place among the great schools of this country ... I am going so far to depart from the rule that I have set myself of not mentioning the names of Old Alleynians as to refer to two, and this for a special reason in each case. The first is Sir Ernest Shackleton, because he was a founder of this Lodge, and the other is [Brother] Stainforth, because he holds the unique record of having travelled at a faster speed than any human being.[57]

The members of public-school lodges were outstandingly successful in the general masonic world. The 1930 *Public Schools Masonic Year Book* shows that the public-school lodges were a Who's Who of empire masonry.[58] The Grand Master of England, the Duke of Connaught, was simultaneously Master of the Old Wellingtonian Lodge.

Imperial connections

As notable as the old school connection is the Indian connection. Indian masonry provided top-ranking English Grand Lodge officers and emphasised the special aura of India, its mystic associations, its civil service imbued with a sense of consecration: 'A corps of specialists in the Indian army and the Foreign Office of the Indian Government, inconspicuously and at times with the sense of carrying a conspiracy or an esoteric rite, secured the continuity of policy ...'.[59] For example, the Old Tonbridgian Lodge included the Assistant Grand Director of Ceremonies of the English Grand Lodge, Sir Maurice Simpson, who headed communications for the India Office as Director-in-Chief of the Indo-European telegraph service. Symptomatic of the umbilical old-boyism that influenced the empire, he always led his list of distinctions in *Who's Who* (Kt, CSI) with 'Tonbridge School, Head boy, 1885'.[60]

The Old Westminsters' Lodge included the Deputy Grand Master for the masonic province of Madras in India, Sir Archibald Campbell. Another Old Westminster was a past Grand Deacon of Grand Lodge, Sir Arthur Knapp. At the same time he was Grand Deacon he was member and Vice-President of the Executive Council for Madras, and his brother and fellow O. W., Campbell, was member of the Board of Revenue. Knapp became a Governor of Westminster and Campbell became Chief Secretary of the

Madras Government (1925–30) while serving as Deputy Grand Master.

Most old-boy lodges had members like Knapp and Campbell who were high-ranking officers of the order overseas. The Charterhouse Lodge boasted the past Deputy Grand Masters for both the Bombay province and Bengal. The Old Shirburnian Lodge included the Senior Grand Warden of the Grand Lodge, Field-Marshal Sir Claud Jacob, who at the same time was Secretary of the Military Department of the India Office, having previously (1920–4) been Chief of the General Staff in India.

The Old Cliftonian Lodge included a headmaster both of Clifton and Rugby and past Grand Chaplain of the Grand Lodge, the Bishop of Liverpool, A. A. David, and the past Senior District Grand Warden for East Africa, Sir Charles Bowring, who was Chief Secretary for Kenya (1911–24) and Governor of Nyasaland (1924–9) as well as a Grand Deacon of the Grand Lodge while holding those offices. The Old Wellingtonians, besides the Grand Master, had the Provincial Grand Master for Lancashire, The Earl of Derby. The Treasurer of the Grand Lodge belonged to the Old Marlburian Lodge, as did the Grand Organist. The Old Rugbeian Lodge included Sir Walter Napier, who was District Grand Master of the Eastern Archipelago. The Old Haileyburian Lodge had the doyen of Middle-East freemasons, Right Worshipful Brother Lt Col Sir A. Henry McMahon, GCMG, GCVO, KCIE, CSI, who was Past Grand Warden of the Grand Lodge and Deputy Provincial Grand Master for Malta. The Old Pauline Lodge included Sir Leslie Wilson, a past District Grand Master for Bombay. The Old Alleynians had a Grand Sword Bearer.

The Old Etonians, as might be expected, were overwhelmed with Grand Lodge officers, including the Earl of Yarborough, the Earl of Shaftesbury, Lord Cornwallis, the Duke of Devonshire, Lord Kensington, the Earl of Harewood and Lord Hailsham. The Old Leysians made do with a Deputy Grand Sword Bearer. Old Harrovians had fewer peers in Grand Lodge office than the Etonians, but listed Lord Lilford, Lord Forester and Lord Tomlin of Ash. Old Lancing Lodge had a past Grand Chaplain, the Bishop of Lewes. Old Rosallian Lodge consoled itself with a District Grand Master for British Guiana.

An old boy could have pursued a distinguished masonic career without belonging to his old school lodge but the public-school lodges had an inordinate number of masonic leaders in their membership holding important masonic offices in different parts of the empire at the same time that they held high government offices.[61] The connections between the empire, lodges and schools are shown by the way references to masonic functions, secret and never appearing in general magazines or newspapers, were openly published in the public-school magazines. This singular exception to the universal masonic rule of 'no publicity' indicated that the school community was regarded differently from the general public, not a masonic audience but not as strangers.[62]

Contributing to public-school freemasonry's strength was the opportunity that senior boys at school had of joining the lodges as lewises, the special category for under-age sons of freemasonry.[63] Candidates are informed of this special class of membership when they take the first degree:

> Lewis likewise denotes the son of a Mason; his duty to his parents is to bear the heat and burden of the day, which they, by reason of their age, ought to be exempt from; to assist them in time of need, and thereby render the close of their days happy and comfortable; his privilege for so doing is that of being made a Mason before any other person, however dignified.[64]

Kipling under this exception became secretary of his lodge in India at the age of twenty.[65] Joining at an early age gave public-school boys advantages because masonic advancement depended heavily on seniority and thus the earlier a man became a mason, the better his chances for preferment within the order.

McMahon and freemasonry

Just as headmasters were simultaneously masters of lodges, prominent British imperial authorities simultaneously held important masonic titles. An example was Old Haileyburian Sir Henry McMahon, progenitor of the McMahon Letters, negotiator of the McMahon Line, first High Commissioner of Egypt (1914–16), 'Kitchener's successor in Cairo ... friend and fellow Grand Master in Masonry of the one-time Commander-in-Chief in India'.[66] McMahon joined the Indian Political Service in 1890, becoming Foreign Secretary to the Government of India (1911–14) and was one of the most important Middle-Eastern figures identified with freemasonry, 'achieving his greatest eminence as Sovereign Grand Commander of the Masonic Supreme Council 33°'.[67] His masonic career shows how a high-ranking British official combined imperial and masonic enthusiasms.[68]

Rituals that McMahon presided over had an exotic and bizarre flavour. Among his innumerable masonic dignities by virtue of being Supreme Head of the Scottish Rite for the Empire was Master of the Lodge of Perfection, whose members wore a special gold ring and were told on receiving it: 'I symbolize the Scottish Rite and, as such, like Aladdin's lamp, I am possessed of miraculous powers, for ... I bring you riches far greater than all the wealth of fabled Golconda: I can summon to you the help and the strength of your Scottish Rite Brethren throughout the nations of our world-wide Masonry...'.[69]

He also commanded the Princes of Jerusalem, a prestigious masonic affiliate which used Middle-Eastern history in its ritual. During the initiation, lengthy reference was made to Cyrus and Darius, and the candidate was made to portray an ambassador to the court of Darius, who received and questioned him. The Princes had a long history in England and America, dating back at least to the eighteenth century, and were partly based on the *Antiquities* of Josephus (lib. xi, Cap. iv, Sec. 9).[70] McMahon added to his dignities by ruling the Masonic Knights of the East and West,[71] whose ritual involved an initiation chamber in the shape of a heptagon hung with crimson, sprinkled with gold stars. In each of the heptagons's angles was a square column on the capitals of which were the initials of Beauty, Divinity, Wisdom, Power, Honour, Glory and Force, and on each base the initials of Friendship, Union, Resignation, Discretion, Fidelity, Prudence and Temperance. As head of the Knights, McMahon was entitled to a throne elevated by seven steps and supported by four lions and four eagles.[72]

Membership of officials like McMahon complemented their involvement with the British secret services and their keen interest in what was happening politically in Middle-Eastern schools and colleges. Lodges in a city like Cairo were good places for picking up information and the British in the Middle East were heavily engaged in the intelligence business, so membership had its useful side. McMahon during his Cairo days regularly received secret reports on the movements and political views of Arab students. As a way of placing those native peoples who became masons under additional obligations and as a source of intelligence, masonry was part of the way the British kept the empire secure. While the brotherhood's power contributed to imperial hegemony, the secrecy had a public schoolboy juvenility to it:

> It seems to the initiates that they go by rules and myths which the inspirers of the other rules and myths could not possibly know or understand, and that this is a game which they may play but which is forbidden to others. Who cannot remember from childhood the attractions of the game in which we would not allow the less favoured children to take part? One of the comments made by its early critics on Freemasonry was that the Masons were like children who want to 'faire la chapelle', which has the meaning of 'playing at church' just as the children 'play at doctors'.[73]

Described as the 'mafia of the mediocre' and 'a practical way of maintaining a closed shop', the masonic orders enabled public-school boys throughout the empire to exercise secret means of control and communication. This was a long-standing function of freemasonry, as Roberts indicates

> ... the Craft played a big part in the internal system of communications of a highly stratified and divided society. The most striking examples of its operation in this way are those provided by masons finding through lodges a mechanism which could introduce them into society in countries other than their own. A well-born young man, Casanova wrote, who wished to travel and see the world without being excluded from the pleasures of his social equals, ought to be initiated a freemason.[74]

One reason for freemasonry's ties with education were controversial was the suspicion that decisions were made in lodges rather than by school governors or faculty. Similar objections were made to public-school old boys in the empire, who used the old-boy network rather than the formal government structure and like the masons were compared with a mafia:

> From being in the human tradition, associated with group loyalty, initiation ceremony, and secret mystery, and possibly, in the Protestant ethic, with martyrdom and the refusal to deny faith in order to escape physical suffering, the idea of honourable silence (the Mafia has a word for it, 'omerta') was a natural pillar of the Victorian public school code. How far it was actually practised, and still is, we can only guess ...[75]

No doubt for some members the craft was a lofty experience with its charities, philosophic doctrines and solemn rituals providing purpose and spiritual refuge. For some it was a wasted lifetime spent on the other side of the looking-glass.[76] The difficulty is when those who have gone through the looking-glass never return, and that was the fate of some of the British in the empire. The abstraction became the reality: 'Life itself has become a myth.'[77]

Undoubtedly some boys learned about the fraternity and joined it because their schools and headmasters were involved; the public-school lodge festivals were a conspicuous advertisement.[78] Though secret, masonry was not adverse to grand displays. Its principal London temple towered over Great Queen's Street and patronage by the Royal Family gave the final imperial accolade, especially when Edward VII was Grand Master.[79] Since imperialism sought *order*, public-school freemasonry was a helpmate in the rationalising of imperial society, imposing its strict hierachy and formality as another means of social control, and with its honours offering another means of reward. Ritualistic fraternalism strengthened the self-confidence with which British administrators exerted cultural domination. 'The Scottish Rite', wrote its Sovereign Grand Commander, 'empowers its candidates and members with a touchstone of spiritual revelation and wisdom *for the guidance of mankind*. As we are told in St Matthew 5: 14-16: "Ye are the light of the world ...".'[80]

It is easy to fall into a trap of thinking that secret societies belong 'on the same level as the fantasies of the Flat-Earthers'; the German SS took the masons seriously enough to form the anti-masonic section which closed lodges and sequestrated membership records.[81] Of the Reich's suppression of the lodges, Roberts says 'This should remind us of the danger of taking the recurrent irrational element in history too lightly.'[82] The situation is that if there is no public school *cum* masonic conspiracy, it is still necessary to deal with the perception that there is: 'Secret-society myths are usually concerned to suggest the existence of small, powerful groups which work invisibly. But the political importance of such myths is their effect on the general currents and atmosphere of public opinion.'[83]

Neither overseas masonry, royalty's connection with masonry, nor the desire of old boys to have their own old-boy lodges is extinct. In April 1986 the notice of the Supreme Grand Chapter of Royal Arch Masons of England, a body conferring higher degrees complementary to the initial ones and with HRH Duke of Kent, KG, GCMG, GCVO, presiding as Most Excellent First Grand Principal, announced petitions 'for a Chapter to be attached to the Enfield Grammar School Lodge, No. 7757, to be called the Enfield Grammar School Chapter' and '... for a Chapter to be attached to the Jubilee Lodge, No. 5582, to be called the Jubilee Chapter, and to meet at Masonic Temple, Kitwe, Zambia'.[84]

The resentment of masonry and the resentment of the public schools focus on the way they helped preserve the *status quo* and divisive social classes,[85] while manipulating the political process.[86] Secrecy makes documentation difficult — the British Library was refused when it requested copies of the *Masonic Year Book* for the Reading Room. Masonry's leaders seldom publicly acknowledged their membership.[87] Nevertheless, the freemasons and the empire recruited from the public schools and the three institutions embraced each other as they rose to dizzy ascendancy during the Victorian era. They are too important to escape scrutiny. Not accidentally in Britain's far realms, one sometimes encountered both fellow old boy, and a *brother* old boy.[88]

Notes

1 'The role of freemasonry in building up the empire, and of its doctrines of brotherhood in sustaining the world-wide activities of traders and empire builders, is not easy to document. Its role in spreading British cultural influences has thus been seriously underrated.' Ronald Hyam, *Britain's Imperial Century, 1815–1914: A*

Study of Empire and Expansion, London, 1976, pp. 152–3. I am grateful to Dr J. A. Mangan and Dr Donald Leinster-Mackay for their comments during the preperation of this essay.

2 John Chandos, *Boys Together: English Public Schools 1800–1864*, Oxford, 1985, p. 20.

3 Frequently freemasonry is used as an example of the fellowship that should exist 'between people who have had a certain degree of education'.John A. Armstrong, *The European Administrative Elite*, Princeton, New Jersey, 1973, p. 234.

4 The fagging system at most schools was a year or more of hazing and servitude.

5 Chandos, *Boys Together*, public schools provided: '... a hierarchically organised environment which stresses mutually reinforcing obligations, an idealisation of the well–rounded man, and a social order that excludes the uninitiated'. Ted Tapper and Brian Salter, *Education and the Political Order: Changing Patterns of Class Control*, London, 1978, p. 20.

6 British masonic bodies insisted on their right to govern masonic affairs in all overseas territories and adopted titles indicating this. Cecil Rhodes was a freemason but considered forming a secret society especially 'to devote itself to the preservation and expansion of the British Empire'. Carroll Quigley, *The Anglo-American Establishment: From Rhodes to Cliveden*, New York, 1981, p. ix. Quigley cites the plans of Rhodes to finance such a society and offers evidence that it actually functioned. *Ibid.* p. 39.

7 'At Eton, and schools that endeavoured to, but did not quite, match it, a boy's steps were set on the first part of that steady and inevitable progress towards the positions of command over the majority. The government of the country, notes Anthony Powell, again of Eton, was somehow made almost a personal matter.' A. P. Thornton, *The Imperial Idea and Its Enemies*, 2nd edition, London, 1968, p. 90.

8 The public schools and freemasonry not only impressed the uninitiated but gave self-confidence to their members. The Colonial Office's Sir Henry Taylor wrote: 'That is no insignificant part of the philosophy of government which calls in aid the imaginations of men in order to subjugate the will and understanding; and so long as man shall continue to be an imaginative being, it will be expedient that those who are to enjoy pre-eminence or to exercise power, should be invested with some ideal influence which may serve to clothe the nakedness of authority.' Sir Henry Taylor, 'The rationale of linking high office to high status'. W. L. Guttsman (ed.), *The English Ruling Class*, London, 1969, p. 230. At least six colonial secretaries, three viceroys, many governors and other imperial figures were active masons. Hyam, *Britain's Imperial Century*, p. 153. The biggest difficulty in determining masonic influence is establishing membership of an individual, given masonic secrecy.

9 Lamb reviews the 'intricacies of Masonic Jurisprudence': 'Whenever possible a lodge should avoid charging a member with a violation of his Masonic oath ... [because] if and when the case is tried anew in a civil or criminal court the contents of the Masonic oath might become the legitimate object of legal discovery procedures. It could be, as we have learned, that a Mason might be ordered by a court to reveal the content of an oath allegedly violated, or since all witnesses are sworn or affirm in court to tell the truth, the whole truth and nothing but the truth, *to reveal which oath he is going to keep!* Discretion has always been the better part of valor!' Newell A. Lamb, *Masonic Trials and Privileged Communications*, Silver Spring, Maryland, 1984, p. 12.

10 I. V. Hansen, *By Their Deeds: A Centenary History of Camberwell Grammar School, 1886–1986*, Canterbury, Victoria, 1986, p. 302.

11 Peter Earle, 'God, the rod, and lines from Virgil', George Macdonald Fraser (ed.), *The World of the Public Schools*, London 1977, p. 39.

12 J.A . Mangan, *Athleticism in the Victorian and Edwardian Public School: The Emergence and Consolidation of an Educational Ideology*, Cambridge, 1981, p. 141.

13 Hansen, *By Their Deeds*, p. 249.

14 Charles Allen, *Plain Tales from the Raj: Images of British India in the Twentieth Century*, London, 1985, p. 286.

15 Mangan, *Athleticism*, p. 145.

16 *Ibid.* p. 146.

17 J. F. C. Harrison, *Early Victorian Britain: 1832–51*, London 1979, p. 196.

18 A. C. F. Jackson, 'Our Predecessors of about the time that Quatuor Coronati Lodge was founded,' *Ars Quatour Coronatorium*, Transactions of Quatuor Coronati Lodge No. 2076, XC, 1977, p. 46.

19 *Ibid.* p. 41.

20 *Ibid.* p. 39.

21 *Ibid.* p. 41.

22 Quoted in Isabel Quigly, *The Heirs of Tom Brown: The English School Story*, Oxford, 1984, p. 150.

23 D. A. Atherton, 'What is Freemasonry?', *The Aldenhamian*, Edition 357, 1985, p. 34.

24 *Newsletter*, St John's Lodge, Boston, Massachusetts, December 1985.

25 *List of Regular Lodges Masonic*, Bloomington, Illinois, 1984, p. 96. This is a list of lodges furnished to the tylers or door guards, useful for analysis of the origins and geographic distribution of lodges. Hereafter *Regular Lodges*.

26 K. W. Henderson, *Masonic World Guide*, London, 1984, p. 94.

27 Stephen Knight, *The Brotherhood: The Secret World of the Freemasons*, London, 1985, p. 36.

28 Henderson, *Masonic World Guide*, pp. 57 and 60.

29 *Ibid.* p. 387.

30 *Ibid.* pp. 151, 162 and 163.

31 *Ibid.* p. 332.

32 *Regular Lodges*, p. 236.

33 Henderson, *Masonic World Guide*, pp. 129–30.

34 Trevor R. Reese, *The History of the Royal Commonwealth Society: 1868–1968*, Oxford, 1968, pp. 105–6.

35 *Ibid.* p. 136.

36 *Regular Lodges*, pp. 51–8.

37 Though not seriously as far as the weight of the argument is concerned. Jackson, for example, states that there were 527 overseas lodges subordinate to the English Grand Lodge in 1885. Jackson, *Our Predecessors*, p. 46.

38 Hyam, *Britain's Imperial Century*, p. 155.

39 A Chief Constable, quoted in Knight, *The Brotherhood*, pp. 79–80.

40 *The Old Melburnians*, No. 23, May 1984, p. 3.

41 *Ibid.* No. 25, February 1985, p. 4.

42 GLE: R. Nott, *The Public School Lodges' Council: 1909–1971* Haslemere, 1971, p. 19. Because of the difficulty in finding privately printed publications, their presence in the Grand Lodge of England Library and Archives is noted by GLE.

43 Jackson, *Our Predecessors*, p. 51, fn. 1.

44 *Regular Lodges*, *passim*.

45 *Ibid.*

46 Knight, *The Brotherhood*, p. 228. For an introduction to the guilds and their public–school connections, see John Kennedy Melling, *Discovering London's Guilds and Liveries*, Aylesbury, 1981.

47 New South Wales: Sydney High School No. 631; King's School, Turramurra, No. 760. South Australia: Pulteney Grammar No. 172, Adelaide; St Peter's Collegiate No. 53, Adelaide. Tasmania: Scotch College No. 80, Launceston; Hutchins Old Boys No. 48, Hobart; Old Holbartians No. 56, Hobart. Victoria: Mt Scopus Collegians No. 827, Burwood; Ivanhoe Grammarians No. 584, Darebin; Malvern Grammarians No. 693, Glenferrie; Scotch Collegians No. 396, Glenferrie; Carey Grammarians No. 810, Kew; Trinity Grammarians No. 500, Kew; Camberwell Grammar No. 615, Glenferrie; University High School No. 517, Kew; Old Melburnians No. 317, Prahran; Melbourne High School No. 759; Wesley Collegians' No. 358, Prahran; Caulfield Grammarians No. 364, St. Kilda. Western Australia: Old Guildfordians No. 298, Maylands; Hale No. 308, Perth. *Regular Lodges, passim.*

48 J. F. Ward, *Prince Alfred College: The Story of the First Eighty Years, 1869–1949*, Adelaide, 1951, p. 130.

49 *Ibid. passim.*

50 Knight, *The Brotherhood*, p. 138.

51 Henderson, *Masonic World Guide*, p. 129. See also GLE: File BE 166 (4165) OLD, GLE: File BEW 166 [52111].

52 *Ibid. passim.*

53 GLE: *Public Schools' Masonic Year Book*, London, 1930.

54 Knight, *The Brotherhood*, esp. pp. 230–69.

55 S. P. Record, *Proud Century: The First Hundred Years of the Taunton School*, Taunton, 1948, p. 307.

56 *Public Schools' Masonic Yearbook.*

57 GLE: *A Short Address on the History of the College delivered by The Worshipful Master of the Old Alleynian Lodge No. 4165 at the Sixteenth Festival of the Public School Lodges*, 11 June 1932, p. 11.

58 Some prominent in their own or inherited right, some obscure and prominent only by virtue of masonic office.

59 Guy Wint, *The British in Asia*, London, 1947, p. 23.

60 *Who Was Who*, Vol. V, 1951–60, p. 1003.

61 For the preceding old-boy lodges and their members, see *Public Schools Masonic Year Book*, pp. 13–18.

62 Masonic reticence about publicity is partly founded in repeated witch hunts by hostile governments, notably in nineteenth-century America and in Germany under Nazism. A current example of anti-masonry is in Iran. Henderson wrote: 'The fate of the Craft in Iran forms the greatest masonic catastrophy since the Second World War. Discovery of oil in Persia brought in many British workers and traders, a percentage of whom were masons. Scotland was the most active in issuing warrants, and it began with *Lodge Light in Iran No. 1191* at Shiraz in 1919 ... The Islamic Revolution in Iran saw freemasonry swept away rapidly, and it would appear that a number of masons suffered execution at its hands.' Henderson, *Masonic World Guide*, pp. 221–2.

63 Knight, *The Brotherhood*, p. 127.

64 Walton Hannah, *Darkness Visible: A Revelation and Interpretation of Freemasonry*, Chulmleigh, Devon, 1980, p. 114.

65 Kipling joined the Lodge of Hope and Perseverance, Lahore, in 1885. Angus Wilson, *The Strong Ride of Rudyard Kipling*, London 1977, p. 414.

66 H. V. F. Winstone, *The Illicit Adventure: The Story of Political and Military Intelligence in the Middle East from 1898 to 1926*, London, 1982, p. 172. McMahon's involvement with intelligence is mentioned by Winstone, including his use of agents to keep watch over Egyptian schools.

67 James Morris *Farewell the Trumpets: An Imperial Retreat*, Penguin Books, Harmondsworth, 1984, p. 272.

68 Despite nearly a column year after year in *Who's Who* listing innumerable details, 'FZS (Ex–Council and VP); FGS, FRGS ... President of Liverpool and Manchester Foot Hospitals', McMahon never mentioned his masonic activities.

69 Henry C. Clausen, *Practice and Procedure for The Supreme Council (Mother Council of the World) of the Inspectors General Knights Commander of the House of the Temple of Solomon of the Thirty-Third Degree of the Ancient and Accepted Scottish Rite of Freemasonry of the Southern Jurisdiction*, Washington 1981, p. 19.

70 *Scottish Rite Masonry Illustrated: The Complete Ritual of the Ancient and Accepted Scottish Rite*, Chicago, 1979, I, pp. 420–30.

71 His membership in the Knights of East and West required that he maintain his affiliations and rank in various subordinate degrees of the Ancient and Accepted Rite, as well as in the Grand Lodge of England. That was no problem for someone who seemed to have an irresistible urge to be an officer in every existing masonic organisation. McMahon was District Grand Warden of the Punjab, Senior Grand Deacon, Senior Grand Warden, and District Grand Master (for Malta), all of the Grand Lodge of England. He was past master of Kitchener Lodge No. 2998, Quetta Lodge No. 2333, and Red Triangle Lodge No. 4000. (Information from handwritten register of Grand Lodge officers in the Secretary's office of the United Grand Lodge of England.) He was a lodge brother of Winston Churchill in Studholme Lodge No. 159 in England. *List of Members of the Studholme Lodge of Ancient, Free, and Accepted Masons*, No. 159, 1926.

72 *Ibid*. pp. 441–2.

73 Peter Partner, *The Murdered Magicians: The Templars and Their Myth*, Oxford, 1982, p. 179.

74 J. M. Roberts, *The Mythology of the Secret Societies*, London, 1972, p. 56.

75 George MacDonald Fraser, 'Mainly little chaps', Fraser (ed.), *The World of Public Schools*, p. 113.

76 '... man needs the alienation of abstraction (i.e. the negation of his reality) to a certain degree. He needs it in order to feel at home again in his traditional, taken-for-granted world. Legends and mythologies about strange people in remote countries or about mythological figures in pre-historic days function as mirrors that enable man to believe more firmly and understand more clearly his everyday reality and taken-for-granted structures. They are a looking glass that offers a magnificent opportunity to wander around in awe-inspiring strange worlds. Such odysseys through abstraction make homecoming desirable and the burdens of everyday life more bearable.' Anton C. Zijderveld, *The Abstract Society: A Cultural Analysis of Our Time*, Harmondsworth, 1974, p. 55.

77 *Ibid*.

78 On becoming headmaster, a man was expected to take an interest in masonry. Tim Heald, *Networks*, London, 1983, p. 183.

79 *Ibid*. p. 185.

80 Henry C. Clausen, *Misconception of the Scottish Rite Mission*, Washington, 1983, p. 8.

81 Roberts, *The Mythology of the Secret Societies*, p. 349.

82 *Ibid*.

83 Partner, *The Murdered Magicians*, p. 177.

84 GLE: *Supreme Grand Chapter Notice*, 18 April 1986, London, p. 4.

85 For a summary of conventional historical views of anti-masonry and a revisionist view of its place in class struggles, see Kathleen Kutolowski, 'Anti-masonry Re-examined'. *The Journal of American History*, Vol. 71, No. 2, September 1984, pp. 269 ff.

86 Hugh Dalton claimed masonry was a factor in Attlee's selection as head of the Labour Party. Knight, *The Brotherhood*, p. 208.

87 *Ibid*. p. 245 and *passim*.

88 For further reading, Knight's *The Brotherhood* is controversial but useful. Heald gives a modern gloss to the old–boy connection. Henderson is indispensable for anyone not familiar with masonic history. A reading of the ritual of the first three degrees is necessary to make sense of masonic publications. An accurate exposé is Malcolm C. Duncan, *Duncan's Masonic Ritual and Monitor, or Guide to the Three Symbolic Degrees*, Chicago, 1974, Revised Edition, Parts I and II. The premier masonic research journal is *Ars Quatuor Coronatorium*.

CHAPTER TEN

Education, emigration and empire: the Colonial College, 1887–1905

Patrick A. Dunae

I

The British public schools and the British Empire represent one of the greatest institutional partnerships in modern history. The reciprocal relationship between the two was especially striking during the late Victorian and Edwardian years, when the empire was at its height and when the schools enjoyed immense prestige. By imbuing young men with a respect for tradition, by teaching them how to excercise power, by lauding physical prowess and loyalty, and by extolling the civilising mission of the Anglo-Saxon race, the British public schools created a spirit which, as A. P. Thornton remarked, came to be 'one of the most potent of the imperial elixirs'.[1] That elixir, in turn, vitalised the public schools in such a way that the spirit of empire and the public schools' ethos were virtually synonomous terms.

Contemporaries were well aware of this relationship and took great pride in it. Their pride — which is evident not only in headmasters' speeches and school magazines, but also in the art, music and popular literature of the period — was not entirely misplaced.[2] Without question, graduates of the public schools did play an important role in the empire and their achievements as military officers and colonial administrators were considerable. But public-school alumni did not distinguish themselves in all parts of the empire or in all the other tropical dependencies; they often experienced difficulties when they emigrated to places like Canada, New Zealand, and Australia. In fact, it was generally conceded that in the wheat fields, sheep stations, cattle ranches and orchards of Greater Britain, the average public schoolboy was apt to be, at least initially, 'a conspicuous failure'.[3]

Cultural baggage contributed to some difficulties the youths faced in the dominions and white settlement colonies. The youths' preoccupation with sport, for example, and their social exclusiveness tended to hamper their progress on the utilitarian, relatively democratic frontiers of the empire. Their ignorance of local geography and economic conditions was also a handicap. In most instances, though, new chums from the Old Country lacked 'knowhow'; that is to say, they were unfamiliar with the basic requirements of agriculture and stock-raising and with the basic skills of settler life.

Many of these handicaps could be overcome at the Colonial College. Located at Hollesley Bay, Suffolk, the college was established in the 1880s for the express purpose of turning classically-educated schoolboys into hardy, independent colonists. To that end, the college offered courses in veterinary medicine, soil chemistry, carpentry, and surveying. It employed instructors who were familiar with colonial agricultural techniques and who could provide students with first-hand knowledge of settler life. But, as this essay will show, the Colonial College was more than just a training centre for middle-class emigrants. It was, in all senses of the word, an imperial institute. In an environment replete with imperial symbolism, the principal of the college and his supporters worked assiduously at developing a heightened sense of empire among students. Emigration within the empire was depicted as an imperial work and students were encouraged to regard themselves as imperial crusaders. By fostering such attitudes, and by providing youthful emigrants with useful skills, the Colonial College went a long way towards reaffirming the imperial importance of the British public schoolboy overseas.

II

Between 1880 and 1914 almost three million adult males emigrated from the United Kingdom.[4] Most of the emigrants were general labourers who were seeking better economic opportunities and a less stratified society. However, a significant portion of this emigrant army — a cadre approximately 300,000 strong — consisted of well-born, well-educated, relatively affluent men known as 'gentlemen emigrants'.[5] Traditionally, gentlemen emigrants included a large number of middle-aged family men who had decided, often reluctantly, to quit the Old Country for financial reasons. Typical of this type of emigrant was the half-pay army officer who was unable to maintain his social position and his large family on his paltry pension. During the last quarter of the nineteenth century, though, the ranks of the gentlemen emigrants came to be dominated by younger men who had recently completed their education in one of Britain's prestigious public schools or universities. Because of the incomplete data, precise figures are impossible to determine, but by all accounts emigration among public-school alumni was substantial. At Rugby, for instance, the number of Old Boys who settled overseas increased from six per cent in the 1840s to thirteen per cent in the 1870s. At Marlborough and Clifton College the proportion of emigrants increased to almost twenty per cent over the same period, and at Uppingham, Haileybury and Bradfield College, the proportion of emigrants among recent graduates was as high as one-third by the 1880s.[6] Why were so many of these youths settling overseas? Some emigrated from a sense of adventure, some migrated in search of wealth. Many emigrated because they were unable to secure places in gentlemanly professions at home.

The growth of the public-school system and the rise of the meritocracy were responsible for many of the difficulties career-oriented youths encountered in Britain. The number of public schools increased from a few dozen in the 1840s to over a hundred in the 1870s. This dramatic increase owed much to the commercial success of the middle classes who wished to provide their sons with the kind of education that had previously been the preserve of the aristocracy. They achieved their goal by founding new schools, such as Cheltenham (1841), Haileybury (1862) and Malvern (1865), and by reviving old grammar schools such as Uppingham (1654). In the spirit and in substance, the resuscitated grammar schools and the new proprietary schools were similar to the Great Schools, such as Eton, Harrow and Winchester. Like the 'Ancient Foundations', the new public schools were character-building institutions, whose main purpose was to produce manly, well-rounded, liberally-educated Christian *gentlemen*.

As the number of recognised public schools increased, so too did the gentlemanly population. In fact, during the middle years of the century, the number of youths attending first-grade public or grammar schools more than trebled.[7] Unhappily, though, the professions which were regarded as being most suitable for gentlemen could not accommodate this greatly enlarged pool of gentlemanly aspirants. Indeed, with the decline of patronage and the advent of competitive entrance examinations, career opportunities for public-school men in the army, the civil service and the liberal professions actually declined.[8] To make matters worse, the schools' archaic curricula (which placed an inordinate emphasis on classical studies) did not prepare youths for new careers involving science and technology. Nor was the 'cult of athleticism', which characterised the late-Victorian public schools, of much practical use to young men seeking places in an industrialised and increasingly specialised society. One result of this situation was the emergence of a new social class — a class of supernumerary gentlemen. It was a class, as one critic observed, made up of 'muscular Christian ... Tom Brown-types'. 'Grown up and growing up, we see them everywhere: bright-eyed, clean-limbed, high-minded; ready for anything and fit for nothing.'[9]

The supernumerary gentlemen gave rise to what the Victorians called 'the younger son question'. The question was debated in the Pall Mall clubs, in the daily newspapers, at meetings of public-school headmasters, and in countless middle-class drawing rooms. It was discussed at length in *Macmillan's Magazine*, the *Nineteenth Century* and in other influential reviews, and in dozens of books bearing such titles as *Our Boys: What Shall We Do With Them?* (1889).[10] The debate inspired several proposals, including one that the government create an élite cavalry regiment, the ranks of which would be comprised entirely of younger sons.[11] But most commentators — Thomas Hughes among them — agreed that the most satisfactory answer to the question was emigration. And so it was that many Tom Browns headed for the colonies soon after they left their schools and colleges.[12]

The majority of the young emigrants took up farming or stock-raising, an understandable choice since agricultural lands in the colonies were free or relatively inexpensive. In colonial parlance, a number of the emigrants 'made good'. A few even became wheat tycoons, cattle barons and shepherd kings. Many others, however, subsisted on marginal holdings, eking out an existence on allowances they received from their relatives at home. Accounts of the latter began to appear frequently in newspapers and travellers' books. 'To speak broadly,' a (London) *Times* correspondent reported, after touring the wheatlands of Western Canada in 1893,

> it must be said that the young Englishman of the better classes sent out to the North-West to be a farmer is not a success. The consensus of opinion which I discovered among practical men upon this point was very striking and the general settlement is not disproved by the many exceptions. The labouring man coming from ... the Old Country to the West with scarce a dollar will in a few years be a fairly prosperous settler, with a good farm and an increasing stock. The young Englishman, coming with the apparent advantage of some capital and a quarterly of half-yearly remittance from home, at the end of the same time has not got nearly so far ...[13]

Similar observations were made by a reporter who had travelled extensively in the United States and Australia. 'Nothing is more strange to the English visitor in a new country than to notice the extraordinary reversal of position which takes place [among British immigrants],' he wrote,

> He sees younger sons of good families leading miserable, hand-to-mouth existences, badly dressed, ill-fed, and in too many cases with that shabby, unshaven appearance which is the surest sign of loss of self-respect. On the other hand, he meets sons of mechanics or farm labourers, men who had never had anything but a board school education, and not much of that, prosperous, well-dressed, and making money hand over fist.[14]

Other reports indicated that young gentlemen tended to be among the most unpopular of settlers — something which was usually attributed to their haughty mannerisms, their tendency to neglect work in favour of sport, and their predilection for drink. It was also noted that the public-school alumni were apt to be dismissed as 'remittance men' — a term of approbation that implied a scapegrace and ne'er-do-well, someone who had been exiled to the colonies and was paid to remain there because he was an embarrassment to his family in Britain.[15]

These reports disturbed Britain's headmasters, who feared that their unsuccessful old boys would bring the much-vaunted public schools into disrepute. The reports worried imperialists and emigration authorities who feared that gently-bred incompetents would blacken the reputations of conscientious British immigrants. Many parties, in fact, including those who had no direct links with the public schools were concerned that steps be taken to ensure the success of emigrant gentlemen. But how was this to be accomplished? How were public schoolboys (whom *The Times* correspondent likened to high-spirited thoroughbreds) to be turned into steady and industrious draught horses? According to most writers, the first step was to ensure that emigrants possessed the right attitude. Prospective emigrants who had been reared in comfortable surroundings were told to prepare for rough conditions and hard physical labour; they were advised to temper their athletic enthusiasms and to dispense with any élitist notions they might have. As one headmaster cautioned, public schoolboys who settled in the dominions would not find themselves among the empire's 'submissive races'. Rather, he said youths would be dealing with 'a people who were not accustomed to obey ... a people entirely free from subservience to rank or wealth, a people intolerant therefore of dictation or condescension'.[16]

A conscientious attitude, an accommodating disposition and a realistic appreciation of local conditions would certainly have facilitated the progress of novice settlers. But even more important was a practical knowledge of agriculture and stock-raising. Without that knowledge, it was said, even well-intentioned emigrants would have difficulty establishing themselves as independent settlers in the developing parts of the empire. Fortunately, the Colonial College was at hand.

The Colonial College was founded by Robert Johnson, a gentleman farmer from Boynton, near Woodbridge, in Suffolk. Johnson had many interests and many talents. He was an astute businessman and an accomplished artist; he was an amateur architect and a pioneer in the field of urban planning; he was a philanthropist, widely known in East Anglia for establishing savings banks and sick-benefit societies for agricultural labourers; he was a penal reformer and a charter member of the Discharged Prisoners' Aid Society. His other main interests were scientific agriculture, emigration and imperialism — causes he combined and promoted through the medium of the Colonial College.[17]

Johnson decided to establish his college after receiving unfavourable reports on young emigrants from friends in the colonies. One correspondent told him of inexperienced youths who, after losing their money and confidence, had become 'idle and reckless' in South Africa. Another friend noted that '*most*... of the young men who are sent out from the Mother Country are miserably unfitted to grapple with the difficulties of a settler's life [in Canada]'. From a third he learned of 'the disastrous and cruel consequences of the too common practice of wrenching a young man suddenly from the comforts of home and throwing him into a new country to make his way without preparation and training'. These reports did not alter Johnson's opinion of the British public schoolboy, whom he regarded highly; rather, they confirmed his opinion that the middle classes were much too casual in their approach to emigration. 'Colonisation,' he asserted, 'is a profession which requires preparation like any other.'[18] To assist youths who intended to enter this profession, Johnson incorporated the Colonial College and Training Farms Limited in 1885. He installed himself as Chairman of the company's Board of Directors and principal of the college. An official from the National Bank of Australia in London and three Suffolk businessmen, along with members of Johnson's family, were invited to act as co-directors.[19]

After incorporating the college, Johnson and his partners set about promoting it among upper and middle-class families. They received considerable assistance from the Major General the Hon. William Feilding, a younger son of the Earl of Denbigh, who had written several articles on the emigrant gentlemen for the *Nineteenth Century*.[20] They also received valuable support from the headmasters of Eton, Westminster, Shrewsbury, Marlborough, Clifton, Haileybury and Dulwich, all of whom agreed to serve as patrons of the college. Other patrons included the agents-general of British Columbia, Tasmania, Queensland, South Australia, Victoria and the Cape Colony, executive councillors of the Royal Colonial Institute, and local members of parliament. Together, they formed a stellar group which readily inspired public confidence in the new academy.

The college site was no less inspiring. Situated behind the River Alde and the shingle banks of Hollesley Bay, the property consisted of almost two thousand acres of arable farmland. The main buildings were of neo-Gothic design and contained offices, lecture rooms, laboratories and dormitories. Beyond the main hall was a modern creamery, an experimental farm with elaborate greenhouses, and workshops for resident blacksmiths, wheelwrights and carpenters. The site also contained a large apiary and extensive stables. The stables provided shelter for the school's celebrated Suffolk Punches, heavily-built, good-natured draught horses. That the Colonial College specialised in developing this breed of horse seemed to underline the founder's intention of transforming thoroughbred youths into sturdy colonists.

Tuition was expensive: annual fees were £175, with additional fees being charged for equipment and extra-curricular activities. But the Colonial College, which formally opened in February 1887, had no difficulty attracting students. On average, fifty new students were enrolled each year and by 1900 over 700 had earned certificates of competency from the college. Most of these young men — or 'Old Colonials'. as college alumni were termed — had previously attended a major public school.[21]

To earn a certificate of competency, students were required to complete a two-year programme. The syllabus varied, but usually involved five hours of 'outdoor instruction' and two hours of lectures per day. The outdoor part of the curriculum was conducted by artisans and experienced agriculturists who provided the students with instruction in metalwork, carpentry, harness-making, horticulture and related subjects. As far as possible, instruction was geared to colonial practices. Thus, students were introduced to western stock saddles and learned how to construct buildings with lumber rather than bricks. The indoor part of the syllabus involved lectures in soil chemistry, geology, botany, veterinary science and land surveying. The lectures were provided by 'professors' who had trained at the Royal Agricultural College, at the Ontario Agricultural College, and other leading technical schools. The Colonial College also offered courses on domestic arts and book-keeping, on the grounds that it was as important for a settler to manage his money and household as it was for him to manage a herd of livestock.

In most of these cases, great emphasis was placed on theory or, as Johnson called it, 'prosaic detail'. Such detail, the principal told his staff, was vital if the college was to produce competent and innovative colonists:

> We have to tell [students] that if they are to be successful owners or cultivators of land, they must study the principles as well as the practice of agriculture; if they are to own flocks and herds, they must understand that the prevention of disease is better than its cure, and that a knowledge of the proper and rational methods of feeding and treatment is of the highest scientific and commercial importance; that if they are to build new houses, to lay out new cities, to reclaim, to plant, to irrigate, to drain, to prospect ... they must bring to bear *informed intelligence* as well as the strong arm and the undaunted will.

Johnson's concern for 'prosaic detail' was indicative of his own interest in scientific agriculture and his abiding faith in the intellectual abilities of the Tom Browns he was committed to train.[22]

The Hollesley Bay Colonial College was not solely devoted to work, though. The 'ideal colonist', in Johnson's opinion, was a 'good, sound all-rounder' — a man who was well-read, well-spoken and well co-ordinated.[23] Accordingly, the college supported a dramatic society and a debating club, and, while the principal was critical of the public schools' preoccupation with organised sports,[24] the Colonial College did not stint in athletics. Colonials, in their distinctive green and gold colours, fielded some of the best football teams in East Anglia; the college had an active lawn tennis club and its XI was well-regarded in cricket circles. Students were equally proficient in aquatic sports, the Colonial College Regatta being one of the highlights of the Suffolk summer.

The Colonial College's reputation as an agricultural school, its success in stock-breeding, and its ability to produce 'good, sound all-rounders' won it unqualified praise from the public. The *Educational Review* commended Johnson for making a 'valuable contribution' to the field of technical education, while the *Army and Navy Gazette* described the college as being 'pre-eminently good'. The college was endorsed by *The Times*, the *Field* and the *Spectator*, and was the subject of feature articles in the *Daily Graphic* and the *Captain* (a magazine devoted to public schoolboys).[25] All of these publications applauded the college curriculum and philosophy; all spoke highly of its informative magazine, *Colonia*, which carried technical articles and reports from graduates overseas. But what most impressed the visitors to the Colonial College was its imperial character. 'The most interesting point in the multifarious energies of the Colonial College,' the *Boy's Own Paper* reported, 'is the consistency with which a real interest in the life of the Empire at large is maintained in every possible manner.'[26]

Indeed, the college's devotion to the empire and its imperial character were its most striking features. This was as Johnson intended when he opened the facility. He envisaged the school as a sister institution to the Royal Colonial Institute and the Imperial Institute. The role of the two institutes, he said, was to disseminate information and popularise the empire; the complementary mission of the college was to 'train the men who will carry forward the flag of the great mother of Nations, sustain her good name the world over, open up new lands, open new markets [and] create new industries ...'. Johnson had also hoped that the colleges would become 'a depository of colonial lore' and that the whole environment at Hollesley Bay would be 'redolent of colonial life'.[27] He succeeded on both counts. Flags, badges and coats-of-arms from the Canadian provinces and the colonies of South Africa and Australia hung in the college dining hall. The walls of the lecture theatres and passageways were decorated with wheatsheaves, fleeces and other colonial products. Maps of imperial possessions and pictures of colonial life graced dormitory walls. The library — which one visitor said contained 'more accurate, reliable and up-to-date information on the colonies than any other place in Britain, including the Colonial Office'[28] – housed an impressive collection of statistical reports and other imperialistic publications. Even the horses that were foaled at the Hollesley Bay stud — Sydney 2783, Tasmania 3205, Winnipeg 3494 — were named so as to underscore the school's devotion to Greater Britain.

And then there were the many dignitaries who came to the college on Speech Days. In 1899 students were addressed by the Marquis of Lorne, former Governor-General of Canada. The next year the Secretary of State for the Colonies, Lord Knutsford, took the podium. He was followed by Sir Napier Broome (former Governor of Western Australia), Sir Graham Berry (Premier of Victoria) and Sir Frederick Young (Vice-President of the Royal Colonial Institute). In subsequent years the speakers included Sir George Parkin, the empire's pre-eminent publicist; Sir Arthur Hodgson, an Old Etonian shepherd king and former Premier of Queensland; Sir Richard Martin, commandant of the British South African Police Force, and a host of colonial agents-general, bishops, ranchers, planters, railway magnates and politicians. All of the speakers emphasised the imperial role of the college. All urged intending emigrants to think of themselves as 'imperial crusaders'.[29]

For many of these visitors, the imperial crusade involved imperial federation. At a Speech Day ceremony in 1890, A. H. Loring, Secretary of the Imperial Federation League, stressed the importance of a cohesive imperial policy and of the economic benefits which would result from preferential trade agreements within the empire. He expressed the hope that out-going colonials would become members of the league and that afterwards, when they had attained positions of influence in their respective colonies, they would work towards realising the league's objectives.[30] The principal of the college expressed similar hopes and continued to advance the cause of imperial federation long after the Imperial Federation League broke up in 1893. Unlike some of his associates, though, Johnson envisaged a federation that would include the United States. 'Then indeed,' he said, in a phrase that recalled Cecil Rhodes, 'might we hope that the Anglo-Saxon race might carry out a great mission to the ends of the earth to maintain the peace of the world.'[31]

Johnson's vision of a united, all-embracing Anglo-Saxon empire was graphically expressed in the Colonial College flag which hung in the main dining hall. The flag was quartered by a broad cross featuring the stars and stripes of the American republic. The upper-left quarter featured the Union Jack and the Star of India; the lower-left quarter contained the armorial bearings of the Dominion of Canada on a red background. The badges of the Australian colonies were shown against a yellow field in the upper-right quarter, while a shield representing the Cape Colony was displayed against a blue background on the fly. Superimposed at the centre was another shield, representing the Royal Standard of Britain. Cluttered though it was, the Colonial College banner was probably the most colourful and comprehensive flag in the empire.

III

The principal's respect for his American cousins notwithstanding, the main purpose of the Colonial College was to direct young men to imperial possessions. 'The Training of Youths for Colonial Life' was, after all, the college motto. In this regard, the Hollesley Bay Institute could claim a very high success rate. According to one report, over seventy per cent of its graduates emigrated and, judging from the school's Old Students' Directories, the majority of them settled 'under the Flag'.[32]

Table 1 is based on available directories for the years 1889 to 1902. The directories are not definitive, for they listed only those graduates who had emigrated and who were willing to provide the editors of *Colonia* with information concerning their whereabouts. Still, in the absence of other records, the directories provide a useful guide to the migratory trends, occupational preferences, and settlement patterns of public-school emigrants during the apogee of empire.

As may be seen in Table 1, the proportion of Colonial College graduates who settled within the empire was consistently high: it increased from seventy-four per cent in the early 1890s to over eighty per cent a decade later. The relative magnitude of Colonial College graduates to destinations within the empire was, in fact, significantly greater than the national average over the whole period, since the majority of British emigrants did not direct their attentions to imperial possessions until after 1906. And even then less than sixty per cent settled within the empire, well below the Colonial College's mark.[33]

The names of Old Colonials who had settled in the various parts of the empire were engraved on plaques which were displayed beneath appropriate flags in the college dining hall. It was a nice touch and added to the patriotic tone of the school. Patriotism, however, was not the emigrants' sole propellent. The young crusaders who emigrated from Hollesley Bay were motivated by economic considerations as well, and to a large extent these considerations determined where they settled within the empire. Hence, few Colonials went to the tropical dependencies in West

Table 1

Period and destination	No. of recorded Colonial College immigrants	Percentage of recorded Colonial College emigrants
1889–93		
Australia	28	18
Brit. South Africa	16	10
Canada	36	23
New Zealand	26	17
Other British:		
India, Ceylon, Burma	7	5
West Indies	2	1
Total empire	115	74
Foreign:		
United States	35	23
South America	5	3
Total	155	100
1894–96		
Australia	35	16
Brit. South Africa	31	14
Canada	45	21
New Zealand	36	16
Other British:		
India, Ceylon, Burma	19	9
West Indies	5	2
Total empire	171	78
Foreign:		
United States	37	17
South America	10	5
Total	218	100
1897–99		
Australia	38	15
Brit. South Africa	42	17
Canada	43	18
New Zealand	43	18
Other British:		
India, Ceylon, Burma	27	11
West Indies	2 ⎫	
Falkland Islands	1 ⎬	2
Egypt	1 ⎭	2
Total empire	197	81
Foreign:		
United States	35	14
South America	12	5
France	1	—
Total	245	100

Period and destination	No. of recorded Colonial College immigrants	Percentage of recorded Colonial College emigrants
1900–02		
Australia	36	14
Brit. South Africa	50	19
Canada	55	21
New Zealand	40	15
Other British:		
India, Ceylon, Burma	28	9
West Indies	4 ⎫	
Falkland Islands	1 ⎬	3
Egypt	2 ⎭	
Total empire	216	81
Foreign:		
United States	36	14
South America	12	4
France	2 ⎫	1
Tunis	1 ⎭	1
Total	267	100

Africa and the West Indies, where opportunities for independent settlers were limited. Similarly, relatively few went to India or Ceylon where, according to one Old Colonial, novice planters received 'a wretched pittance' from the large tea companies who employed most of the European settlers.[34] Instead, the majority of Old Colonials migrated to the dominions and the white-settlement colonies. There, with a modest amount of capital, they could put their training to good use.

Canada, as Table 1 shows, attracted the greatest number of Colonial College graduates. The dominion's favoured position was due in part to its proximity to Britain and to the aggressive advertising campaign waged by Canadian government immigration authorities. An accessible frontier, a booming economy, and the availability of free homesteads were inducements to Old Colonials like Arthur Headlam, one of Johnson's first graduates. Headlam arrived in Manitoba in 1889 and spent his first year working on a large wheat farm near Brandon. He then established his own farm at Portage la Prairie, where he devised a method of refrigerating dairy products. 'I am getting on famously and am quite used to the work,' he wrote in the first of many letters he sent to *Colonia*.[35] William Fraser got on famously too. Having graduated from the Colonial College in 1890, Fraser made his way to Cannington Manor, an aristocratic community in Assiniboia (Saskatchewan). Cannington Manor had its own hunt club and racecourse and was known as one of the sportiest places in the West. But, like other gentlemen's colonies in North America, it was a rather frivolous place where residents played, rather than worked, at farming. Realising this, Fraser moved on to Alberta where he established a cattle ranch. A pioneer in the use of cattle vaccines, Fraser became one of the leading stock growers in the territory. Before relocating in British Columbia (another area much favoured by Old Colonials), Fraser also introduced the Suffolk Punch to the Canadian Prairie West.[36]

Several of Fraser's classmates — including Trollope's son, Frederick — began their careers in Australia. Of those who immigrated 'down under', most settled on sheep stations in Queensland and orchards in Tasmania. The Taranaki region on the North Island of New Zealand also attracted several dozen Old Colonials, the majority of whom took up dairy farming. But by the late 1890s, as Table 10.1 indicates, the Antipodes had lost its place as a favourite destination to southern Africa. The agricultural districts of the Cape Colony and Natal were the most popular, although a few Old Colonials were engaged in mining in the Transvaal. The largest single employer in the region, however, was the British South Africa Company which hired a number of Hollesley Bay men as assayers, surveyors, building inspectors and veterinarians in Mashonaland and Matabeleland (Rhodesia).

As might be expected, the Old Colonials who had settled in southern Africa were among the first to enlist at the start of the Anglo–Boer War in 1899. It was not long before they were joined by their confrères from other parts of the empire. Arthur Headlam, for example, left his farm in Manitoba to join an imperial regiment headed for the Cape. He subsequently transferred to a colonial unit and saw out the war as Superintendent of Police in Pretoria. Other Old Colonials came out with the Canadian Mounted Rifles and with various units raised in Australia and New Zealand. The letters they sent to *Colonia* reveal a tremendous élan and the kind of imperial fraternity that inspired Kipling's Boer War poem, 'The Parting of the Columns' (1903):[37]

Think o' the stories round the fire, the tales along the trek —
O' Calgary an' Wellin'ton, and Sydney and Quebec.

Their letters also indicate a continuing appreciation for the training they received at Hollesley Bay. 'Since I turned my ploughshare into a sword I have been in many queer places and played many parts,' a former student who had joined the South African Field Force wrote, '[and] I can assure you I found all I learnt at the College of the greatest use to me...'[38]

Understandably, Johnson was immensely gratified by these letters, for they indicated to him that the spirit he had fostered at the college had taken root with his students. A peaceable man, he was even more pleased with the reports he received from Old Colonials who were making their way as ranchers, dairymen, farmers and horticulturalists. Their success was proof of the efficiency of his system. Johnson's former students, in turn, appreciated the interest which he took in their endeavours; indeed, if the letters he wrote to William Fraser are representative, Johnson continued to stand as mentor, friend and confidante to his boys long after they had left Hollesley Bay.[39] For many of these Old Colonials, Johnson's death at the age of sixty-five in 1901 must have been a great loss.

Certainly his death was a great blow to the Colonial College. As well as being the founder of the institute, Johnson had been its sustaining force. Without him the college floundered. The other directors of the Colonial College and Training Farms Limited seemed to lack Johnson's energy and organisational abilities. They also lacked his financial skills and in 1905, after a record deficit, the college was forced to close. The following year the property was auctioned and acquired for £36,000 by the Central Body for London. Re-named the Hollesley Bay Farm Colony, the facility was used to retrain unemployed urban labourers.[40]

The Colonial College closed at a time when public-school emigration was increasing and almost immediately efforts were made to fill the void it had left. Modifying the curriculum which Johnson had developed, the Royal Agricultural College established a special six-month programme for intending emigrants. The Headmasters' Conference organised a Public Schools' Emigration League, while at least two public schools — Bradfield College and Berkhamsted — established residential training farms and ranches for their old boys overseas.[41] Although these initiatives were valuable, none was as comprehensive or as wide-ranging as the programmes the Colonial College had offered.

IV

Robert Johnson is not remembered today as a reforming educationalist, nor is he remembered by historians as one of the leading imperial propagandists of the late-nineteenth century. Clearly, he deserves to be recognised as both. Like Welldon of Harrow, Moss of Shrewsbury, Thring of Uppingham and the other imperially-minded headmasters of the period, Johnson was responsible for raising the imperial consciousness of public-school alumni. With them, he reinforced the bond between the schools and the empire and helped to make the imperial elixir more potent. But unlike many of his contemporaries, Johnson was a pragmatist. He realised that imperial enthusiasm and a public-school education were not by themselves passports to success. On the agricultural frontiers of the empire at least, young Britains had to be well-prepared and adequately armed with theoretical knowledge and practical skills. In other words they had to be 'professionals'.

By depicting colonisation as a skilled profession, Johnson helped to make overseas settlement a respectable and exciting career for many erstwhile supernumerary gentlemen. 'Bright-eyed, clean-limbed, and high minded', the Tom Browns who followed his regimen were ready and fit for a great many careers which might otherwise have been denied to them. Thanks to the patriotic catechism of the Colonial College, the young emigrants who answered Johnson's call could also begin their careers secure in the knowledge that they were part of an important imperial crusade. With Johnson's help they were able to play a part that was expected of them. They became empire-builders, whose success in the fields and forests of Greater Britain did much to reaffirm the imperial traditions of the British public schoolboy.

Notes

1 A. P. Thornton, *The Imperial Idea and Its Enemies*, London, 1966, p. 90.

2 See J. A. Mangan, 'Images of empire in the late Victorian public school', *Journal of Educational Administration and History*, 12, January 1980, pp. 31–9 and Mangan, '"The grit of our forefathers". Invented traditions, propaganda, and imperialism' in John M. Mackenzie (ed.), *Imperialism and Popular Culture*, Manchester, 1986. Many other studies — including Rupert Wilkinson, *The Prefects*, London, 1964 and L. H. Gann and P. Duigan, *The Rulers of British Africa*, London, 1978 — have dealt with the relationship between the schools and the empire. But perhaps the best statement on the Victorians' view of the subject is Lady Butler's celebrated painting, *Floret Etona!*, 1882.

3 Herbert Branston Gray, *The Public Schools and the Empire*, London, 1913, p. 30.

4 Brinley Thomas, *Migration and Economic Growth*, Cambridge, 1954, pp. 59–63.

5 This estimate is based on figures provided by Thomas, *Migration and Economic Growth*, pp. 59–63, Frank Musgrove, *The Migratory Elite*, London, 1963 and W. A. Carrothers, *Emigration from the British Isles*, London, 1929, p. 315.

6 T. W. Bamford, *Rise of the Public Schools*, London, 1967, p. 210; Musgrove, *Migratory Elite*, pp. 21 and 173; W. J. Reader, *Professional Men*, London, 1966, pp. 212–14.

7 Bamford, *Rise of the Public Schools*, pp. 18–36.

8 Musgrove, 'Middle class education and employment in the nineteenth century', *Economic History Review*, 2nd ser., 12, 1959, pp. 99–111.

9 S. H. Jeyes, 'Our gentlemanly failures', *Fortnightly Review*, 61, 1 March 1897, p. 388.

10 James Aspdin, *Our Boys: What Shall We Do With Them? or, Emigration — The Real Solution of the Problem*, Manchester, 1889. Other examples of the genre include W. Stamer, *The Gentleman Emigrant: His Daily Life, Sports, and Pastimes in Canada, Australia and the United States*, London, 1874; John J. Rowan, *The Emigrant and Sportsman in Canada*, London, 1881; 'Outlying professions', *Blackwood's Edinburgh Magazine*, 136, November 1884, pp. 579–91, and 'Gentlemen emigrants', *Macmillan's Magazine*, 58, May 1888, pp. 30–40.

11 J. Henniker Heaton, 'An imperial corps d'élite: a suggestion', *Pall Mall Magazine*, 4, October 1894, pp. 334–41; Jeyes, 'Our gentlemanly failures', pp. 392–3.

12 A more detailed discussion of the factors and circumstances which prompted public schoolboys to emigrate is to be found in my *Gentlemen Emigrants: From the Public Schools to the Canadian Frontier*, Manchester, 1982. Although the discussion centres on the dominion, it is equally applicable to other parts of the empire.

13 *The Times* (London), 31 January 1894.

14 T. C. Bridges, 'On training boys for colonial life: advice to parents of public schoolboys', *Empire Review*, 15, February 1908, pp. 62–4.

15 The term 'remittance man' originated in Australia in the 1880s and by the 1890s was a common expression in many parts of the empire. See Edward E. Morris, *Austral English*, London, 1898, and D. Wallace Duthie, 'The remittance man', *Nineteenth Century*, 46, November 1899, pp. 827–32.

16 Gray, *Public Schools and the Empire*, pp. 20–1.

17 Dunae, *Gentlemen Emigrants*, p. 200; *Annual Register*, 1901, p. 138.

18 Robert Johnson, 'The origin of the Colonial College', *Colonia: The Colonial College Magazine*, 1, April 1889, pp. 4–5; 'The ideal colonist', *Colonia*, 4, August 1896, p. 175.

19 Public Record Office. Great Britain. Board of Trade. Registrar of Companies. BT 31/3492/21224. Colonial College and Training Farms Limited Memorandum and Articles of Association.

20 See William Henry Adelbert Feilding, 'What shall I do with my son?', *Nineteenth Century*, 13, April 1883, and Feilding, 'Whither shall I send my son?', *Ibid*. 14, July 1883.

21 *Boy's Own Paper*, 23, 17 November 1900, p. 111.

22 *Colonia*, 3, April 1895, p. 325.

23 *Ibid*. 1, August 1890, p. 165.

24 Johnson felt that J. E. C. Welldon, headmaster of Harrow, attached 'undue value to the influence of athletic sports' in the formation of Britain's national character in a speech which Welldon gave in 1895. In support of his contention, Johnson noted that 'men of business in the colonies' complained that English public–school men were 'inordinately concerned with sports and were disappointed unless they could play their half time'. *Colonia*, 3, April 1895, p. 322. Welldon's address, entitled 'The imperial aspects of education', was printed in the Royal Colonial Institute *Proceedings*, 26, 1894–95, pp. 322–49. On the schools' preoccupation with sport generally, see J. A. Mangan, *Athleticism in the Victorian and Edwardian Public School*, Cambridge, 1981.

25 *Extracts From Press Notices of Colonia*, Woodbridge, 1896; *Daily Graphic*, 6 January 1890; *Education*, January 1891; *Captain*, September 1899; *The Times*, 2 September 1901.

26 *Boy's Own Paper*, 23, 17 November 1900, p. 111.

27 Johnson, 'The Colonial College: a retrospect and a forecast', *Colonia*, 3, April 1895, p. 228; 'Origin of the college,' *Ibid*. 1, April 1889, p. 7.

28 R. E. MacNaughton, 'Emigration: a plea for state assistance', *Economic Review*, 8, January 1898, p. 20.

29 Speech Days were held in July of each year and reported in the August numbers of *Colonia*.

30 'Imperial Federation', *Colonia*, 1, April 1890, pp. 81–4.

31 *Ibid*. p. 79.

32 *Boy's Own Paper*, 12, 17 November 1900, p. 111.

33 Carrothers, *Emigration from the British Isles*, p. 314; Thomas, *Migration and Economic Growth*, p. 57.

34 *Colonia*, 5, December 1898, p. 140.

35 *Ibid*. 1, December 1898, p. 10.

36 Foothills Historical Society, *Chaps & Chinooks: A History West of Calgary*, Calgary, 1976, II, p. 288.

37 Rudyard Kipling, *The Five Nations*, Toronto, 1903, p. 175.

38 *Colonia*, 6, April 1901, p. 217.

39 I am grateful to J. A. W. (William) Fraser's daughters, Miss Daphne and Miss Diana Fraser of Sidney, British Columbia, for providing me with access to the letters Johnson wrote to their father. The Misses Fraser also provided me with copies of the Colonial College prospectus and other ephemeral publications used in this study.

40 *The Times*, 17 December 1906. The Hollesley Bay property changed hands a number of times over the following thirty years, until it was acquired by HM Prison Commissioners. Since 1938 it has served as a borstal home and rehabilitation centre for juvenile offenders. The facility still raises Suffolk Punches and a copy of the Old Colonial College flag adorns one of the stables.

41 Dunae, *Gentlemen Emigrants*, pp. 206–14.

CHAPTER ELEVEN

British colonial education policy: a synonym for cultural imperialism?

Clive Whitehead

In the late 1930s W. K. (later Sir Keith) Hancock warned historians to steer clear of the term 'Imperialism' because the emotional echoes it aroused were too violent and too contradictory and it had no precise meaning.[1] His warning has gone unheeded, especially among contemporary neo-Marxist revisionist writers, who rarely use the term cultural imperialism in other than a pejorative sense — the *conscious* and *deliberate* imposition of alien cultural values and beliefs on hapless indigenous peoples. One can, of course, argue that most colonial schooling was conducted initially by missionaries who were primarily concerned with religious conversion. That inevitably led them to attempt to reform some of the more objectionable aspects of indigenous cultures like polygamy, female circumcision and the power of witchcraft. In that sense the schools were culturally imperialistic, i.e. they encouraged the adoption of Christian (European) moral ideals, but an important distinction needs to be drawn between the missions' motives, which were largely dictated by a desire to improve the quality of human life, and those attributed to colonial governments by neo-Marxists who argue that colonial education policies were expressly designed to perpetuate European cultural and political hegemony. It is the latter interpretation of the term cultural imperialism, implying an obvious negative value judgement, which is questioned in this chapter.

Two aspects of British colonial education policy have been condemned by revisionist critics. The first was the concept of adaptation, which justified the provision of a form of education closely related to the local environment and to the rural lifestyle that most Africans and other colonial subjects seemed destined to lead in the 1920s. The second was the Western literary education provided for a small number of the indigenous population. Revisionists argue that the adaptation concept was deliberately fostered to maintain the subordinate status of the indigenous population, while the few who did receive a Western education were taught to accept the superiority of European culture and, by implication, their subordinate role in colonial society. In both instances it is claimed that indigenous intellects were colonised, i.e. they were taught to accept the inherent dominance of British culture and political control. In 1926 L. S. Amery, the Secretary of State for the Colonies, addressed the Imperial Conference in the following terms:

> Our whole endeavour now is to substitute for a purely literary education, not suited to the needs of the natives, a type of education more adapted to their mental aptitude — a type of education which, while conserving as far as possible all the sane and healthy elements in the fabric of their own social life, will also assist their growth and evolution on natural lines and enable them to absorb more progressive ideas; it aims, above all, at the building up of character on the part of the native, at giving him an understanding of his own environment, at making him useful in his own environment rather than at giving him the kind of education which is really only suitable in the environment of a country like Great Britain.[2]

Did this statement represent a genuine concern for the welfare of colonial peoples, or was it nothing more than a clever ploy to deny most of them a Western type of schooling in order to preserve Britain's cultural and socio-political dominance? I wish to argue that British policy was not a synonym for cultural imperialism in the pejorative sense. In retrospect, Amery's statement seems more like an expression of the confused nature of British colonial education policy in the 1920s than a blueprint for the perpetuation of British rule.

Martin Carnoy's celebrated study *Education as Cultural Imperialism*,[3] published in 1974, strongly condemned colonial schooling as part of a deliberate policy to perpetuate British imperial rule. His theoretical standpoint was challenged at the time by Mary Jean Bowman,[4] but recent articles by Udo Bude[5] and Marjorie Mbilinyi[6] suggest that there is no lack of contemporary support for his original thesis. Carnoy argued that considerations of power and conflict are central to all educational processes. In capitalist societies, schooling and education policy are instruments for the legitimation and maintenance of the ruling bourgeois class, and schools serve to channel youth into status and occupational roles that support the existing power structure. They also 'colonise' the minds of students to accept designations of inferiority that serve the capitalist class system. The application of this thesis to a colonial setting implies that education policy was designed primarily to preserve European hegemony. This *structuralist* view of education currently enjoys widespread support amongst many left-wing academics who are disenchanted with the liberal progressive or *incrementalist* approach, which has traditionally accepted the legitimacy of the existing economic order and an emphasis on the role of the school as a vehicle of individual enlightenment and as an agent of social reform.

A more scholarly and potentially damning indictment of British colonial education policy is contained in a doctoral study by D. G. Schilling, an American scholar, who traced the development of African education policy in Kenya during the period 1895-1930.[7] He argued that education policy was rooted in political and economic realities of life in Kenya which were influenced primarily by the aim of the British settlers to create a 'white man's country'. By the 1920s there was general support for African education but only, Schilling claimed, if it stressed discipline and the virtue of work and was not seen as a means to social advancement and growing political awareness. African education policy in Kenya was designed to nurture and sustain a colonialism in which Europeans retained the reins of power.

It is certainly true that British colonies containing significant numbers of European settlers posed major problems for the Colonial Office during the inter-war years — Schilling's criticisms of African education policy in Kenya applied equally to Southern Rhodesia and possibly also to Northern Rhodesia, with its strong European mining interests. European settlers were naturally keen to extend their political and economic influence, but they were thwarted by successive British governments which felt obliged to uphold the concept of trusteeship, with its clear emphasis on protecting the interests of indigenous or native peoples. Schilling provided strong evidence in support of his Kenya thesis, but the extension of his argument to include the activities of the London-based Advisory Committee on Education in the Colonies is much less convincing. He claimed that by attempting to avoid the earlier mistake made in India, i.e. the uncontrolled expansion of Western academic education through the medium of English, the Committee had an overtly political objective — to stifle African nationalism in order to perpetuate British rule. 'From its very inception the Advisory Committee had an overtly political object; and, while many of the issues with which it dealt over the years appeared to be purely educational, this political object formed the general context of its considerations.'[8]

Schilling's scholarly analysis contrasts with the passionate and often vitriolic criticisms levelled at colonial schooling by many colourful but nevertheless ardent neo-Marxist writers. The late Walter Rodney, for example, claimed that colonial schooling sought to instil a sense of deference towards all that was European and capitalist:

Colonial schooling was education for subordination, exploitation, the creation of mental confusion ... an instrument to serve the European capitalist class in its exploitation of Africa. Whatever colonial educators thought or did could not change that basic fact ... with regard to colonial education policy one comes closest to finding the elements of conscious planning by a group of Europeans to control the destiny of millions of Africans.[9]

Samir Amin, writing in a leading Unesco journal in the mid–1970s, likewise suggested that colonial education had the merit of being consistent in its 'cynical brutality'.[10] He claimed that it had two basic goals; the destruction of traditional or indigenous forms of education 'with a view to uprooting the national culture and consciousness', and the training of an élite of subordinate servants. Other prominent critics of colonial schooling sharing a similar ideology include Ivan Illich,[11] Albert Memmi,[12] Paulo Freire,[13] Franz Fanon[14] and Abdou Moumouni.[15]

Their type of criticism may have served a political purpose in the aftermath of independence when anti-colonial passions were uppermost, but a more dispassionate assessment is surely called for now, involving a more impartial consideration of what the situation looked like at the time to those responsible for making decisions. As H. A. Gailey, the American historian, has remarked, the British Empire should be judged by the standards and aspirations of the period and not by the beliefs of present-day society.[16] Professor A. Fajana likewise remarked, in his inaugural address at the University of Ife in 1982, that it is easy to criticise Nigeria's former colonial education system from the standpoint of the present including, one might add, current 'theories' of history, but it is only realistic to do so in the light of a full understanding of the best of contemporary educational thought of the period and the *range of choices that were open*[17].

In reviewing Carnoy's work, Mary Jean Bowman of the University of Chicago wondered just what sort of evidence he would conceivably accept as running counter to his argument and what policies he would endorse today as having other than socially pernicious effects on all but a privileged segment of the population. She suggested that empirical evidence to support or refute Carnoy's position would require assessments of both motivation or intent in the formulation and implementation of education policies and of the actual societal effects of education systems and their operations. An analysis of that magnitude lies beyond the bounds of this chapter. Instead, I propose to confine myself to the more limited task of examining the stated policy which theoretically guided the development of schooling in British colonial territories in the years between the two world wars and reactions to it. In particular, I wish to highlight the idealism and the confusion of purpose in the determination of education policy, both in London and in the colonies. This was brought about mainly by a determination on the part of many colonial officials to avoid a repetition of the mistakes commonly acknowledged to have been made in India in the preceding century, and also by the controversial nature of the principle of trusteeship as embodied in the League of Nations' mandates. I wish to argue that the evidence derived from official sources and from men and women who were influential in the formulation of British policy casts serious doubt on any suggestion that education was deliberately used as a means of enforcing British cultural hegemony in the colonies. Most colonial schooling certainly mirrored schooling in Britain, but there is ample evidence to suggest that this was more a reflection of local demand on the part of indigenous peoples themselves, than an indication of any deliberate British policy to colonise the indigenous intellect.

During the inter-war years British colonial education policy was characterised by what amounted in practice to an essentially *laissez-faire* philosophy. At the local level, widespread adherence to the voluntary principle ensured that most schools were established and operated by a varied assortment of missions and other local interest groups, while in Whitehall, policy statements emanating from the Advisory Committee were never meant to constitute binding directives on colonial governments. They were thought of rather as guiding principles which local officials were free to modify or, if necessary, even reject outright in the light of local circumstances. It is not surprising, therefore, that there were often significant variations from one territory to another in the nature, extent and purpose of schooling. These facts, combined with chronic shortages of trained administrative and teaching staff in all colonies, provide no support for the belief that the Colonial Office was intent on promoting a deliberate and sustained policy of cultural imperialism as argued by revisionist critics.

Professor D. K. Fieldhouse has stressed the fact that initially colonial rule was understood to involve a strictly limited liability but that over time, largely for practical reasons, it became total.[18] He likewise claims that colonisation was not a rational or planned condition but rather the product of a unique set of circumstances that resulted, quite unpredictably, in the formal partition of the world between the Great Powers. Having acquired their empires, few of them seemingly had any coherent, preconceived idea of what they would do with them or any enlightened appreciation of the problems they would create. Fieldhouse has likened colonial rule to a 'complex improvisation',[19] often characterised by confused goals. This is a

[215]

H

definition which accurately describes the nature of British colonial education policy in the 1920s and 1930s. It also highlights the essentially pragmatic nature of British colonial administration which relied heavily on the judgement of local officials in preference to formal policy statements issued from the Colonial Office.

Prior to the First World War, the British Government took only a fitful interest in the development of schooling in its overseas dependencies, largely because education was considered a matter for local initiative and voluntary effort. Even within the colonies, local administrations were content, for the most part, to confine their educational activities to the routine and largely unimaginative disbursement of local revenues to voluntary agencies. However, the attitude of the British Government underwent a marked change in the early 1920s, in response to the new concept of trusteeship and the growing scale and complexity of the problem of native education in Africa. In 1923, the Colonial Office established the Advisory Committee on Native Education in British Tropical Africa.[20] The Committee subsequently issued a series of statements outlining various guiding principles, but in each case the final determination of education policy was left to 'men-on-the-spot' to make in the light of local conditions.

After the First World War, the British colonial empire embraced more than three million square miles of territory and in excess of fifty million people, representing virtually every known racial type and culture, but it was the African colonies, comprising almost seventy per cent of both the total population and land area, which constituted the principal preoccupation of the Colonial Office in London.[21] By the 1920s the nature of imperial debate on Africa had shifted ground. It was no longer a question of whether Britain should acquire an empire, but how it might best be governed and in whose interests.[22] There were no simple answers to these questions, but as Sir Charles Jeffries remarked many years later, the mere act of entering upon the African scene set in motion forces which were bound to press forward with irresistible momentum.[23]

There was the obvious need, once law and order was established, to encourage economic activity to enable each territory to become financially self-supporting. Traditionally all British colonies were treated as separate and distinct administrative and economic units. Moral concern for the welfare of native peoples was a further important consideration. Critics of British colonial rule frequently scoff at the notion, but the evidence of moral considerations had long been present in British policy in South Africa and elsewhere.[24] By the end of the nineteenth century humanitarian concern clearly gave a moral justification to the expansion of British economic interests in Africa. Humanitarians accepted the spread of commerce as a potent civilising force, while the likes of Cecil Rhodes had no qualms about 'philosophy plus five per cent'. Concern for native welfare was, however, complicated by white settlement, and the future of both Kenya and Southern Rhodesia posed vital questions regarding the long-term aims and methods of British native policy.

Humanitarian influence was evident in the composition and work of the Advisory Committee on Education in London. The redoubtable J. H. Oldham, Secretary to the International Council of Missions, played a leading role in the formation of the Committee and also exerted a profound influence on its subsequent deliberations.[25] The Committee was established initially, to provide the African colonies with advice on how they might go about organising and expanding their educational services, at a time when there was little or no such expertise available locally. At the Committee's inaugural meeting, the Chairman, the Rt. Hon. W. G. A. Ormsby-Gore, opened proceedings by referring to the great unease being felt about education policy, especially in India, where it was freely admitted that mistakes had been made in the past.[26] The object of the Committee would be to avoid a repetition of such mistakes in Africa. Ormsby-Gore then mentioned the problems which had arisen from the growing African demand for education. These included the need for an adequate system of financing education, a clearer understanding of the relationship between local government and the missions in the running of schools, and the place of the Muslim religion in relation to native education, especially in Nigeria and in East Africa. He concluded by suggesting that the best policy for the Committee to follow was 'to devote itself to the consideration of problems as they arose', a clear endorsement of what was an essentially pragmatic approach to British colonial education policy.

Schilling's belief that the primary objective of the Committee was to stifle African nationalism is based presumably on Ormsby-Gore's remarks about mistakes made in India. The British were clearly anxious to prevent the proliferation in Africa of a disaffected pseudo-intellectual or 'babu' class, such as had arisen in India as a result of the uncontrolled spread of sub-standard English-medium, academic schooling. It is equally true that throughout the inter-war years British colonial policy in Africa was strongly influenced by the concept of indirect rule which provided little or no scope for a critical native 'intelligentsia'. But this did not mean that the Advisory Committee was opposed, in principle, to the growth of secondary education in Africa. On the contrary, it gave strong backing to the establishment of Achimota College in the Gold Coast and the upgrading of Yaba College in Nigeria. Later, in the 1930s, it was in the forefront of moves to initiate the upgrading of Gordon College in The Sudan and Makerere

College in Uganda, and played a leading role in the events of the early war years, which led to the development of colonial universities after 1945. Clearly, opinions may differ as to the most desirable time and speed at which to expand educational opportunities — the depressed economic conditions of the 1930s were not the most propitious of times for rapid expansion — but the record of the Advisory Committee simply does not support the belief that it deliberately blocked or retarded educational development in Africa for political reasons, as Schilling claims.

The Advisory Committee consistently opposed educating large numbers of young Africans for white-collar employment which did not exist but it was equally concerned about the possible adverse effects on African tribal society if Western academic schooling was allowed to proliferate too quickly. This was a fear that was endorsed by many leading anthropologists in the 1920s. Throughout most of the inter-war period the Advisory Committee remained wedded to the belief that the basis of future life for most Africans would remain agrarian. It followed, therefore, that one of the primary tasks of African education policy should be to assist in the growth of stable rural communities securely established on the land.[27] This was the main reason why the principle of adaptation was so readily endorsed by the Committee. To suggest that the policy of adaptation was part of a deliberate political ploy to stifle African nationalism is surely to credit British colonial officials with greater foresight than they deserve and to ignore the genuine concern expressed at the time for the future wellbeing of traditional African society. Far from wishing to destroy indigenous culture, as many neo-Marxists assert, British education policy in the 1920s was expressly directed towards preserving it.

The Advisory Committee was financed initially by the British Government and by contributions from the colonies that sought its advice. In the early 1930s, the Committee ran into financial difficulties and survived only through the generosity of the American Carnegie Corporation.[28] The British Government would surely have placed the Committee on a more secure financial footing if it had been intent on using education to assert cultural hegemony in the colonies. It is also unlikely that American philanthropic support would have been forthcoming if there had been any suggestion that the Committee performed a political function. It is true that most committee members belonged to what might loosely be termed the 'Establishment' but many, like Sir George Currie, and later Professor W. M. Macmillan and L. J. Barnes, were frequently outspoken critics of British colonial rule. British colonial policy changed radically after 1945 but in the field of education, the Advisory Committee signalled many of the policy changes years before. Far from being a reactionary body, as

Schilling seems to imply, hindsight suggests that the Committee was generally in the forefront of more enlightened thought about the future of the colonies, especially in the late 1930s and thereafter.

Colonial administrators had no choice initially but to work in partnership with the various voluntary bodies in determining education policy. The conference convened by the Government in Tanganyika in 1925 was a classic illustration of this fact.[29] Local officials could exert financial pressure on missions by threatening to cut off grants-in-aid but in the last resort the Government could not order missions to implement official directives. Government involvement in the provision of schooling made limited but nevertheless significant progress in most colonies between the two world wars but it was forever bedevilled by acute shortages of finance and trained staff and the manifold problems which arose from having to deal with numerous and often antagonistic voluntary agencies. If the British had been serious about using the schools as agents of a deliberate policy of cultural imperialism they would surely have made more determined efforts to overcome these problems.

Throughout the inter-war years, African education policy was based theoretically on the principle of adaptation. In practice, there was much confusion, especially in the colonies, as to what it meant and how it should be implemented. The concept was first outlined in the now celebrated Advisory Committee memorandum *Education Policy in British Tropical Africa*, published in 1925.[30] This statement was strongly influenced by the first of the two Phelps-Stokes reports on education in Africa, published in 1922.[31] In an oft-quoted extract it was stated that education should be adapted to the *mentality, aptitudes, occupations and traditions of native peoples*. It was the educational corollary to the concept of indirect rule.

In practice, it was interpreted to mean that Africans should be encouraged to develop *along their own lines* in order that they might be better able to handle their changing environment. Exactly what this meant was never made clear. In general, the adaptation principle resulted in a reinforcement of the rural emphasis which characterised the curriculum of many primary schools and the strong sense of paternalism evident amongst many colonial officials in the 1920s. Subsequently, it also gave rise to widespread and growing resentment from African and European critics alike, who argued that it was a deliberate means to perpetuate European dominance because it denied most Africans access to formal academic schooling. It has already been suggested that this was not the underlying motive, but it was only to be expected that Africans should increasingly view it in this light as the pressure for academic secondary schooling intensified in the 1930s.

Hindsight suggests that the 1925 Memorandum was a product of the confused educational thought of the period. It was agreed that colonial governments should promote the economic and social development of native communities but there was no consensus on how this might best be achieved or how rapidly changes should be encouraged. Some indication of the confusion over education policy can be gauged from the remarks of Sir Donald Cameron, the Governor of Tanganyika. He was strongly opposed to westernising the African and thereby turning him into a bad imitation of a European. Instead, he wanted to make him into 'a good African', but it was never clear what he meant by the term.[32] A. G. Fraser, the outspoken foundation Principal of Achimota College, was well aware of the dilemma when he posed the question of how Africans were to be educated without detribalising them or taking them clean away from their people. It was, he said, a question often asked by educationists of each other in sad searching of heart, and by administrators, often in scorn and fury.[33] Sir Hugh Clifford, the Governor of Nigeria, likewise sounded a note of warning about likely African reactions if their education was restricted to a practical or vocational nature.[34] The radical *Gold Coast Times* left its readers in no doubt about the need for Africans to receive a sound intellectual training if they were not to be educated to remain forever inferior to the European — 'The education that Africans need is the kind that will fit them to take their rightful place in the counsels of the nations in the fullness of time.'[35] The same writer also stressed the importance of consulting Africans about any educational policy intended for their benefit — a practice noticeably absent at the time. Professor W. M. Macmillan, a prominent colonial critic, was equally forthright in demanding that Africans be given liberal access to western education: '... there is this set against making him [the African] a pale copy of a European, we forget that the African himself wants our education and will himself adapt it. We spend too much time wondering what we are going to do about adapting education to our own ideas of his needs.'[36] In practice, British policy was ambivalent. In Whitehall, there was a strong commitment to prevent the undue exploitation of native races by Europeans. This was evident not only in Africa but also in places as far afield as Malaya and Fiji, where attempts were made to preserve tribalism by wrapping native races in what amounted to a cultural cocoon. At the same time, however, it was impossible to stem the forces of change, as Julian Huxley saw for himself when he visited Africa in the early 1930s:

The mere presence of the white man in Africa makes it impossible for the primitive condition of things to continue ... Every motor car, every mission, every packet of cigarettes or yard of cotton print, every book to be read, every black man who can write — these and a thousand other things are altering the conditions in which and the ideas by which African natives live.[37]

Ultimately, the theory of cultural adaptation proved to be fallacious. Experience proved that it was not possible to control social change and somehow fuse the best of the old ways with the best of the new;[38] nor was the African a lump of clay or stone that could be fashioned to fit some predetermined shape.[39] Hindsight also suggests that laudable as the principle of adaptation may have seemed in the abstract, it came too late to shape events because it was rapidly outdated by the gathering pace of social and economic change and by the attitudes of Africans and Asians alike, who soon perceived that any type of schooling which was not conducted in English and academic in content was deemed to be second-rate and leading nowhere. By the 1920s, Western education was already firmly rooted in West Africa, where it was widely recognised as the principal means to salaried employment. The rapid extension of this belief to Central and East Africa subsequently fuelled the insatiable drive by many Africans for Western schooling in the 1930s and thereafter. In retrospect, it might well be argued that the British colonial educators were more the victims of pressures and circumstances often beyond their control than the architects of any deliberate and coherent policy of cultural imperialism.

This fact was never recognised by the vociferous critics of colonialism who dominated many of the early Unesco debates on education. W. E. F. Ward, who was Deputy Educational Adviser at the Colonial Office immediately after the Second World War has recalled his personal impressions of some of those early meetings.[40] In the aftermath of war it was widely assumed that colonial rule was inherently evil because it was based on the subjection of one race by another and maintained solely for the convenience or profit of the Colonial Power. It followed, therefore, that education policy was determined solely according to the needs of the colonial administrators rather than the interests of the local people. Ward, a former teacher at Achimota College in the Gold Coast and an acute observer of the African colonial scene, considered this reasoning to be a gross oversimplification of the nature of colonial rule. In his view British colonialism was in no sense a deliberately planned system in which schools played their allotted role, nor was British rule in the colonies established and maintained solely for the benefit of Britain.[41]

There were numerous educated Africans who were bitter and outspoken critics of British rule, especially in the 1930s, but their presence was not the chief determinant of education policy. The British traditionally discriminated between the education of the masses and that of a minority who were given a Western academic schooling in order that they might fill posts in the administrative and technical services. The problem, as one writer has pointed out, was to keep a balance between the two.[42] The growing wave of African criticism in the 1930s was mainly due to lack of suitable employment opportunities and also to the fact that there was no provision in the system of indirect rule for meaningful participation by an African intellectual élite.

Most British colonial educators do not appear to have been opposed in principle to the spread of English-medium schooling. What they objected to was poor teaching of the language and a sub-standard product. 'It [was] very undesirable', said Albert Isherwood, the Deputy Director of Education in Tanganyika, 'that Africans should be given a mere smattering of English. When English is taught at all, it must be taught thoroughly and completely and only to such pupils as are undergoing a period of school life long enough to enable English to be learnt properly.'[43] In retrospect, it would seem that the acute shortage of competent English-speaking teachers, evident in all colonies, was as much to blame for the restricted access to English-medium schooling as any overriding socio-political considerations.

The secondary school curriculum was, likewise, closely geared to British examination syllabuses, not for reasons of cultural imperialism, but because the colonial peoples themselves insisted that they follow the British model. Anything less would have been considered second rate.[44] By the late 1930s, H. S. Scott, the former Director of Education in Kenya, considered it was too late to reverse the trend. African political development was proceeding at such a pace that any attempt to provide anything other than a purely Western academic form of education was doomed to failure. It would be no exaggeration, he claimed, to say that the educated African does not recognise education except in its Western garb.[45] Ormsby-Gore likewise criticised the dominance exerted by external examinations on the curricula of colonial schools, but he saw little hope of reversing a trend in which educated Africans graded themselves into those who had passed the Cambridge Overseas School Certificate, those who had passed the Junior Certificate, those who had tried but failed, and finally, those who had not even tried.[46]

Both the theoretical and practical difficulties facing British colonial educators in the 1920s were readily acknowledged by Julian Huxley, who doubted whether the British had any clear long-term notion of what they were trying to achieve in Africa.[47] He was equally sure, however, that it was not possible merely to preserve a human zoo or anthropological garden. The mere presence of the European in Africa made that impossible in the long term. He also warned against any attempt to restrict Africans to technical or 'useful' education designed to fit 'the labouring classes to their station in life'. Scott likewise commented on the lack of positive direction in colonial education policy and practice.[48] There was, he claimed, general agreement that the African should be developed morally, socially and economically, but no clear indication of how this should be done or the pace to be set. He also commented on the apparent lack of appreciation by most Europeans of growing African feelings for education as a means of advancement.

Professor Fred Clarke, of the London Institute of Education, expressed his deep concern 'about the sinister uses to which a quite innocent advocacy of educating the native 'on his own lines' might be put.[49] He called for a rigorous self-examination, 'for a relentless dragging into clear consciousness' of all the motives underlying British efforts to 'civilise' the African native by systematic education to avoid the danger that policy would be derived uncritically from a dominant sense of British rather than African interests.[50] It would be no easy task, he concluded, at a time when the West was unsure about its own educational needs and still more so about those of Africa. Clarke's comments, perhaps more than those of any other observer, highlighted the confused and often contradictory nature of British colonial education policy in the inter-war years.

The mid 1930s were marked by growing social unrest in many colonies, especially the West Indies, where the economic depression caused a major slump in sugar prices. Bernard Porter has referred to this period as one of stagnation, when a territory like Tanganyika 'lay in mothballs' and development of any sort was little more than a pious wish.[51] It is significant, however, that most of the criticism levelled at British colonial policy at that time focused on Britain's apparent neglect rather than exploitation of the colonies. This was largely attributable to the widespread indifference in Britain towards the colonies in the 1930s, which resulted in the lack of a firm government commitment towards colonial development and the confused nature of colonial education policy generally. As the Marquess of Dufferin and Ava, the Parliamentary Under-Secretary of State for the Colonies, remarked in 1939: 'In our tradtional colonial education policy ... *we have not made up our minds early enough or firmly enough on the precise* type of educated native we desire to produce; we have left too much to the missions and not taken sufficient initiative ourselves...'[52]

The onset of war hastened a reappraisal of colonial policy and resulted in new initiatives to stimulate economic and political development.[53] Education policy, in particular, changed direction. The principle of adaptation was officially abandoned and replaced by a strong emphasis on the rapid expansion of Western schooling as the principal means of preparing the colonies for self-government. The policy of indirect rule was also jettisoned and colonial officials were exhorted to work closely with educated Africans in preparing for the future.[54]

There was never any published statement akin to the 1925 Memorandum, which outlined post-war education policy for the colonies. The nearest approach was a Colonial Office paper prepared for the Conference of African Governors, held in London in November 1947.[55] It stressed the need for a vigorous drive to expand educational opportunities, and urged that special attention be focused on the training of as many African men and women as possible for senior posts in the government service, the professions, and in business. Emphasis was also placed on strengthening cultural links between Britain and the colonies, mainly through expanding opportunities for colonial students to study in Britain and by the recruitment of British expatriates to teach in colonial schools and institutions of higher learning. Nowhere in the document, which ran to some twenty typed pages, was there any hint that education should be used for any purpose other than to facilitate the rapid social and economic progress of the African territories, on the understanding that self-government and eventual independence would follow. In the aftermath of war, colonial education policy was increasingly caught up in a race against time to produce an adequate pool of skilled manpower to sustain essential services once independence was granted. This was especially noticeable in the more politically advanced colonies like the Gold Coast, Nigeria and Malaya.

It might conceivably be argued that the establishment of new university colleges in the colonies after 1945, based on the Asquith formula, which closely mirrored the Oxbridge model, constituted a direct attempt by the British to instigate a deliberate policy of cultural imperialism.[56] The University College of Ibadan, the first of the new colleges, certainly embodied all that was thought best in the British academic tradition, but it is equally true that the Africans would not have accepted anything else. Moreover, when it was initially announced that there was to be only one university college, at Ibadan, to cater for the needs of West Africa, the people of the Gold Coast reacted so strongly that the British Government was obliged to revise its plans, and to include provision for a second college, based on the same Oxbridge formula, to be sited in the Gold Coast.[57]

In the 1950s, Sir Christopher Cox, the Chief Educational Adviser to the Secretary of State for the Colonies, and his staff at the Colonial Office, were increasingly aware of growing American academic influence in the African colonies.[58] Indeed, Cox's memorable address to the British Association in 1956 was delivered with the Americans very much in mind.[59] The American presence might have caused acute concern in Whitehall if colonial policy had been geared to maintaining solely British cultural ties with the colonies, but this was not the case. Even if it had been, there was, by then, little the British could have done to isolate the colonies. Many of them were close to independence and increasingly responsible for determining the future of their own education systems. In fact, Anglo-American cooperation, especially in fostering the development of tertiary education and teacher training, became a notable feature of British education policy in Africa in the 1960s.[60]

In addressing the British Association, Cox spoke of the impact of British education in the colonies.[61] He referred, in particular, to the 'peculiar' situation which confronted Britain after 1918, of being 'ultimately responsible for the education of other peoples of very different stock in other parts of the globe'. It was, he suggested, a formidable responsibility which had fallen to few peoples, and to none on quite such a scale as the British. He dwelt at length on the clash of cultures and the role of Western education as an instrument of social change and pointed out how in India, Burma, and elsewhere in the Far East, British education had opened up new career opportunities for the indigenous population without destroying their culture. He also stated that after the First World War, there was a deliberate attempt in Africa to graft Western schooling on to indigenous stock but that it was unsuccessful because the Africans rejected it. Cox suggested that this fact emphasised a fundamental, though often underrated truth about colonial education generally; that policy was determined less by the government than by the attitude of the governed.[62] In a memorable sentence he proclaimed that in the long run Africa would take what it wanted, digest it slowly, and assimilate what it did not spit out again.

Cox went on to say that in the inter-war period Africans increasingly wanted Western education, identical with that of their British rulers and guaranteed by common examinations. What set fire to the imagination of the Gold Coast, he claimed, was the founding of Achimota College, not, he felt sure, because Achimota broke new ground in secondary education by seeking to build on indigenous tradition but because it led on to the highest qualifications and became the symbol of advance. By the mid-1950s, the demand for Western education in Africa had reached a stage of intensity, at times almost obsessional in its strength, which far outstripped the capacity of the territories to meet it. Cox believed that the demand for purely Western education would ultimately abate. Then, certain elements of the traditional culture would reassert themselves as a prelude to *the achievement of that distinctive national identity, cultural as well as political, which has for so long been the implicit objective of our educational policy.*[63]

The clash of cultures and the nature and impact of British colonial education policy were also subjects of central concern to Professor Margaret Read when she was Head of the Colonial Department at the University of London Institute of Education immediately after the Second World War. She, too, emphasised the essentially pragmatic and often confused nature of British colonial policy: 'The winds of doctrine blowing from Britain to her colonies have been fitful and changeable, unlike the steady trade winds from France and Portugal which have consistently carried French and Portuguese culture and orthodox methods of teaching it to their respective colonies.'[64] She readily admitted that this pragmatic approach had resulted in 'a store of trouble in the educational field'.

One of the strongest denials of any deliberate attempt by the British to use education as a means of cultural imperialism was voiced by A. J. Loveridge, a former Chief Commissioner in Ashanti, Ghana, who subsequently lectured at the Institute of Education in London. On the basis of wide experience in the design of school texts and involvement in community development, he claimed that British officialdom was remarkably diffident about changing the minds of colonial peoples. He, likewise, had no hesitation in claiming that Britain's colonial presence 'was not established for the purpose of changing men's minds'.[65]

In this chapter I have endeavoured to expand upon what Professor Macmillan termed 'the confusion of counsel'[66] amongst those who were responsible for determining British colonial education policy between the two world wars, and thereby provide an alternative perspective on a subject of widespread academic controversy. Lord Hailey once described British colonial policy as being based on the principle that the maximum of initiative and responsibility should rest with the colonial administration. Education policy was characterised by the same 'lack of system'.[67] Hailey attributed this partly to the predominance acquired at an early stage by the missionaries, and partly, also, to the projection into the colonial field of the traditional disinclination of the British to subject education or any other intellectual movement to State control. If there was any major distinguishing feature of British colonialism, Hailey argued, it was surely its piecemeal or *ad hoc* nature.

Professor Macmillan likewise highlighted the absence of any high-handed imposition of doctrinaire principles in British colonial administration but pointed out that policy was seldom strong or determined as a result.[68] He also berated the British for the paucity of education in most of their colonies and argued that colonial governments should have assumed greater responsibility for expanding education in the 1920s. W. R. (later Sir William) Crocker, the outspoken Australian critic and former British colonial official in Nigeria, also highlighted the confusion in British colonial education policy:

> British education practices — it has hardly been possible to speak of a British education policy — have mingled every approach and every attitude that could be disastrous, disaster itself normally being warded off only because of the inspired muddle which resulted in nothing getting very far and in what was done in one direction being cancelled out by what was at the same time being done in the opposite direction.[69]

He added, somewhat ironically, that the main opposition to the reform of colonial education — in particular the undue emphasis placed on literary education and the subsequent neglect of technical education — came from Africans who saw any suppression of English norms as a trick to fob them off with something second best. Crocker's comments, together with those of Hailey and Macmillan, cast still further doubt on any deliberate British policy of cultural imperialism.

By the early 1950s, any initiative that the Colonial Office might have exercised over the direction and content of colonial schooling had passed. 'It is in the territories themselves', said Sir Philip Morris, the chairman of the Cambridge Conference on African Education, 'that policies must be framed, their cost calculated and provided for, and the understanding and cooperation of organisations and people sought and secured.'[70]

The problems created by the clash of cultures in the 1920s had not disappeared, nor were they any less difficult to solve. Morris defined education as the process by which people were acclimatised to the culture into which they were born, in order that they might advance it, but what was the culture of modern Africa? African life was constantly changing and tribal life was unstable. E. B. Castle, Professor of Education at the University of Hull, writing in the early 1960s, referred to the young African being caught between two worlds, 'the one dying, the other not yet defined; and he has no firm footing in either'.[71] Nor was the cultural problem confined to Africa. The New Zealand and Australian governments found no easy solutions to the problems of cultural adjustment encountered by Maoris and Aborigines respectively, while in American Samoa, the administration likewise found it difficult to know what education policy to adopt on behalf of the local Samoan people.[72]

The colonial experience will doubtless long remain the subject of ongoing controversy because of its paradoxical or contradictory nature. There are critics who argue, like Carnoy, that education was a means to perpetuate subservience through the promotion of a colonial mentality, but others claim with equal conviction that Western schooling was the means of promoting enlightenment and the growth of modern societies, even though the process was fraught with much uncertainty and confusion of purpose. In a recent study of financial management in British crown colonies, R. M. Kesner argues strongly that the British Government acted, in the main, in the interests of the colonies and not on behalf of metropolitan interests, but he readily concedes that many critics will remain unconvinced. 'They will argue that the official record disguises the real intentions of British political designs which were to subjugate economically the Crown Colonies making them captive markets for British goods and cheap sources of raw materials for British industry.'[73] He concluded by saying that 'One cannot of course label British activities in the colonies as purely altruistic but it would be equally incorrect to characterise them as simply exploitative.'[74] The tenor of his remarks applies equally as well to British colonial education policy.

Notes

1 W. K. Hancock, *Survey of British Commonwealth Affairs*, Vol. 2, O.U.P., 1940, p. 1.
2 *Imperial Conference 1926*, Appendices to the Summary of Proceedings, Cmd. 2769, p. 123.
3 Martin Carnoy, *Education as Cultural Imperialism*, New York, Longman, 1974.
4 M. J. Bowman, Review, *Economic Development and Culture Change*, 24 (July 1976), pp. 833–41.
5 Udo Bude, 'The adaptation concept in British colonial education', *Comparative Education*, 19, 3 (1983), pp. 341–55.
6 M. J. Mbilinyi, 'African education during the British colonial period 1919–1961', Chap. 7 in M. H. Y. Kaniki (ed.), *Tanzania Under Colonial Rule*, Longman, 1980.
7 D. G. Schilling, 'British policy for African education in Kenya 1895–1939', Ph.D. thesis, University of Wisconin, 1972. An abbreviated version of Schilling's thesis is included in E. M. Harik and D. G. Schilling, *The Politics of Education in Colonial Algeria and Kenya*, Ohio University Centre for International Studies, 1984, pp. 49–102. For an alternative viewpoint, see S. P. Abbott, 'The African education policy of the Kenyan Government 1904–1939', M.Phil. thesis, University of London, 1970. Abbott argues that deficiencies in education policy were due to fallacies inherent in contemporary educational theory rather than to any deliberate attempt to perpetuate European dominance.
8 Schilling, 'British policy', p. 298.
9 Walter Rodney, *How Europe Underdeveloped Africa*, London, Bogle L'Ouverture Publications, 1972, pp. 264, 275 and 281.
10 Samir Amin, 'What education for what development?', *Prospects*, V, 1, 1975, p. 51.
11 Ivan Illich, *Deschooling Society*, New York, Harper and Row, 1971.
12 Albert Memmi, *The Colonizer and the Colonized*, Boston, Beacon Press, 1965.
13 Paulo Freire, *Pedagogy of the Oppressed*, Harmondsworth, Penguin Books, 1972.
14 Frantz Fanon, *The Wretched of the Earth*, Harmondsworth, Penguin Books, 1972.

15 Abdou Moumouni, *L'Education en Afrique*, Paris, François Maspero, 1964.
16 H. A. Gailey, *Clifford: Imperial Proconsul*, Rex Collings, London, 1982, p. 185.
17 A. Fajana, *Educational Policy in Nigeria: A Century of Experiment*, University of Ife, Inaugral Lecture Series 55, 1982, p.4. (Author's emphasis.)
18 D. K. Fieldhouse, *Colonialism 1870–1945. An Introduction*, London, Macmillan, 1983.
19 *Ibid*. pp. 41–2.
20 For the establishment and early history of the Committee, see F. S. Clatworthy, *The Formulation of British Colonial Education Policy 1923–1948*, University of Michigan School of Education, 1971.
21 Figures derived from *Colonial Office List 1924*.
22 J. E. Flint, 'Frederick Lugard: the making of an autocrat 1858–1943', in L. H. Gann and Peter Duignan (eds.), *African Proconsuls*, New York, Free Press, 1979, pp. 309–10.
23 Charles Jeffries, 'Recent social welfare developments in British Tropical Africa', *Africa*, XIV, 1943–4, p. 4.
24 Ronald Robinson, 'The trust in British Central African Policy 1880–1939', Ph.D. thesis, Cambridge University, 1950.
25 Clatworthy, *British Colonial Education Policy*. The archives of the Joint International Missionary Council and the Conference of British Missionary Societies (IMC/CBMS) are the source of Oldham's correspondence. These have been microfilmed and published by the Inter Documentation Company AG, Zug, Switzerland, 1979.
26 Minutes of the first meeting of the Committee on Native Education in Tropical Africa, 9 January 1924, CO 879/121.
27 For elaboration of this theme, see the Committee's *Memorandum on the Education of African Communities*, Colonial No. 103, HMSO, 1935.
28 Clatworthy, *British Colonial Education Policy*, pp. 57–60.
29 Tanganyika Territory, *Report of Education Conference, 1925*.
30 Cmd. 2374, 1925.
31 *Education in Africa*, Phelps Stokes Fund, New York, 1922.
32 B. T. G. Chidzero, *Tanganyika and International Trusteeship*, London, 1961, p. 118.
33 A. G. Fraser, 'Aims of African education', *International Review of Missions*, 14, 1925, pp. 514–22.
34 Sir Hugh Clifford to J. H. Oldham, 4 May 1923, IMC/CBMS Archives, Box 275.
35 *Gold Coast Times*, 16 February 1924, IMC/CBMS Archives, Box 219.
36 W. M. Macmillan, 'The importance of the educated African', *African Affairs*, January 1934, pp. 137–8.
37 Julian Huxley, *Africa View*, London, Chatto and Windus, 1932, p. 299.
38 Philip Foster, *Education and Social Change in Ghana*, Chicago, University of Chicago Press, 1965, p. 165.
39 A. V. Murray, 'Education under indirect rule', *African Affairs*, July 1935.
40 W. E. F. Ward, 'My Africa', unpublished manuscript, Rhodes House Library, Oxford, and Reid Library, University of Western Australia, Perth.
41 *Ibid*.
42 A. R. Thompson, 'The adaptation of education to African society in Tanganyika under British rule', Ph.D. thesis, University of London, 1968, p. 41.
43 *Report of Education Conference 1925*, p. 18. See also Walter Morris-Hale, 'British administration in Tanganyika from 1920 to 1945', Ph.D. thesis, University of Geneva, 1969, p. 53.
44 Michael Omolewa, 'The adaptation question in Nigerian education 1916–1936: a study of an educational experiment in secondary school examination in colonial Nigeria', *Journal of the Historical Society of Nigeria*, VIII, 3, 1976, p. 109.

45 H. S. Scott, 'The development of the education of the African in relation to western contact', *The Year Book of Education 1938*, London, Evans Bros., pp.697–8.

46 *Oversea Education*, 111, 1, October 1931.

47 Huxley, *African View*, p. 374.

48 John Anderson, *The Struggle for the School*, Longman, 1970, p. 42.

49 Clarke to Professor Percy Nunn, 16 October 1931, 'Sir Fred Clarke File', University of London Institute of Education Archives.

50 Fred Clarke, 'The double mind in African education', *Africa*, 5, 2, 1932, pp. 158–68.

51 B. J. Porter, *The Lion's Share: A Short History of British Imperialism 1850–1970*, London, 1976, pp. 281–2.

52 *Oversea Education*, XI, i, 1939, p. 5. Author's emphasis.

53 *Statement of Policy on Colonial Development and Welfare, 1940*, Cmd. 6175.

54 Ronald Robinson, 'Andrew Cohen and the transfer of power in tropical Africa, 1940–1951', in W. H. Morris-Jones and George Fisher (eds.), *Decolonisation and After*, London, Cass, 1980, pp. 50–72.

55 Education Policy in Africa (Revised Version), CO 987/12.

56 A full account of the founding of the new colonial universities is found in I. C. M. Maxwell, *Universities in Partnership*, Scottish Academic Press, 1980.

57 C. Whitehead, 'The two-way pull and the establishment of university education in British West Africa', *History of Education*, 16, 2 1987, pp. 119–33.

58 Personal remark to the author, New College, Oxford, November 1979.

59 *Ibid*.

60 E. J Murphy, *Creative Philanthrophy*, New York, Teachers' College Press, Columbia University, 1976.

61 Sir Christopher Cox, 'The impact of British education on the indigenous peoples of overseas territories', *The Advancement of Science*, 50, September 1956, pp. 125–36.

62 For a similar conclusion see Godfrey Brown, 'British educational policy in West and Central Africa', *The Journal of Modern African Studies*, 2, 3, (1964), pp. 365–77.

63 Author's emphasis.

64 Margaret Read, *Education and Social Change in Tropical Areas*, Thos. Nelson, 1955, p. 74.

65 A. J. Loveridge, *British Colonial Experience in Education Development*, University College, Cardiff Press, 1978, p. 15.

66 W. M. Macmillan, *Warning from the West Indies*, Faber and Faber, 1936, p. 141.

67 Lord Hailey, 'British colonial policy', *Colonial Administration by European Powers*, London 1947, p. 122.

68 W. M. Macmillan, *Africa Emergent*, Faber and Faber, 1938, p. 265.

69 W. R. Crocker, *On Governing Colonies*, London, Allen and Unwin, 1947, p. 55.

70 Memorandum on *African Education*. A statement to launch the published record of the Cambridge Conference, Colonial Office, 11 March 1953. ACEC 13/1953. CO987/18.

71 E. B. Castle, *Growing Up in East Africa*, O.U.P., 1966, p. 18.

72 Edward Beauchamp, 'Educational policy in Eastern Samoa: an American colonial outpost', *Comparative Education*, 11, 1, 1975, pp. 23–30.

73 R. M. Kesner, *Economic Control and Colonial Development*, Clio Press, 1981, p. 223.

74 *Ibid*.

INDEX